MAKING LIFE WORK

MAKING LIFE WORK

Freedom and Disability in a
Community Group Home

JACK LEVINSON

University of Minnesota Press
Minneapolis
London

Material in this book previously appeared in Jack Levinson, "The Group Home Workplace and the Work of Know-How," *Human Studies: A Journal of Sociology and Philosophy* 28, no. 1 (2005): 57–85.

Published by the University of Minnesota Press
111 Third Avenue South, Suite 290
Minneapolis, MN 55401-2520
http://www.upress.umn.edu

Library of Congress Cataloging-in-Publication Data

Levinson, Jack, 1965–
    Making life work : freedom and disability in a community group home /
Jack Levinson.
        p. cm.
    Includes bibliographical references and index.
    ISBN 978-0-8166-5081-1 (hc : alk. paper) — ISBN 978-0-8166-5082-8 (pb : alk. paper)
    1. Group homes for people with mental disabilities—New York (State)—
Case studies. 2. People with mental disabilities—New York (State)—Case studies.
I. Title.
    HV1569.2.U52N495 2010
    362.3′8509747—dc22

                                                        2009016340

Printed in the United States of America on acid-free paper

The University of Minnesota is an equal-opportunity educator and employer.

17 16 15 14 13 12 11 10   10 9 8 7 6 5 4 3 2 1

To the memory of my uncle,
Martin J. Price

The Puritan wanted to work in a calling;
we are forced to do so.

—Max Weber

CONTENTS

PREFACE

The Self-Organized Life

Making Life Work: Freedom and Disability in a Community Group Home examines the nature of freedom and authority in a setting often taken as the opposite of freedom: a group home for adults with intellectual disability (or mental retardation, a term still used commonly in the United States). The book is based on more than a year of fieldwork conducted at Driggs House, a group home in New York City with fifteen residents. Rather than taking the familiar approach to the group home simply as a setting of social control, I consider Driggs House essentially as a workplace in order to understand how it is also organized by the dilemmas posed by individual freedom and autonomy. Driggs House *is* a workplace, of course, providing a livelihood for the counselors. Yet it is a workplace in more than the conventional sense, because, although their work is an important dimension of this study, counselors are not the only group home workers. Residents are group home workers, too, and my aim is to demonstrate how Driggs House depends on the voluntary and skillful participation of all those who live and work there.

For the residents, group home work primarily involves the work they do on themselves to "become more independent." The chapters that follow will make sense of this phrase. For now it points to a cultural insight I offer here in broad strokes as a backdrop to the empirical analysis. In a world where *work* is a primary metaphor for all of life, what the residents do is not so different from what we all do: in places like the United States, living well, living right, is defined by the attention we pay to ourselves. My concern is not the familiar moral one about egoism, social atomism, or the erosion of community but one about how we actually do work on ourselves—how we know and act on ourselves in terms of our own potential and individuality. This is the ethic of autonomy Nikolas Rose describes as a fundamental orientation to life that emerged over the latter half of the twentieth century. Rose argues that an ideal of autonomy, of the self as autonomous, underlies the ever-encompassing emphasis on the individual and on individuality in the culture and politics of modernity today. The work of group home residents is but one example. The ideal of self-regulation through personal autonomy guides conduct not only for those of us who live independently—"out in the community," as we said at Driggs House—but also for those of us whose autonomy is always in question.

We all work on ourselves. We work to overcome personal obstacles and to strengthen or cultivate the capacities that we believe will prevent problems before they occur, problems for which we are ostensibly at risk even in the absence of trouble. For many of us, the absence of trouble is precisely what warrants the greatest diligence. Health and happiness are understood and experienced less and less as good fortune than as outcomes of personal choice that we feel responsible, obliged even, not simply to enjoy but also to preserve and maintain actively. This involves the systematic and sustained effort to understand, manage, and enhance our most ordinary capacities and experiences; we see ourselves as resources, each harboring within us both the potential and the limits to surpass.

At the start of the twentieth century, Weber used the phrase "social ethic of capitalist culture" to describe how the instrumental orientation of the market had rationalized all aspects of life through a confusion of means and ends. He perhaps never imagined the degree to which individuals would in time become responsible for their own freedom, or the shape freedom would take: that duty would lie in the limitless pursuit not merely of one's personal goals but also of one's own *self*, striving for happiness, staying healthy, discovering who one truly is and who one can be, and always trying to be the best one can be.

Is it true that "out in the community" many choose to work on themselves, whereas in the group home residents are forced to do so? This distinction is true enough on its face but fails to account for the cultural dimension that makes group home residents not so different from the rest of us after all. What residents apparently *must* do is precisely what everyone in one way or another just *does*. Though *Making*

Life Work is a case study of a single group home, it is, in a sense, as much about "us" as about "them." This reflects a principled aim to persuade readers not that the distinction between us and them is morally questionable (though it certainly is)—that residents are people too or that "labels are for jars"—but that it is socially untenable. For all of us, making *life* work somehow involves making *work* of life itself.

Group homes emerged in the United States by the 1970s as the main alternative to the large, segregated custodial institutions that for nearly a century served as home to many people with mental and physical disabilities. The popular and professional consensus for decades was that these institutions spared families the burden and shame of their disabled children, who were uneducable and too vulnerable to live in society, and protected society from the dangers they posed. By the early 1970s, mounting criticism together with shocking media exposure made it impossible to ignore the despicable conditions, negligence, and abuse that had long become routine. When the clinical and moral failure of the institutions was finally acknowledged (by the courts as well as parents, professionals, and the public), community group homes offered a solution. Yet, beyond the asylum walls, providing services to citizens rather than inmates posed a new kind of problem. Group homes assumed what in effect is the task of cultivating the capacities for autonomy that enable individuals to live in the community, albeit in supervised settings.

Unfortunately, community-based residential services in the United States have not delivered in a variety of ways on the promises of rights, self-determination, and integration made more than thirty years ago. It is only for clarity that I indulge here the misleading and simplistic, if common, opposition between institutions and the community. The closing of institutions has actually been a slow, inefficient process, with great variation nationally. In many states, facilities still operate on a scale far too large to be considered anything other than institutional, despite what they may now be called (such as New York's "developmental centers").

My question, however, is neither whether residents are truly free nor whether services in the community have succeeded or failed. Instead, *Making Life Work* is a study of how a group home accomplishes its task of supervising individuals who are thought of as free yet incapable of freedom. This produces a tension between freedom and authority that, although perhaps more easily seen in the group home, does not make the group home unique: in the liberal individualist ethos of modern societies, this tension is inherent. What I ask is how residents and counselors actually manage this tension every day. The book, in one aspect, is also a study of the capacity to act. I show how Driggs House is organized by the ongoing effort to cultivate the capacity in all residents for the kind of systematic and voluntary orientation to their own conduct that is the practical shape freedom takes today.

The group home is one organizational realization of freedom in contemporary society. At least, I argue that it should be considered this way. In the popular imagination, however, a group home is antithetical to the freely lived life that is the promise and presumption of liberal individualism. To live in such a home means that freedom is apparently beyond one's reach. For those of us who do not live in such places—social scientists and "normals" alike—and who understand social control simply in terms of the incapacity to act, it may be difficult to accept the participation of residents as either voluntary or skillful. Yet among the most fundamental theoretical insights from the turn of the twentieth century is the idea that the opposition between freedom and control is a false one, that "liberty," in one of Durkheim's formulations, "is the fruit of regulation." For Weber, as well, if in a different way, this insight was a cornerstone of an inquiry offered in contrast not only to economic and psychological individualism but also to the coercive determinisms that more than a century later still variously grip the imagination of many social scientists. These issues are perennial concerns in social theory but require no further elaboration to make the basic point. For Durkheim and Weber, at least, it was precisely *social* analysis, which was both enabled and required by the conditions of modern life, that could yield concepts of freedom and authority uniquely adequate to it.

My insistence on this foundational insight requires qualification in the particular context of intellectual disability, however. Especially in America, the history of professional classification and treatment is one of crushing brutality. From the mid-nineteenth century until the walls began to crumble in the early 1970s, institutions harbored the vulnerable by incarcerating them and, at the same time, protected society from the threat of violence and moral corruption the vulnerable were seen to pose. More than a metaphor, these walls demarcated the narrow boundaries of life for many with disabilities and, in the utter separation of the worlds on either side, concealed the professional practices that decade after decade not only tolerated but perpetrated unspeakable abuse and exploitation. The policy of segregation that hid what went on inside justified the routine exclusion and domination of people with intellectual disability that went on outside: for example, varied forms of persecution in school as well as discrimination in employment from the nineteenth right into the twenty-first century. Even the issue of forced sterilization persisted well into the 1970s and was still embattled in the courts as late as the 1980s.

Disability researchers and activists, for good reason, continue to focus on the unrealized goals of deinstitutionalization and community integration: neither professional transparency nor the self-determination of individuals with intellectual disability has been adequately achieved. Community services are thus often seen merely to have replaced the direct coercion of institutions with the normative control of expertise. Barring outright abuse—which occurs all too frequently—many of the settings mandated to ensure the rights and autonomy of individuals are dominated by the professional agenda of psychologists, educators, and bureaucrats. In some states, what defines an institution versus an integrated community residence is still in contention, and many facilities look more like small hospitals than homes. Even when an intimate scale has been achieved, the institutional character of service delivery has been hard to shake, however far from the world of the asylum. Dreary decor and mundane regimentation indicate the distance yet to go before achieving the self-determined independent life envisioned early on for community integration.

It is this vision, nonetheless, that is expressed in the regulations and rhetoric of professional services. And, despite a greater cultural and political acceptance of intellectual disability in American society since the 1970s, discrimination and basic misconceptions persist. No doubt deinstitutionalization and integration, however circumscribed, have contributed to the common assumption that community services have righted the wrongs of an unenlightened, if recent, past. Many still believe not only that intellectual disability refers to a clear-cut identifiable condition but also that it is equivalent to social incompetence. I have been slightly surprised, I'll admit, to encounter such attitudes in academic circles and to have experienced on occasion the cavalier way social scientists dismiss an issue that does not fit neatly into a familiar framework. This dismissal reflects ambivalence about the status of disability as a category of social analysis and experience, as well as certain ideals social scientists hold about their profession and about themselves. Colleagues have often presumed that if intellectual disability is a problem at all, it is merely a problem of policy and clinical service. For some who are old enough, vague memories of the galvanizing events at the Willowbrook State School in New York City are invariably tied up with a comforting (though oddly selective), technocratic faith that the plight of the unjustly incarcerated was essentially solved decades ago. In casual discussion about my research, especially while I was in the field, I was met with unembarrassed, if heartfelt, remarks such as, "How depressing," "How frightening," and the most puzzling sentiment of all, "How wonderful of you." It seems that people diagnosed as intellectually disabled are simply too alien, too unknowable, too pathetic. Even for many self-described "critical" social scientists, "the retarded" apparently just don't rank among the researchable oppressed.

My own experience in the early 1990s working as a counselor in two group homes suggests that more must be said about these places than the usual concern about the social control function they most certainly serve. I have known a good number of residents over the years. With few exceptions, they have never appeared to experience group home life only as a limitation or the participation required of them only as a cost. The residents are not just simple and content. Nor are they gloomy, institutionalized, or detached from life. In the group homes where I have spent time, life's difficulties, as for most people, do not generally preclude its pleasures and comforts. I am not suggesting that these (or any) group homes are desirable places to live or would be the choice of the people I have known, if there really were a choice. Nor do I claim about Driggs House that substantial constraints are not imposed on the residents. My point is that living in this professionally structured and supervised world does not make residents quite as different as is commonly believed, even by many residents themselves.

Surely, none of us in American society is immune to the pervasive fear of being perceived as stupid. Lewis Anthony Dexter made this point in his 1964 polemic against how narrowly we had come to understand intelligence in terms of academic achievement. There was little concern in education at the time with arguments about different forms of intelligence (a notion that happens not to be so recent, after all). Dexter charged that schools ultimately teach "some students little more than that they are stupid" and the rest "to fear stupidity and despise the stupid." Since the 1970s, education's "intellectualistic values" have broadened somewhat to encompass different kinds of learners. First, children with physical disabilities were "mainstreamed" in regular classes. By the early 1990s, mainstreaming was seen to reinforce rather than reduce differences among students. It was replaced by "inclusion," a policy of integration that, in principle, extends to children with cognitive and learning difficulties.

Paradoxically, as the approach to learning has broadened, the use of quantitative testing in education has expanded substantially. Dexter's criticism is as trenchant today as it was in the early 1960s. Consider those adults who are deeply opposed to the vast proliferation of educational testing yet believe all the activities of children, both prior to and in addition to formal schooling, should be "educational." Determined parents pack the schedules of their toddlers and preschoolers with classes in not merely music and art but also music and art appreciation, not to mention early reading and writing and, for "tech tots," science and computer skills. For older children, weekends and after-school hours are filled with yet more lessons, costly hobbies, and "structured play." It seems fair to say that middle- and upper-middle-class Americans, at least, "suffer from . . . nervousness and worry" more than ever because stupidity is still perceived as "equivalent to failure." In Dexter's view, academics suffered, too, but they saw a problem of values elsewhere. He took David Riesman and others to task for "looking down" on what they considered a middle-class preoccupation with "being liked as an end in itself," because "the fear of being stupid plays, for many intellectuals, the same role as the fear of being unpopular does for many whom *they* would stigmatize as unduly 'other-directed.'" Today, parental nervousness about stupidity and failure is perhaps matched only by that of academics, given their ever-specializing, downsizing, and increasingly output-oriented industry.

Even the disability rights movement in the United States, which emerged in the 1960s, was dominated by the agenda of physical disabilities and actively distanced itself from the concerns of people with mental and cognitive problems. Only in the 1980s did activists and academics succeed in gathering all experiences of disability under one political banner. The accomplishments of disabled people's movements cannot be overstated. Nor can the accomplishment of establishing disability as a legitimate category of analysis and scholarly field. It was in the 1980s, along with the burgeoning interest in identity in the academy, that disability studies was, so to speak, institutionalized. This field has kept on the radar entrenched cultural misconceptions and the failure of policy and services. A now-substantial body of research documents the experience of stigma, discrimination, disempowerment, and unyielding professional domination in an arena in which political and personal autonomy have for some time been the central ideals.

I share these political and intellectual commitments, and though my aim in this book was not motivated by them, the foundation laid by critical researchers and activists is what enabled me to pursue a different kind of question altogether. In *Making Life Work* I do not ask about the often great distance between actual practice and the ceaseless pervasive rhetoric of autonomy and integration. What I do ask is how these ideals are realized practically in the ongoing problems of group home life that must be solved every day. The study offers an additional insight into the way services in the community are organized—and in some accountable fashion *must* be organized— by the problem of each resident's individuality. This is why, insofar as the tension between supervision and the autonomy of residents reflects the essential dilemma of liberal authority, that tension is routine. It is in this inherent tension, and its ongoing routine resolution, that I examine the social order of a group home and how its goals are actually defined and accomplished.

For this reason I regard Driggs House as a workplace and the participation of residents and counselors alike as equally competent and skillful. It is organized as a workplace by three different but inseparable kinds of work: first, the work of counselors and other group home staff; second, the self-work of residents; and, finally, from a phenomenological perspective, everyday life itself. The reader will not be surprised to discover that much of my description affirms certain asymmetries one might expect between residents and staff in a group home. Yet these same examples also illustrate in one way or another the residents' capacities for competence, capacities which the group home aims to cultivate and on which it fundamentally depends. And though the research setting cannot be considered representative, the principle of autonomy now at the heart of all social services means that the dilemmas faced and resolved every day at Driggs House likely capture the experience in a variety of workplaces.

Although *Making Life Work* is based on fieldwork, it does not contain some of the features that have come to be associated with a good deal of qualitative and ethnographic research. The reader who seeks simply a moving story of life at a group home will be disappointed. I have not aimed to provide an overarching narrative about Driggs House and the people who live and work there. Nor have I aspired in the writing to the popular realism that is now too often taken as a measure of qualitative research independent of the analysis it offers. Rather, the book is organized by the practices that emerged as salient during my fieldwork in relation to my particular concerns about authority and knowledge. Further, I do not seek to uncover the genuine experience of residents or elaborate a perspective that is uniquely theirs, because I do not regard what they do and say simply as an adaptation to the group home's inescapable demands. Nor have I sought to "give voice" to the residents, a task which presumes the very model of power and political objectives I have chosen to bracket. Actually the residents of Driggs House manage pretty well in their own ways to have their say, despite at times being manipulated and even stifled by staff (not to mention each other). At the same time, the brutal history and persistent stigma of intellectual disability does haunt both those who bear the label and, in different ways, those who work with them. These burdens shape the whole enterprise, and, although I don't approach them as problems to be solved, they are part and parcel of the group home life I aim to understand.

Finally, I do not seek to clarify the nature of such a thing called intellectual disability, and I do not address directly the long-standing theoretical controversies about how intellectual disability (or disability in general) should be defined. These issues, however, and the unusual history of nomenclature in this field, warrant an explanation of my own terminology. By the mid-1990s, "mental retardation" was too stigmatizing, having lost any semblance of clinical or diagnostic neutrality. The term had been abandoned in the United Kingdom, much of the anglophone world, and most of Scandinavia in favor of more general categories such as learning difficulties or learning disabilities. American self-advocates and critics in the field for years pressed for such a change, and after much deliberation the American Association on Mental Retardation in 2007 became the American Association on

Intellectual and Developmental Disabilities. Throughout the book, I use the singular form—"intellectual disability" rather than "disabilities"—simply for ease of writing. More important, my use of the term in no way refers to any specifiable biological, cognitive, or developmental condition or state, but in the same way that the terms "disabled," "resident," and "counselor" may function: as shorthand for kinds of persons, both historically, in an abstract sense; and sociologically, in the group home research site.

My overall aim in *Making Life Work* is to capture certain aspects of how life is lived at Driggs House, not to suggest how it could be lived better. Of course, to live better, in another sense, is precisely what the endless work at Driggs House is all about. Whether or not readers appreciate the empirical project itself, I hope they will recognize that, however different group home life appears from our own, the residents are very like us. That is, in some specific and perhaps unfortunate ways, and more thoroughly than most of us are willing to acknowledge, we organize our own lives much as the residents must organize theirs.

ACKNOWLEDGMENTS

Of course, I could never have made this work without the help of others. I am indebted to Paul Attewell, David Goode, Barbara Katz Rothman, and the late Lynn Zimmer for their tireless intellectual support for this project. To Barbara I owe special thanks for her guidance and encouragement as I prepared the book. I am also very grateful to Ivan Karp, who made an extraordinary impact on my thinking and writing over many years and during crucial stages of the project.

To the friends, colleagues, and teachers whose critical conversations, editorial suggestions, and special counsel were invaluable along the way, I offer my thanks: Henry Abelove, Phil Alcabes, the late Bob Alford, Andy Beveridge, Claudia Center, Patricia Clough, Martha Copp, Tim Costelloe, Jack Cuddihy, Anne Dunham, Cynthia Epstein, John Eyck, Judy Filc, Rebecca Gallager, Josh Gamson, Martha Gever, Rachel Grob, Mark Halling, Dan Hood, Robin Isserles, Marcia Jacobs, Lynn Keslar, Bill Kornblum, Cary LaCheen, Matthew Lindholm, Mike Lynch, Kelly McKinney, Jill Morawski, Robert Perinbanayagam, Maritsa Poros, Polly Radcliffe, Nikolas Rose, Randi Rosenblum, Rob Sauté, Don Scott, Marvin Scott, Jen Smith-Maguire, Andy Stewart, Evalyn Tenant, Harry Thorne, Shelley Tremain, Alex Vitale, Matthew Weiss, Charles Winick, Mike Wood, and Julia Wrigley. I am also grateful for the support and assistance of my colleagues in the sociology departments at Hunter College and The City College of New York.

I am indebted to my editor, Richard Morrison, at the University of Minnesota Press, for his extraordinarily thoughtful and intelligent guidance. Many thanks also to Tammy Zambo for her remarkable work on the manuscript and to Adam Brunner for sorting out some of the technical problems. I benefited greatly from the very constructive comments and criticisms made by the reviewers for the Press.

I am grateful to the administrators at the agency where I conducted this research. I was fortunate to find such intellectual openness and trust in me as a researcher. Above all, I reserve my deepest gratitude for the residents and staff at Driggs House, who welcomed me into their work. And, of course, boundless thanks to my family—John, Jeralyn, Jeremy, Simone, Helene, and Robert—for their love and support.

INTRODUCTION

Welcome to Driggs House

DRIGGS HOUSE IS A LARGE APARTMENT in a modest building on a quiet side street near a busy commercial area in one of New York City's outer boroughs. Driggs House has fifteen residents and is categorized as a community residence (CR), which specifies the number of residents, staffing patterns, staff-resident ratios, and on-site services (14 N.Y.C.R.R. § 686.3).[1] For the most part, CR residents are able to come and go without supervision, and there are fewer program requirements for a CR than for the kind of group home just prior to it on the continuum of services, an intermediate-care facility (ICF). ICFs have a larger staff and more intensive programming, because residents presumably require more supervision and assistance.

At Driggs House, space can sometimes be tight, but its routine negotiation, especially in the common areas, is generally taken for granted and not perceived as a limitation of the group home setting itself. There is no doubt, however, that the size and layout—with the living room at one end and the staff office at the other—contributes to the bustle and energy of the place in the evenings, when nearly everybody is home and the residence is going full steam. In addition to the living room, dining room, and kitchen, the staff work areas—the medication, staff, and supervisor's offices—also variously serve as common areas. The staff office, just across from the front door, is the administrative heart of the group home and serves as the base and gathering place for counselors over the course of a shift. It is also a prime social gathering place for residents. People are always coming and going. Residents and counselors sit at or on the long desk that lines the left wall or just opposite, on a low cabinet next to the large bookcases, chatting, talking on the phone, or looking at the paper. Depending on the time of day, one can easily find a mix of people and activities there: staff doing paperwork or sending a fax; residents, alone or alongside a counselor, preparing a weekly budget; and people discussing group home business or just hanging out.

Every room serves multiple purposes, and in the evening there is constant movement as residents and counselors go about their routines. There is no spot at Driggs House which does not sometimes function as a venue for work. The medication office is a small room next to the staff office and contains the regulation locked medicine cabinet, a chair and small desk, a low file cabinet, and mounted shelves. Its size makes it less amenable to the routine comings and goings that turn the staff office into a social hub. When not in its specified use, however, the "med room" offers a place with fewer interruptions: counselors catch up on paperwork there or hold small meetings and counseling sessions that require privacy.

The living room is the central social gathering place for everyone as well as a place where matters of work are continuously and variously addressed: in the residents' discussion of group home operations, in the routine interventions of counselors, and in the ongoing negotiation of schedules. On Monday nights, the residents' meeting makes the living room a formal work setting, if only for an hour or so. The same is true of the small shared bedrooms, which provide residents both a relative haven of privacy and, at times, a setting to work on their goals, alone or with a counselor. Goals, or goal plans, are the clinical plans written for each resident and constitute the heart of the group home's individual work. They identify some aspect of conduct for a resident's modification or cultivation—from toothbrushing to room cleaning to budgeting to problem solving—and specify systematic techniques for both residents and counselors.

Confidentiality Issues in This Research

That the identity of both the agency and individuals must be concealed are the two usual issues of confidentiality in this kind of research, but they are uniquely intertwined in this context. Given the legal history of deinstitutionalization and the establishment of community-based services, intellectual disability is a highly regulated arena, especially in New York State, because of the terms of the Willowbrook Consent Decree. The residents at Driggs House are known within overlapping networks through various sites that involve services as well as vocational and recreational activities. In New York City, the density of services and number of recipients do not appear to reduce the likelihood that individuals are known to staff and fellow recipients at multiple agencies and settings. Individuals who were ever institutionalized anywhere are considered Willowbrook Class members and are protected by additional regulations and monitoring. Though this has changed over the years and is done largely at the agency level and not in the group home, the status of formerly institutionalized residents means they are likely to be known in yet another well-connected network of providers, state officials, and legal advocates. Given these facts, apart from changing names, assuring confidentiality required me to alter, omit, or combine certain personal details, but I have done so only in ways that are inconsequential to the empirical analysis. Finally, the regulations of the New York State Office of Mental Retardation and Developmental Disabilities (OMRDD) allow voluntary agencies latitude in implementing standards of certification and in the structure of reporting. This means that each agency can have its own distinct jargon, job titles, and so on; I use a version of the regulatory language when it differs from the terms used at Driggs House.

Who Are the Residents?

Of the residents of Driggs House, six are women and nine are men. Nine are white, four are African American, and one is Puerto Rican. Five are Jewish; three are Protestants; and one who is Italian American, the Puerto Rican, and one African American are Roman Catholic. The residents come from a variety of class backgrounds, but the majority can be categorized loosely as working middle-class or middle-class. Three are from poor backgrounds (one white, two black); and one white resident is from a wealthy family. These are some of the categories that, for sociologists, organize the world. At Driggs House, however, they do not structure life in any regular observable way. Certainly the cultural diversity of residents—as well as staff—gives the residence the flavor of New York City itself. But in my research, gender, racial/ethnic, and class differences provided only occasional explanations and they were never quite adequate.

Evelyn and Diane were friends, for example, and that they are both black women no doubt had something to do with it. Nevertheless, they also shared interest in the same weekday program, a fondness for music, and an attachment to their portable cassette players. Both were also religious. They were roommates when I began the research but had some sort of falling out and wanted to switch around, which was possible because Donna and Ruby were agreeable to switching. The counselors could not figure out why they were not getting along. Evelyn and Diane gave general answers about "being angry with" or "sick of" the other but provided few details. The staff speculated that there was a sexual element to the relationship, but this was not confirmed and, as far as I know, the question was never put directly to either of them. After a few weeks, in any case, though they were no longer roommates, the friendship was repaired, or at least back to normal, as far as anyone could see.

Evelyn, fifty-three years old, was talkative and friendly, and full of enthusiastic greetings. She tried to cheer up people who seemed down, laughing and joking in the office. She had a solitary side, too, and often could be found in the laundry/utility room with her headphones on, gazing out the window, cassette tapes spread out on the top of the storage freezer. When she was upset, there could be fireworks. By contrast, Diane, thirty-nine years old, was reserved, even shy, but usually sweet and obliging. She was not actively social but enjoyed being in the presence of others and would often hang out quietly in the middle of the action, sitting in the living room, headphones on, listening to her cassette player. The personalities of the two women complemented each other. Diane was friendly with other more lively residents, like James, just as Evelyn paid special attention to other shier residents, like Donna.

Very rarely, racial differences were angrily thrown into relief. I am aware of two instances in the thirteen months I spent at Driggs House; both involved conflict between a resident and a counselor. The first time, a substitute counselor (a regular but not permanent member of the staff) who was West Indian crossed Theresa, a sixty-eight-year-old Italian American resident, by pressing everyone to get their evening chores done. Theresa apparently perceived him to be tampering with the evening's natural rhythm and, in this matter, stepping on her turf. Her anger flared and tears flowing, she yelled, "Get off my back, you fuckin' black nigger!" She ran into her room and slammed the door. The second time, Carlos, a regular counselor, was doing room maintenance with Paul, which involved straightening his side of the room and sorting and discarding things he had collected that day. Paul, a sixty-one-year-old Jewish man, detested this daily surveillance, and it often generated conflict. On this particularly stormy evening, he called Carlos a "fat Puerto Rican bastard." Carlos, aged twenty-four, was Paul's primary counselor, and they generally got along quite well. (Each counselor had a caseload of three or so residents for whom he or she was primarily responsible day to day, although all counselors assumed the responsibilities for residents not on their caseload in the absence of the primary counselor.)

These rare incidents indicate how racial difference was made visible in a negative way. The counselors described them as "inappropriate," but there were many things at Driggs House that, in the moment, counselors regarded as inappropriate (a term that meant anything unacceptable, wrong, scandalous, embarrassing, over the line, out of control, and so on). These racial epithets, for the counselors, were evidence not of Theresa and Paul's racism but of their level of anger in these moments. The day after the incident involving Theresa, she agreed with Angela, a morning counselor, that what she had said was hurtful and wrong. However, the bulk of the discussion, held casually in the presence of another counselor and me, was about how to express anger appropriately, an issue on which Theresa had worked for some time and for which she had a behavior plan. It was notable to me that the two residents involved in these incidents were the oldest white residents at Driggs House. Angela was the only one to comment on this, adding casually, with a knowing laugh that indicated her own background, that Theresa's family was "probably as old-fashioned Italian as they come." No one described Theresa and Paul as racist. This may not need to have been said, because there may be a presumption among counselors of certain kinds of racism or racist expression among residents. What also went unsaid, perhaps for the same reason, was that no equivalent incident had ever occurred between counselors and the black or Latin residents or between residents.

Race was observably relevant in a less divisive way for the black women residents and counselors in relation to familiar issues related to hair (Banks; Byrd and Tharps; B. Rothman). In my time at Driggs House, I saw Susan, a thirty-year-old black counselor from Trinidad, often do Diane's, Evelyn's, and Ruby's hair. This was motivated less by cultural affinity than by Susan's effort to save them the cost, especially Diane and Evelyn, who both had longer hair and often wore braids. Susan always did their hair in the staff office; occasionally Ruby, Evelyn, and Diane would do each other's hair in the living room, talking and chatting and watching TV, and it seems that the energy and focus of a beauty shop is generated wherever hair is being done.

At first sight, class background appeared to determine the kind of relationship residents had to their families: families with fewer resources likely had less contact, and those with more resources, perhaps because it might be easier, were more likely to have a sustained relationship with an adult child or sibling living in the group home. Chris, aged forty-eight, who is white, and James, aged thirty, who is black, had no family contact, and their poor backgrounds no doubt contributed, if in different ways, to the same experience for both men. Chris was physically and mentally abused as a child in his rural home and was placed in a state institution from which he was released in the mid-1970s. Neither Chris nor the staff were aware of whether any members of his family were even alive. James had grown up in a New York City housing project, living at home with his parents. In his early twenties, he was living alone with his mother when she died suddenly. The exact story of his family, his mother's death, and his placement in residential services was unclear. He had no contact with his father and older brother, neither of whom was involved in finding him residential services or ever made any contact. For his part, James did not actually want to see them and had refused offers from staff to try to locate them. By contrast, Kenneth, thirty-seven years old, who is from a middle-class family (his late father was a manufacturing supervisor), regularly spent Jewish holidays with his widowed mother, who still lived in the apartment where Kenneth grew up. The same was true for Diane, who frequently visited her aging mother, a retired schoolteacher, and always attended family gatherings.

Yet the association between class background and family contact was not consistent. Jennifer, aged forty-six, moved into the group home at age thirty, when her father died (her mother had died years earlier). Raised in a well-to-do Jewish family in Manhattan, she had infrequent contact with her brother and an aging aunt, and would have liked more. Johnny, twenty-nine years old, moved into Driggs House at twenty-seven, when his parents became too ill to keep him at home; they both died within the next year or so (only shortly before I began the research). Johnny is from a struggling working-class Puerto Rican family and spent many weekends and holidays at the home of his sister, brother-in-law, and young nephews.

The age range among residents is great—from twenty-three to sixty-eight—but age also did not appear to determine relationships between people at Driggs House. The exceptions were Theresa and Paul, who moved to lighter weekday program schedules, but this reflects the way age is becoming a factor in services. For younger residents, institutionalization or the prospect of it was not a factor growing up. Ruby, aged twenty-three, is the only resident under thirty. Like the residents in their thirties and forties (Johnny, Kenneth, James, Diane, Evan, aged forty-three, Marty, aged thirty-six, and Jennifer), Ruby had grown up at home and attended public school. Although it was only in 1975 that the federal Education for All Handicapped Children Act (Public Law 94-142) mandated "mainstreamed" special education in public schools, in many states such programs were already in place when the older residents attended school. The age at which each moved into residential services (at Driggs House or elsewhere) depended on varying circumstances. This group, all in all, came of age in an era when attitudes toward intellectual disability and services were changing. Even so, in the group home generational experience does not distinguish in any social way these residents from the older ones, even those who had been institutionalized.

It happens that most of the older residents at Driggs House also grew up at home, even those few who ended up living for a time in a state institution. This may be one indication of the role that class played earlier in their lives. Then again, as James Trent suggests, after World War II the swelling institutional population in America can be attributed in part to the greater number of middle- and upper-middle-class families willing to place their children in institutions. Nevertheless, it is important to remember that even during periods when institutions dominated the perception and treatment of disability, the majority of people who could be considered disabled by current professional standards actually remained at home and in their communities (Brockley 1999). In the 1950s and 1960s, though placement was the recommended course of action for a child with a disability, children who had physical disabilities were identified and therefore often placed earlier than those with intellectual disabilities. This possibly explains why Irving, who wears leg braces, was institutionalized as a very young child. Chris was the only other resident of Driggs House who had been institutionalized as a child, at about the age of eight. Given what was known about his background, the staff speculated that he was likely removed from his parents' care by the state. Paul, Theresa, and David, aged fifty-nine, were all raised at home. Theresa and David, however, were institutionalized as young adults when their parents died in the 1960s. Remaining family members (adult siblings in both cases) saw the institution as a viable option because there were no alternatives; they did not take them in for whatever reason—resources, shame, indifference, or, however unlikely, therapeutic concerns.

Moving out of the family home as an adult and into community residential services was the most common experience of residents at Driggs House. Paul lived with his widowed mother until her death, in the late 1970s, at which time he moved into the newly opened Driggs House. For Ruby's and Kenneth's families, despite the fifteen years' difference in their ages, the explanation they provided was that it would be infantilizing to remain at home after a certain age and would make their own aging more difficult. They both moved to Driggs House in their early twenties, because it was important for them to "move on." In this way, access to residential community services defines for some how adulthood can be envisioned. A number of others moved into residential services from their family homes even later in life, in some cases because they wanted to and in others because families could no longer keep them at home for reasons of age or illness. Diane, Donna, aged fifty-four, Evan, aged forty-three, Evelyn, and Jennifer were all raised with their families, but changes in the household played some role in the decision to place them.

And the Counselors?

The counselors also reflect the diversity of New York's racial and ethnic communities. Of the main counselors and staff, four are West Indian, and all the rest are American-born: four Protestant whites, two African Americans, two Jews, two Puerto Ricans, and one each Greek, Italian, Dominican, and Indian. Seventy-five percent are women; all are from working- or middle-class backgrounds; and all but three have bachelor's degrees or are attending college part-time, some the first members of their families to do so. Of the ten main counselors, five are in their early twenties, three are in their late twenties and early thirties, and two are in their midforties.[2] Sonia, the supervisor at Driggs House, is

Puerto Rican; her boss, Mike, the regional supervisor, is Irish American; and Beth, the nurse, is Jewish. All were born and raised in New York. The gender ratio, age distribution, and class background of the Driggs House staff and counselors are consistent with the demographics of the direct-care workforce in the United States (Hewitt and Larson, Jaskulski and Ebenstein). That half of the counselors are in their early twenties and about one-third in their early thirties reflects that the counselor position is considered an entry-level direct-care job. Eight of the ten are decided about pursuing a career in social services: Susan is attending a master's program in social work part-time, and two are planning to pursue master's degrees in social work or psychology. The counselor position is also regarded as having potential for advancement, and many voluntary agencies encourage promotion from within to contend with the problem of retention and recruitment that is characteristic of the direct-care workforce in the United States. Though these problems tend to be more serious with personal care and home service positions (such as providing assistance with eating, washing, toileting, and dressing), retention is always an issue in residential services (Hewitt and Larson; Light).

As with the residents, neither class nor racial or ethnic background structures the counselors' relationships with each other or with the supervisors in any obvious way. Age plays an interesting but minor role, in that the supervisors and nurse are in their late forties and fifties. This highlights their seniority but surely is not unique to Driggs House. The two counselors in their forties in some ways have different orientations to the work than do their younger colleagues. Angela has worked at Driggs House for eight years and is married with teenage children, so the morning schedule suits her family life. Daniel, who is also married with teenagers, formerly worked in several other fields, mostly involving business or sales, and said that he "wanted to make a change and . . . do something important for once." Daniel's age occasionally formed the basis for his understanding of how to deal with residents and, at times, justified his taking on an informal teaching role with new younger counselors.

Can Difference Be Interesting but Not Relevant?

That sociological categories of difference are eclipsed by the other ways life gets organized at Driggs House seems to me both perfectly sensible and a bit too pat. When I began the research, I did not presume that the conventional sociological categories of difference would be particularly relevant, based on my past work experience in similar settings in New York. Also, I did not presume that the presence of certain differences necessarily had social relevance, however relevant they might be in other contexts.

There was one kind of individual difference that was observably relevant at Driggs House: the complex range of individual competencies among residents. For the counselors, these differences could be clinically relevant and at times shaped the kind of time and attention they devoted to certain residents. There is no point in indicating these differences by listing the specific individual features that ostensibly warranted residents' placement at Driggs House or the unique aspects of their personalities that frustrated, annoyed, or endeared them to counselors. For more than fifty years, research has demonstrated that professional categories of disability emphasize deficits rather than capacities and preclude recognition of certain kinds of competence at the expense of others. The situated capacities of individual residents, which interested me, are not to be found in the pathology orientation of the records in the staff office. I treat these differences as the observable object and outcome of the governing practices that organize life at Driggs House, and it is in this way, in the chapters that follow, that readers will learn about the individuality of residents.

The varied capacities of residents may be clinically and socially relevant to staff, but they are also relevant to residents. Some are regarded as more capable, as "smart"; others are regarded not conversely, as stupid, but in terms of the practical limitations of everyday life. Interestingly, the distinctions recognized by residents are rarely associated with overt exclusion or cliquishness. For example, three residents—Evelyn, Donna, and Diane—were not permitted to leave the residence alone but might go out with a resident who was independent "out in the community," the phrase used to refer to being away from the group home but not at another services setting. All the residents were aware of who might or might not go out in the community on their own. Often this meant that Evelyn, Donna, and Diane were invited by others on their way out for a walk, a coffee, shopping, and so forth.

The shier, more reticent residents were often coaxed into participation or assisted in various ways by residents who were "more capable" insofar as it was defined by the activity or task at hand. Theresa almost always helped Evelyn with her laundry, because Evelyn was vexed by the machines. James might remember on his way out the door that Donna probably wanted to "go down for coffee," too, and went to find her. Chris offered to assist Diane when he saw her trying to fix her cassette player. If they were going out, Chris, James, Theresa, Ruby, and Jennifer would often pick up a magazine for Marty (who was allowed out only with staff), batteries for Evelyn, or a snack for Donna. I do not mean to portray some idealized community characterized by harmony and cooperation. My hunch is that this routine (and, I'd guess, genuine) thoughtfulness reflects residents' recognition of who they are and where they live, a recognition of their lot in life: they're stuck with each other, at least for the time being, so differences in capacity do not, for most residents, produce division or exclusion. The differences are real to many residents in specific ways but do not form the basis of a fixed exclusionary hierarchy. Perhaps it is the very diversity of Driggs House, in the more conventional sense, that makes these differences less relevant than they might be elsewhere.

Those residents who were naturally reserved stuck more to themselves but might be amenable to joining in, whether going on organized outings or just chitchatting in the house. Jennifer and Irving, however, chose to keep to themselves most of the time. At times, this was because they did see differences in capacity as socially significant and as evidence that they shouldn't be in the group home. At other times, it was expressed simply as a matter of fact. In any case, I never observed them making such distinctions with other residents in any systematic way. Once Jennifer and I were talking about an argument that had occurred at a residents' meeting, and she quickly dismissed its significance by exclaiming, "Look at these people here. What do you expect?" By the same token, though Jennifer was regarded as terribly irascible, she was also known as "smart," and residents often asked for her assistance. If she couldn't provide an answer, she often made a skillful referral to someone else, either a counselor or a resident who she judged could handle the problem.

Jennifer was one of three residents with her own room and spent a good deal of time there alone with the door locked, listening to music, watching television, or looking at magazines and old photos. Theresa and Irving also had rooms of their own. Irving, too, spent much of his time alone in his room or hanging out with Ruby. He was explicit with me about the "level" of most of the other residents and pointedly refrained from participating in most all social activities, even watching television in the living room. He was quite involved in the residence, however, and ruffled feathers at times by giving unwelcome advice and instruction to others. Irving resented living there, something that he related to his experience of institutionalization, but he recognized frankly, at least in our conversations, that there were no real alternatives. The counselors, however, accounted for his resentment as a problem of denial—his refusing to accept that "he's here for a reason, he's disabled"—and occasionally they expressed this view to Irving outright.

Though sociology's usual explanatory suspects may not be all that helpful for my questions about how resolving the ongoing practical dilemma of freedom organizes life at Driggs House, it is undoubtedly true that the racial/ethnic traditions represented, as well as the personal style of individuals, give the place its particular flavor. Chris spent a lot of time in the dining room listening to the radio or cassette player and working on his craft projects. Although the radio was in a common space and anyone might turn it on if Chris wasn't around, it was his radio and when he was around he controlled it. James was known for his knowledge of music, especially disco and funk, and had an impressive collection of cassette tapes, which Chris would sometimes ask him to haul out of his room. The two of them would sit together and play the tapes some evenings and weekend afternoons, not talking much more than was required for deciding on the next selection.

In a similar, if less collaborative, way, Paul's love of short movie serials from the 1930s and 1940s meant that *Flash Gordon* and *Tom Mix* were often playing on the living room television. He owned a sizable collection of videotapes and also regularly borrowed them from the library. Though his unflagging determination to get one of his videos into the machine would elicit occasional outcries from others in the living room, many of us pretty regularly watched with him. Westerns were his favorite, and he was often costumed in cowboy hat and vest, six-shooter at the ready. Any given video was always accompanied by his running commentary about the characters, the action, and sometimes the history of the series. It was soon a regular joke that when Paul's narration promised to give away the story before it unfolded on the screen, I would put my fingers in my ears and sing.

Not everyone appreciated the aesthetic of Paul's cherished videos. Residents had their own powerful memories of time and place, exemplified by James's pleasure in popular music from the 1970s. Though these memories sometimes invoked nostalgia for a past gone, they were not what Goffman called "sad tales," because they were never explicitly about what and who the residents once were or really could be. Jennifer was fascinated with the Kennedy family and had numerous books about them, as well as old magazines, most with Jacqueline on the cover. In addition to other childhood memories of the 1960s, a time which she emphasized was before her mother's death from cancer, she had vivid memories of the president's assassination. Her father, who died much later, was apparently a Republican, but the television vigil following the president's death was seared in her memory, as is true for so many families. Jennifer's keen interest in the Kennedys also had to do with the family's connection to mental retardation. My time at Driggs House was during President Clinton's second term, and Jennifer was well aware of the tribulations at the White House. She watched the news and looked at the newspapers around the staff office, and though she did not (and perhaps could not) follow the issues in detail, her convictions were clear. One evening when she and I were talking together in the living room, the Clintons appeared on television. Jennifer interrupted our conversation to declare, "I hate them." When I asked why, she did not refer to the then-current scandal about Monica Lewinsky (though Jennifer regarded that matter as wholly unsavory), but said, "They don't care about the retarded. They've never had any retarded people at the White House."

Music, movies, politics, religion. For Diane and Evelyn, attending church together was a sustained aspect of their friendship. What being religious meant, however, was a practical matter at Driggs House, as it is everywhere. For Diane, who was Catholic, it meant 5 p.m. Mass every Sunday at the church down the block. Because it was so close and attending was so important to her, the church was the one place where she had been "travel trained" to go on her own. She rarely had to go alone, however, because Evelyn had a standing invitation and most often went too. For Evelyn, however, being religious meant largely the experience of her late father's evangelical ministry. Evelyn could often transform herself into a preacher and the staff office into a revival meeting, largely for laughs and the warmth of it. If a bunch of us were hanging out there, with only the slightest encouragement she'd distribute blessings, sing hymns, and lay hands on her impromptu congregation, joyful and laughing all the while. I asked Evelyn once what it was like going to Mass and whether it was different from her father's church. "Oh, I know," she said with a wave of her hand, "no talking, no screaming, no saying anything!" Sonia, the supervisor, had told me that during the first Mass Evelyn attended, her ecstatic inclinations earned her a friendly chat with the priest, apparently a kind man who already knew Diane and was aware the women lived at Driggs House.

One late Sunday afternoon in summer, I was in the office chatting with Linda, aged twenty-seven, a New York Puerto Rican woman who is a regular weekend counselor, when the front door of the residence burst open. Evelyn and Diane were home from church. Evelyn rushed into the office first, full of questions that were difficult to understand in her energetic excitement. Linda said, "Slow down so we can hear you!" When she extended her hand to indicate the chair, Evelyn promptly deposited into it the source of her agitated curiosity: the host. Linda froze. The exchange continued:

LINDA: Why do you have this?
EVELYN: He gave it to me? What is it?
LINDA: Why didn't you eat it?
EVELYN: I didn't know what it was.

The pink wafer rested gently on Linda's upturned palm. Flustered, she looked down at the wastebasket and then over at me, and gestured.

LINDA: Please get rid of this. Dispose of it. I just can't do it. You know . . . it's my religion—
JACK: Yes, of course.
LINDA: I mean, it's, you know, it's—
JACK: I understand. Here, let me take it.

I stood up and removed it from her hand. Linda looked at Evelyn, who was still standing above her.

EVELYN: I didn't know what it was!
LINDA: Why did you take communion? You're not supposed to. Did you ever do that before?
EVELYN: I think?
LINDA: (slightly incredulous): The priest gave it to you? Did he put it in your mouth?
EVELYN: My hand. He gave it to me in my hand.

It was not clear, after all the times Evelyn had attended Mass with Diane, why on that day she was faced with this dilemma. It is possible that Evelyn regularly approached the altar during the call for communion but the priest did not give her the host. Linda speculated that perhaps the regular priest had not officiated, but before she thought to ask, Evelyn and Diane had left the office: Diane apparently unfazed by the sacrilege she had witnessed, and Evelyn apparently satisfied at having discovered what she needed to know about the thing she wouldn't eat. It took Linda a few minutes to recover, and then she said, in surprise at being surprised, "I'm not even religious!"

Movies, music, politics, religion. And, of course, food. The cultural flavor of Driggs House was often literal. Susan prepared an astonishing chicken curry; Angela's manicotti was her Neapolitan-born mother's recipe; and for special occasions Nicky made Greek almond-flour cookies dusted in confectioners' sugar. Eating Nicky's cookies at the holiday party was easy, but pronouncing them required some assistance. Nicky stood like a conductor before a little group of us as we repeated over and over, "Kourambiedes," our mouths full.

I. Locating the Problem

1 INTELLECTUAL DISABILITY

A Brief History

AFTER THE SECOND WORLD WAR, institutionalization was, in effect, the professional consensus about how to deal with people diagnosed with intellectual and other developmental disabilities (such as cerebral palsy). Physicians explained to parents that "nothing could be done" for their disabled children but provide custodial care, which was too great a burden at home and held potentially serious consequences for normal siblings. In many institutions, visits were limited or prohibited for a period following admission so as not to exacerbate the difficulties of adjustment for both patients and families.

Within this context, some parent groups focused on creating a larger role for families in the care of their institutionalized children. Others pressed for expanded special education in schools and social and vocational programs in communities that would enable certain children to grow up at home. In fact, a good deal of the community services that were available in the 1950s were provided by parent-based organizations. The intention was to broaden the repertoire of options, not to encroach on or replace institutions; in fact, these groups largely supported the expansion of institutional resources because of overcrowding and long waiting lists.

These initial postwar efforts to broaden and expand existing services, by 1960, incorporated the aim of reforming conditions in institutions. Parent organizations laid the groundwork for what, within a decade, would emerge as a movement to transform both the nature and location of services. In the 1940s, only occasional but searing professional criticism of institutions gained press attention. Likewise, only a minority of professionals were aligned with parent reform efforts through the 1950s, but this soon changed. By the end of the next

decade, several widely publicized scandals at large state facilities galvanized the movement against the institutions. Popular media gave
unprecedented attention to the abominable conditions, neglect, and
abuse in institutions, portraying them as a fundamental moral failure
of American society.

No scandal symbolized this more, both politically and visually, than
the horrors at the Willowbrook State School in New York City. In January 1972, a staff physician and a social worker were fired, apparently
for their persistent complaints about conditions on the wards and for
effectively organizing the parents of patients to do the same. The day
after they were dismissed, the physician, Mike Wilkins, contacted
someone with whom he had worked at the U.S. Public Health Service
and elsewhere. The former colleague, a lawyer involved with health
advocacy issues, had changed careers: by 1972 Geraldo Rivera was a
television news reporter for New York's ABC affiliate. Wilkins took
Rivera and his film crew into Ward B of Building 6 at Willowbrook,
which contained about eighty children in various states of undress,
some manacled to radiators, some soiled, and some rocking alone in the
middle of the room (Rivera; Rothman and Rothman). The images of
gruesome neglect they recorded were broadcast that evening and immediately picked up by national and international media. This foot-
age had a revelatory impact, decisively shifting the climate of opinion
among the public, professionals, and politicians against the very idea
of institutionalization.

The conditions at Willowbrook and other institutions, in New York
and elsewhere, were not exactly news to parent groups, advocates, and
the growing body of professionals arguing that institutions be closed
and services be provided in the community. The rhetoric of community services had come to dominate policy at a number of levels, and
in some states challenges to institutional authority were already wend-
ing their way through the courts. In New York, the dearth and quality
of services for people with disabilities was an ongoing political problem mired in multiple conflicts over state-federal financing schemes,
turf issues among state agencies, and issues of economic development
at the local and state levels. As Paul Castellani argues, the confused
priorities of New York state officials unwittingly fostered the move
toward a clear anti-institutional agenda among the very parent and
advocacy organizations that had been so willing to work with public
officials for reform. These organizations were well represented on

various state task forces established in the early 1960s to address New York's lack of coordination and future direction of services, as well as the institutional conditions increasingly being called into question across the country. By 1965, it was clear to advocates of people with mental retardation that, despite the rhetoric of community integration, their recommendations had largely been ignored (Castellani). This disappointment resulted in the final disaffection from New York's reform efforts by parent-based groups. Their long-established organizational network was easily mobilized and formed the base of what became the movement to close the institutions for good. In this sense, the shocking exposé of Willowbrook was not so much the cause of changes to come but a catalyst that brought a lingering and complex political problem into the public eye and galvanized the anti-institutional forces already in place (Castellani).

From Schools to Institutions in Nineteenth-Century America

Trent argues that the emergence of large, segregated, custodial institutions in America through the latter half of the nineteenth century had to do with a number of factors both external and internal to the institutions themselves. Their origin was the small, privately run schools opened in the 1830s and 1840s that sought to educate trainable "idiots" and return them to their communities able to be productive members. The founders were effectively reformers who traveled the country promoting establishment of the schools and, in the process, developing new ideas about both education and idiocy. They contributed to a recasting of the problem of idiocy, in part, by distinguishing it from lunacy (Radford; Trent) and, more broadly, by identifying idiocy as an overlooked but widespread problem that extended beyond the responsibility of family and became a proper matter for the state (Trent). These reformers argued that intelligence and the limited capacity to learn were barriers to social adaptation and integration that could be overcome through systematic occupational training and the social learning that only the environment of a school could provide. Such claims echoed European approaches in education, including sign-language training for the deaf and mute and, with idiots, teaching techniques that formed the basis of, and are still used in, what in the twentieth century came to be called special education.

The educational aim to return students to their own communities depended on economic conditions robust enough to absorb them, a lesson learned when the labor market shrank with the economic downturn in the 1850s. The result was a transformation of the schools' initial aim, not only because of limited job opportunities for graduates but also because of the substantial increase in requests by families and local authorities that schools admit their unemployable idiots. The schools began accepting more and more children and young adults with multiple disabilities, and by the Civil War had effectively redefined the educational mission. As the ranks of students swelled, the aim was less and less to return pupils to their communities and more and more to provide a presumably permanent custodial arrangement that would still provide training and social learning but now in the very operation of the expanding and ultimately segregated schools.

In contrast to prior historians of mental retardation, Trent emphasizes that practices which constitute care cannot easily be separated from those which constitute control. The transition of the schools' function to permanent, segregated custody through the end of the nineteenth century is not adequately explained by the idea that idiocy came to be seen as "incurable," nor that its increasing association with danger simply justified growing concern about social containment and control (Trent). The initial educational ideal of self-sufficiency was not simply abandoned but redefined in the schools' adaptation to changing economic and social conditions. Trent argues that what were in large part strategies of institutional survival and growth resulted in a reversal in the educational function of facilities from temporary training to permanent custody. This can be understood broadly as a reversal of means and ends: that institutional work qua training became the end in itself.

The very meaning of productivity changed in relation to the changing character of schools, and this was encouraged by and realized in the architectural model used widely to expand facilities and build new ones. The cottage or colony plan featured large central buildings for administrative offices, an infirmary, laundry, and common rooms, surrounded by landscaped grounds dotted with residential cottages, each of which functioned in essence as a ward. This arrangement was understood to create a microcosm of American society, a self-sufficient social order in which education consisted of working in the various operations that maintained the institution itself. Many had farms, workshops, and other modest commercial enterprises that provided for the school's own needs. Given their increasingly varied ages and kinds of disability, capable inmates worked in the kitchen and laundry, and provided other basic services, including personal and bedside care for those who required it. The use of inmate labor quickly became fundamental to the running of institutions and would prove especially crucial during periods of fiscal constraint, such as the Second World War.

The professionalization of medicine from the middle of the nineteenth century onward was part and parcel of these changes. Disability was one arena in which regular (that is, medically trained) physicians were able to expand the authority of medicine. By the late 1860s, almost all the superintendents of state schools were regular physicians. They justified their role in the adaptation and growth of institutions partly in terms of the complex needs of the rapidly swelling population of multiply disabled children and young adults, and the expansion of extant facilities often involved the incorporation of medical services and staff. This was so despite the marginal influence that medical superintendents of institutions had among their physician colleagues. Like alienists, superintendents were regarded as not strictly medical, given the nature of their patients. Even alienists, however, refused to support the establishment of the Association of Medical Officers of American Institutions for Idiotic and Feebleminded Persons (AOM), in 1876. Nonetheless, the lunatic asylum provided a model for the emerging institutions, and, through the 1850s, the educational goals of the earlier schools were largely supplanted by medical concerns with pathology, typology, and degeneracy. The idea that idiots were incurable actually reinforced rather than undermined medicine's expanding authority. Because idiots were increasingly seen as victims of modern life (Foster; Trent; Radford), John Radford (13) suggests that the very idea of incurability posed a challenge to the "curious mixture of optimism and hopelessness" that characterized the particular enlightenment ethos of the late nineteenth century. Trent argues that the new definitions of education, training, and productivity were reconciled in part by the fit between the custody function of the asylum model and incurability as a medical problem. This in turn reinforced the claim that incurability posed a serious social problem for which the institutions were a solution.

Fundamental to the medicalization of disability—and to the broader cultural consequences of the professionalization of medicine—was the concern to develop new, more refined yet encompassing diagnostic categories (Tyor and Bell; Foster). The focus on classification was spurred on by institutional expansion (Tyor and Bell), and the architecture of the cottage model encouraged the differentiation and refinement of types—of persons by diagnostic grade, of specialized wards, of tasks and work assignments (Trent). What had long been known as idiocy was incorporated into "feeblemindedness," a broader category not just derived from but central to the evolutionary logic of emerging fields such as hereditarianism and eugenics. These scientific approaches reinforced the legitimacy of medical authority and provided a basis for recasting disability as a new kind of social problem, one understood in relation to the predominant concern with typology and classification (Foster). The superintendents contributed to public fear of the feebleminded and portrayed institutions as a medical solution to a vast new social problem, though what they described as treatment amounted simply to containment (Trent). In the 1870s, along with the AOM, the Conference on Charity and Corrections promoted the idea that social degeneracy, moral depravity, and criminality made feeblemindedness a serious and widespread problem, especially in relation to a host of other threats to social order (Trent; cf. Gelb 1995). Such claims were compelling in the context of the anti-immigrant and nativist movements that thrived in the economically turbulent last few decades of the nineteenth century. In Reconstruction, increased government funding was a factor in the initial growth of the schools and in the transformation of their mission. Even the rapid dwindling of this support, however, did not deter the proliferation of institutions, partly because of the growing fear of the feebleminded and partly because of the substantial resources institutions were extracting from the labor of their own inmates. By century's end, all types of feebleminded were regarded as beyond trainable, and between 1876 and 1890 the institutionalized population in the United States tripled (Trent, 9).

The Twentieth-Century Sciences of Danger and Progress

The advent of mental testing at the turn of the twentieth century reinforced the association between intelligence and moral degeneracy in the idea of mental defect. "Mental deficiency" became the broad diagnostic category—and an ostensibly more suitable, scientific one than "feeblemindedness"—and captured starkly the notion of absence, of lack, of mental *and* moral incapacity, that characterized the period in which disability was perceived most acutely as a social threat. When the AOM became the American Association of Mental Deficiency (AAMD), in 1910, it established a new classification of "mental age" based on IQ score. The new, objective measure provided a resource in the continued effort to demonstrate that feeblemindedness was a more widespread social problem than people realized. However, the rapid proliferation of such techniques in the second decade of the twentieth century also provided a scientific basis for the mental hygiene movement's ideas about the role of education in the community. By the 1920s, the influence of hereditarian and eugenic perspectives was on the wane (despite their prominent place in emerging movements of European fascism), this time because of a growing emphasis on social adjustment and adaptation. The developmental and moral importance of community integration, as well as the establishment of the first special education classes in public schools, reflected the economic flush and technocratic optimism of the period. The institutional population declined, and the rate of admissions slowed. It wasn't long before economic depression again eclipsed the policy focus on community adjustment, but some parents and professionals never abandoned its aims.

Nonetheless, after the Second World War, institutions once again dominated the landscape of mental deficiency in America. As in the 1860s and 1870s, the successful expansion of institutions in the late 1940s and 1950s reflected changing and "mutually profitable" relationships between the state and those professional fields competing in this arena (Foster, 16). Psychology and education had gained a substantial foothold in mental deficiency through the 1920s, but medicine—in the form of psychiatry in the late 1940s—retained the position it had held more or less since the 1860s. Soon, however, medicine would lose its dominant position in the field to psychology. Psychology's growing influence through the 1950s was evident in the increasing emphasis on behavior. When "mental deficiency" became "mental retardation," in 1959, the change in nomenclature was in part a strategy to address the issues of confusion and credibility that arise when technical terms become schoolyard epithets. But the adoption of "mental retardation" was also the mark of psychology's success: by 1960, psychologists and educators made up 60 percent of the membership of the American Association of Mental Deficiency (Trent, 244). The new term involved an important expansion of the diagnostic classification itself: mental retardation required a behavioral assessment in addition to the IQ score, which had been the sole basis of diagnosis for decades. The incorporation of "adaptive behavior" reflected a recognition that previous classifications had largely ignored the influence not only of setting but also of individual variation and development.

With mental retardation, the incorporation of a behavioral assessment elevated the diagnostic importance of the qualitative experience and capacities of individuals. The irony, as Trent points out (238), is that institutionalization expanded rapidly after 1950 despite the agenda to include a behavioral component and the presence of parent groups that sought to raise their children at home. By 1970, "75 percent of the public facilities housing mentally retarded people had been built after 1950." In part this reflects the effectiveness of the claims of medical authority in the postwar period and the entrenchment of the standard recommendation to institutionalize disabled children. As Susan Bannerman Foster argues, however (13), the institution also "survived by redefining itself." The physician-superintendents "dominated the reform measures" and crafted a different role for the institution by extending it into the community. In this way, institutions became the "locus of control" in relation not only to expanding programs for special education but also to a broader "network of social welfare and mental health systems." These organizational changes increased both the power of the state and professional authority over disability.

Parents, Families, Professionals

By the mid-1940s, the conditions in institutions had started to come under fire for the same reasons that would justify closing them by the early 1970s. As early as the 1940s, searing criticisms of psychiatric institutions as "snake pits" (Ward) and "the shame of the states" (Deutsch) did not overlook the so-called schools for the mentally deficient, and stories echoing these concerns circulated widely in the popular press. Though parent-based groups turned out to be a major force in deinstitutionalization, their postwar agenda was not at odds with institutional care. During this period, parents of institutionalized children pressed for more family involvement, and parent-based groups generally supported expanded resources for institutions as well as a greater range of resources in the community and public schools. A few of these organizations, such as the Association for the Help of Retarded Children (AHRC), established in 1948, were already providing the kind of community socialization programs and vocational training that they thought warranted greater state support. In addition, a growing number of popular accounts of disability (some in well-known families), such as books by Pearl Buck (1950) and Dale Evans Rogers (1953), personalized the issue. In retrospect, Trent (238) argues, the popular literature and parent associations helped families rationalize the institution as an option, because there was "no shame in placing a retarded child in a public facility." He suggests that one reason the institutional population swelled in the mid-1950s was the inclusion of children from more well-off families for the first time since before the First World War.

At the same time, the personalizing of disability experience in the 1950s also contributed to growing criticisms of professional authority and the role of institutions. Dale Evans Rogers's 1953 book, *Angel Unaware*, largely about the experience she and Roy Rogers had at home with their daughter with Down syndrome until she died at age two, was also an account of their refusal to follow the medical recommendation to institutionalize her. The book was reissued ten years later (with an introduction by Norman Vincent Peale), just as community care was being established as a national political issue.

Some experts on mental retardation expressed concerns not only about the conditions in institutions but also about the moral justification for such facilities, and they advocated anew for a focus on adjustment and community integration. John Kennedy's election to the presidency promised attention to a problem that had barely been on the radar of mental health professionals and policy makers. Edward Berkowitz suggests that the Kennedy family's personal concern played a major role in making mental retardation a national issue. Their efforts were motivated and styled in part on earlier examples in which greater public awareness of conditions resulted from the personal experience of the famous, notably Franklin Roosevelt's initiatives with polio. Mental retardation was made a focus during Kennedy's presidential campaign, spearheaded by the candidate's sister Eunice Shriver, who continued to work closely with executive initiatives on the issue after the election. The president defined mental retardation as a matter of national political import and in October 1961 convened the Task Force on Mental Retardation, in which Shriver was a highly involved member. It was additionally composed of prominent experts in the field and a few supportive legislators, some of whom had children with mental retardation. The task force's criticisms of institutions were based on arguments about cultural deprivation, on the one hand, and civil rights, on the other, and the final report, issued in October 1962, strongly recommended support for community-based services in lieu of institutionalization (Berkowitz).

It was no accident that, just weeks before the report was released, an article by Shriver entitled "Hope for Retarded Children" appeared in the *Saturday Evening Post*. In the article, she disclosed the truth about Rosemary, the Kennedys' mentally retarded sister, who had been the subject of public speculation through the 1950s, especially during John's political campaigns. The press had uncovered, and the family had circulated, various stories accounting for Rosemary's absence from the highly visible Kennedy family (Shorter). Shriver used the story of the family's experience with Rosemary to describe educational and vocational approaches and to champion the expansion of "sheltered workshops," which provided employment in conjunction with private industry. According to Shriver, her sister had lived at home happily until her teens, when she began to recognize that she was not doing the same things as her older siblings and was treated differently, especially outside the family. Echoing the reformers who founded schools for idiots in the 1830s and 1840s, Shriver's article is indicative of the way parent groups and other advocates drew attention to mental retardation by defining it as a social problem that warranted the country's attention. "We are just coming out of the dark ages," she wrote, "in our handling of this serious national problem" (72).

That the president's own sister was mentally retarded meant that any family could be affected. Institutionalization, Shriver argued, only reinforces commonly held prejudices. Notwithstanding her rhetoric of progress, one problem Shriver faced was central also for the educational reformers of the 1830s and 1840s: distinguishing mental retardation from mental illness. This was seen as a major hurdle and, for the task force, was a main concern. Addressing the moral failure of institutions was also an important part of the campaign to accept mentally retarded people for who they were. Shriver used her own family's dilemma to describe institutions as brutal anachronisms in the modern world. Rosemary was institutionalized in her early twenties, when the family decided she could no longer live at home. "It fills me with sadness," Shriver wrote, "to think this . . . might have been unnecessary if we knew then what we know today" (72–74). Eventually Rosemary was moved to a facility that emphasized "rehabilitation rather than indefinite confinement." This contrast between educational potential and mere custody was not Shriver's only criticism. What we know now about mental retardation means that "there is no excuse for these people having to live neglected lives in dark garrets and medieval institutions which are hangovers from yesteryear." Although "the public and the governments they support are slowly wakening to the needs of the retarded . . . less is being done for them at the community level than for any other afflicted group."

In the president's 1963 report to the Congress, he looked ahead to a time when "reliance on the cold mercy of custodial isolation will be supplanted by the open warmth of community concern and capability" (quoted in Berkowitz, 134). The recommendations in the report stirred turf conflicts among federal agencies and other problems with the states (Berkowitz). As had happened a century earlier, federal funds for constructing institutions were not followed in the 1960s by support for upkeep, which was left to the states. The result was the deterioration of already terrible conditions, which by decade's end contributed to the mounting criticism. What had started earlier among parents and some professionals as a call for institutional reform became a charge "that no innovation could alter the fundamentally custodial and abusive nature of these facilities" (Foster, 13). Through the 1960s, the movement for deinstitutionalization gathered steam in the context of momentous organizing for civil rights, challenges to the authority of expertise in a range of areas, and the emergence of intellectual trends that made social analysis central to political and cultural transformation.

The Social Character of Competence

The goals of community adjustment and integration that had been revived during the 1920s may have been difficult to pursue, given changing economic and political priorities through the Depression and war, but they remained important concerns for parent-based groups and for some professionals working in mental deficiency. Actually, the role of social context and the nature of professional authority emerged after the war in criticism across fields. Within psychiatry, for example, the therapeutic community approach emphasized social setting and interaction, arguing for the clinical value of democratic participation in treatment and equality between hospitalized patients and medical staff (Jones 1953). R. D. Laing (1959), David Cooper (1967), and the antipsychiatry movement argued that mental illness was not merely an individual but a social affliction born of the intense alienation of modern life and family. Thomas Szasz (1960, 1963) called into question what he argued was the extraordinary authority accorded psychiatry, given its questionable scientific basis and negligible clinical efficacy.

Sociologists also produced studies of hospitals and mental institutions that showed how organizational demands shaped professional goals and practice (Goffman 1961; Roth 1963; Stanton and Schwartz 1954). From differing historical perspectives, Michel Foucault (1965) and David Rothman (1971) traced the emergence and character of various kinds of institutions not merely as features of developing professional fields but in relation to complex social, economic, and cultural dimensions. Goffman's *Asylums* (1961) offered a social rather than psychological account of the self and, in what he identified as a commentary on the organizational character of modern life, demonstrated how the imperatives of institutional control determined the ostensibly professional setting of a large psychiatric hospital. Caplan's *An Approach to Community Mental Health* (1961) argued that community mental health should be at the heart of psychiatry. Published in the same year, Caplan's book and *Asylums* were read widely by policy makers involved in efforts to establish community care.

Into the 1960s, these intellectual trends encompassed both new political and academic approaches to criminality, mental health, homosexuality, race, sex roles, and physical and mental disability. What Howard Becker (1963) called "labeling" shifted sociology's analytic focus away from deviant persons or behaviors and onto the social processes by which deviance was defined and enforced in a wider range of settings. Thomas Scheff (1966) argued that psychiatric authority could best be understood as a practice of labeling.

In this context, it is no surprise that the presumably natural character of and relationship between intellectual and social competence would be called into question (Dexter 1964; Edgerton 1993). Robert Edgerton's groundbreaking 1967 book, *The Cloak of Competence* (issued in a revised edition in 1993), was based on a large-scale qualitative study of people who had been tracked from special education classes into institutions and then released as adults during the 1950s.

Edgerton found that these people were as capable of living independently as others with the same socioeconomic indicators, though they
depended on certain kinds of assistance from intimates. He referred to
a "cloak" of competence because the subjects underplayed or aimed
to conceal various strategies and the crucial assistance of spouses,
friends, or siblings. Edgerton was later criticized for not adequately
questioning the diagnosis itself and for questioning the veracity of his
own subjects' accounts (Bogdan and Taylor 1982). Though Edgerton
emphasized the concealment rather than the social competence that
such strategies represent, his analysis helped put the social character
of mental retardation on a broader intellectual map.

     Questions about the situated and social character of competence
were not limited to the everyday life of pathologically defined groups
but extended to that of professionals as well. Influential books by Braginsky and Braginsky (1971) and Mercer (1973) underscored the fundamental injustice of institutionalization by challenging the very category
of mental retardation. This research, along with Edgerton's, did in the
arena of mental retardation what others had been doing in the critical study of deviance generally: showing how many things taken for
granted as identifiable features of individuals were actually contingent on specific social and institutional settings. Braginsky and Braginsky's comparative study of children in institutions and in schools
showed that mental retardation was merely "a labeling process . . . a
function of a social order" (29). Given the category's few and unreli-
able biological features, they argued, mental retardation was made
"objective" through the "mythical power" of mental testing, which
experts "refuse to reject" (14). Mental retardation was nothing more
than a "crude metaphor" that served the single purpose of justify-
ing incarceration (29). Mercer also demonstrated substantial limits to
the validity of mental testing and, though she was more circumspect
about the category of mental retardation, criticized the use of a statistical conception of normal to explain biological difference. She also
studied children in an institution and in the community, contrasting
these clinical and social "systems" to show that mental retardation is
an "achieved status," describing behavioral differences as features of
each system to demonstrate that the constitution of normal "depends
on system specific role performance, conformity and expectations" (22).

     In 1959, the incorporation of adaptive behavior in the new classifi-
cation, "mental retardation," marked the beginning of a trend that

continues today toward greater emphasis on qualitative, contextual, and individualized assessment and services. The incorporation of behavior in the new diagnosis was motivated by "the variability in everyday functioning of retarded persons of the same mental age or IQ" and the realization that, because an individual's score could change, "it became obvious that IQ was not immutable" (Grossman, 10). Ironically, along with adding adaptive behavior, the AAMD increased the IQ threshold for diagnosis from two standard deviations below the mean to one—that is, from a score of roughly 70 to 85 on the most commonly used tests—to create "borderline" mental retardation. The authors of the change were well aware that this "made it possible to include 15 percent of the total United States population in the group identified as retarded" but did not regard it as a "major concern" because the diagnostic process now also required a behavioral assessment (Grossman, 6). Never without controversy, the borderline classification was eliminated in 1973 and the IQ threshold changed back to 70, where it had been for most of the century. In part, this was a recognition of exactly what motivated the new 1959 classification: the limited diagnostic utility of an IQ score. In the context of widespread popular and professional criticism of mental testing, lowering the cut-off score was also a recognition that having a low IQ has less impact on a person's functional capacity than the stigma of being diagnosed. This was not a small matter, because, at the time, 80 percent of people considered to have mental retardation were borderline (Zetlin and Murtaugh).

Despite the entrenched investment certain fields have in psychometric techniques even today, criticisms throughout the 1970s had some impact on how mental testing was used and understood in general. The 1959 classification has remained at the core of all subsequent changes in the official definition of mental retardation, which have elaborated and expanded the importance of qualitative assessment and the contextual character of functioning in relation to quantitative measures. One emphasis in the AAMD's 1983 revision was further standardization of diagnostic practice through increasing the availability of appropriate scales of adaptive functioning across multiple settings, a concern expressed in 1973. Also, the 1983 revision acknowledged the concerns raised by the "large-scale attack on intelligence tests . . . in the 1960s and 1970s" that equated classification with labeling (Grossman, 7). Although this was attributed to "lack of understanding of test construction" by "the lay public as well as users of test results," the authors of the revision advised cautious and informed application of scores. They emphasized that the validity and clinical utility of a score can be assessed only in relationship to other kinds of diagnostic measures and with proper knowledge of the nature of statistical error with particular tests.

The official definition of mental retardation issued in 1992, by what was then called the American Association on Mental Retardation (AAMR), further refined and expanded the diagnostic categories of functioning that were both contextual and individual. In contrast to the explicit qualifications in the 1983 manual about how mental test scores should be applied, in 1992, specific "assumptions . . . essential to the application of the definition" were highlighted alongside the definition (AAMR, 1). These assumptions indicated, further, the trend toward expanding, at the same time, diagnostic refinement and the contextual and individual character of mental retardation. Most notably, the 1992 definition explicitly rejected the "view of mental retardation as an absolute trait expressed solely by an individual" and, in what was described as a "paradigm shift," adopted a view of mental retardation "as an expression of the interaction between the person with limited intellectual functioning and the environment" (AAMR, x). This is in line with what elsewhere has been called a deficit versus a developmental model (Sandieson), which recognizes that with appropriate "supports over a sustained period, the life functioning of the person . . . will generally improve" (AAMR, 1). The trend toward individualization and individual experience is reflected in the recognition that the 1992 definition took into account changing meanings of mental retardation over time and the stigmatizing affect of the diagnosis. The authors noted that they retained the term "mental retardation," despite calls for its elimination by "many individuals with this disability," because of its widespread established use in research and practice. The trend toward both context and individualization was also reflected in the expansion and refinement of categories in 1992: "rather than requiring subclassification into four levels of a person's mental retardation (mild, moderate, severe, and profound), the [1992 diagnostic] system subclassifies the intensities and pattern of support systems into four levels (intermittent, limited, extensive, and pervasive)" (AAMR, x).

The focus on "systems of supports" rather than "services," and on individual needs rather than stock interventions, is considered one of the innovations of the paradigm shift represented by the 1992 manual and developed further in the official definition issued in 2002. Now referring not to "mental retardation" but to "intellectual disability" (since the renaming of the American Association on Intellectual and Developmental Disabilities [AAIDD], in 2007), the 2002 definition is considered current. It reflects the increasing elaboration and development of the issues established by the 1959 classification: the qualitative, context-bound, and individual character of the diagnostic process and of the diagnostic entity itself. This trend began accelerating in the late 1970s but can be illustrated just in the difference between the official definitions issued in 1992 and 2002. From 1992:

> *Mental retardation* refers to substantial limitations in present functioning. It is characterized by significantly subaverage intellectual functioning, existing concurrently with related limitations in two or more of the following applicable adaptive skill areas: communication, self-care, home living, social skills, community use, self-direction, health and safety, functional academics, leisure, and work. Mental retardation manifests before age 18 (AAMR, 1).

The 2002 definition incorporates, among other things, an emphasis on mental retardation as an interactional feature of individuals and environments:

> Mental retardation is a disability characterized by significant limitations both in intellectual functioning and in adaptive behavior as expressed in conceptual, social, and practical adaptive skills. This disability originates before the age of 18. A complete and accurate understanding of mental retardation involves realizing that mental retardation refers to a particular state of functioning that begins in childhood, has many dimensions, and is affected positively by individualized supports. As a model of functioning, it includes the contexts and environment within which the person functions and interacts and requires a multidimensional and ecological approach that reflects the interaction of the individual with the environment, and the outcomes of that interaction with regards to independence, relationships, societal contributions, participation in school and community, and personal well being (AAIDD).

Conclusion

By the time the Willowbrook scandal hit the press, in June 1972, various lay and professional groups were already lined up behind the aim of shutting down institutions and locating services in integrated community settings. The courts proved a crucial resource and, in a judicial climate relatively favorable to civil rights, there were already class-action challenges to institutionalization in a number of states (DiPolito). Legal precedents were unclear during this period, however, and though the distinction was rarely made between settings for mental retardation and mental illness, case law was used interchangeably in major decisions related to institutions and involuntary confinement (Perlin). Various cases laid the groundwork for findings of rights specifically for individuals with mental retardation that were being denied in institutions. Notably among them: in *Wyatt v. Stickney* (1972) the court found that a person had the right to treatment in the least restrictive environment and, in *Pennhurst State School v. Halderman* (1974) that the only justifiable basis for confinement was treatment and habilitation as opposed to custody.

The consensus among families and professionals by the early 1970s was that institutions were inappropriate, both anachronistic and cruel. When *ARC v. Rockefeller,* the class action on behalf of Willowbrook's inmates, was filed, in 1972, New York State mounted what, in effect, was a modest defense focused largely on moving toward the consent decree signed in 1975—not that this process was absent of conflict over strategy among state agencies and over the role of the federal courts (Castellani; Rothman and Rothman). *Wyatt* had established standards for the right to treatment and the provision of normal living environments that influenced the New York decree. Also included was a timetable for closing New York's institutions and the establishment of a separate state agency—which became the Office of Mental Retardation and Developmental Disabilities (OMRDD)—to implement, certify, and monitor standards of services in community settings. In addition to the OMRDD's regulatory safeguards to prevent the emergence of institutional conditions in community settings, the consent decree established an additional surveillance system specifically to monitor and protect the rights of former inmates—Willowbrook Class members—living in the community.

Despite the rapid transformation of policy and services in the late 1970s and early 1980s, especially in New York, this is no simple history of progress. The term "deinstitutionalization," once a watchword of progress, soon developed negative connotations, largely as a result of criticisms that psychiatric facilities at this time released inmates en masse without adequate assistance in communities. Andrew Scull called it "decarceration," arguing that it was largely a fiscal maneuver by the state dressed up in the rhetoric of rights and autonomy. Though the shift toward community for people with intellectual disability has had a different history, even now deinstitutionalization can hardly be considered a settled matter. It is broadly misleading, historically and socially, to frame the story as the simple opposition between institutions and community, however adequate that may be for my purposes. In nineteenth-century America, for example, there was substantial regional variation in the development and role of both the early schools and the later institutions (Noll and Trent). In fact, most people who could have been characterized as disabled at any given historical point actually remained at home or in their local communities (Brockley 1999). Nonetheless, the number who were incarcerated is impressive.

So is the number today, despite what may be considered progress. In 1992, 77,600 people still lived in state institutions in America, a number that was nearly halved by 2004, to 41,214. At the same time, the number living in facilities with six or fewer residents increased from 128,129 in 1992 to 336,073 in 2004 (Braddock et al.). Deinstitutionalization, such as it is, grinds on slowly. And the failed promises of community integration continue to be an important focus of political activism and social research.

Even so, the discovery that people with intellectual disability are citizens has had extraordinary ramifications. Criticisms notwithstanding, the orientation toward community has transformed the arena of intellectual disability not only for former inmates but also for many who never lived in institutions. One way this can be seen is in the proliferation of services in the community—of which Driggs House is but one example—that ideally are organized to promote and encourage independence in each individual resident. This is what I mean by "governing" disability. It is what being out in the community requires.

2 GOVERNING DISABILITY IN THE COMMUNITY

The citizen is construed and addressed as a subject actively
engaged in thinking, wanting, feeling and doing, interacting with
others in terms of . . . psychological forces. . . . In the family, the
factory, and the expanding systems of counseling and therapy,
the vocabularies of mental hygiene, group relations, and
psychodynamics are translated into techniques of self-inspection
and self-rectification. These techniques are taught by teachers,
managers, health visitors, social workers, and doctors. Through
the pronouncement of experts in print, on television, in radio
phone-ins, they are woven into the fabric of our everyday
experience, our aspirations and dissatisfactions. Through our
attachment to such technologies of the self, we are governed by
our active engagement in the search for a form of existence that is
at once personally fulfilling and beneficial to our families, our
communities, and the collective well-being of the nation.

—Nikolas Rose, *Inventing Ourselves*

ON MORAL GROUNDS THERE WAS NO DEBATE—especially after
Willowbrook—that abuse and coercion were integral to institutions
for people with intellectual disability. As a legal matter, too, there
was little argument that the rights of inmates were being violated in
the most fundamental and egregious ways. This emerging consensus
accounts for the readiness of New York and some other states to sign
consent decrees. Apart from the honorable goals they laid out, such
decrees avoided costly legal proceedings the states would have had to
mount on indefensible positions. But the transformed climate of opinion is one thing. It is quite another matter to accomplish the actual
task of providing services in the community, supervising individuals
who are free but considered incapable of living independently.

Group homes in principle are no different from other settings that aim to mobilize individuals to act freely for themselves in specific ways. This is what Foucault (1991) called the "government" of conduct and argued was the defining strategy of ruling in liberal societies. I use the term "liberal" in the broad classical sense, to refer to liberal individualism and the form of rule in which authority, for the most part, is exercised indirectly and depends on the consent and participation of the governed. Many writers now use "neoliberal" to emphasize the increasing role and changing forms of individuality in policy, politics, and culture over the last three decades. The term "liberal" is adequate here, because my purpose does not require a comprehensive theoretical and historical account of these issues. My aim is to demonstrate some of the situated and practical ways they are realized in and organize a specific group home. Similarly, I do not take up debates about the meaning of concepts such as rights, freedom, and liberty, but use them in the general sense. This is how such concepts are used both as legislative and regulatory ideals and in the course of everyday life at Driggs House.

Although group homes are often portrayed as an exception to a liberal form of rule, ideally they are an organizational realization of the problem and strategy of rule that defines liberal societies. Like most professional settings, Driggs House is organized by the tension between authority and the freedom of individuals inherent in liberal societies. This ongoing tension is managed—and *must* be managed—by enabling individuals to govern themselves. The very notion of providing services to citizens in the community presumes that even those whose capacity for freedom is always in question are somehow able to govern themselves.

In this sense, the question of citizenship, for me, is practical rather than theoretical. Other writers draw on the theoretical literature about social citizenship to address intellectual disability (Barnes), use disability to highlight the conceptual limits in the literature and problems of policy (Rummery), or examine the relationship between forms of citizenship and social movements (Barnes and Oliver; Beckett). I rely on the concept of government, because it encourages a focus on practice. Government, in this sense, does not refer to liberalism as a political program or theory of the state. It is a "rationality" posed by the dilemmas of liberal forms of ruling between the liberty of the individual citizen and the legitimate boundaries of state authority (Rose 1998a, 1999b). Having recourse to direct coercion only in specific situations, authority is exercised indirectly for the most part, and the practical resolution of this dilemma is the measure of its legitimacy. Government also does not refer just to the activities of the state, because the modern liberal state itself took form historically in relation to the range of new problems and interventions that defined its purview in the late eighteenth and the nineteenth centuries (Dean 1999; Dean and Hindess; Foucault 1991; Gordon; Hindess 1996; Rose 1999b). The development of statistics, for example, was a necessary condition for the development of the modern state, among other things enabling population to be conceived as a definable, measurable object that could be monitored, managed, and improved (Foucault 1991; Hacking 1990; Rose 1999b). That population came to be understood as an object of knowledge and intervention did not imply a need for uniformity of individual conduct. On the contrary, the governing of populations depends on the individuality of individuals (G. Burchell). It may be that the comprehensive, precise disciplining of docile bodies in prisons or the military is considered one of modernity's historical signatures, but the "total institution"—and on this point Goffman and Foucault agreed—has furnished only a limited metaphor for the nature of authority and control in twentieth-century life.

The aim of governing is not to achieve total regulation but to structure the possibilities for action; to create conditions in which individuals may conduct themselves freely in particular ways. Human conduct, in this sense, is thought of "as a resource" that must be both "unlocked" and "harnessed" (Dean 1996, 60–61). Governing involves the systematic attempt to "act on the actions of others," or, in Foucault's concise phrase, the "conduct of conduct" (1991). It is necessary, for this reason, to know and understand the governed, because taking into account their nature and capacity preserves the very autonomy on which effective government depends. Acting effectively on the actions of others occurs through the protection and enhancement of individual health, happiness, and wealth. This is what Foucault called "bio-power," in contrast to forms of ruling that operate coercively by crushing or compromising the aspirations and ideals of individuals. What liberal government presumes is that it is through life's fundamental biological, economic, and psychological processes that individual goals can be aligned with the needs of the community, the nation, and society itself. Governing involves the effort to shape the capacities of individuals to act freely for their own benefit in ways that are also of benefit to all.

As Culturally Normative as Possible

The question of personhood, as both a legal and a cultural status, has defined the dilemma of liberal authority at the heart of community services for individuals with intellectual disability. This dilemma was central to "normalization," which emerged in the early 1970s as the dominant professional perspective. Normalization can be seen as a systematic attempt to synthesize the emerging legal and clinical concepts of personhood. With deep historical roots in moral treatment and community adjustment, normalization provided both a criticism of the institutions—designating them deforming as well as cruel—and a paradigm for services in the community.

In his landmark 1972 book, psychologist Wolf Wolfensberger (1972, 28) described normalization as the "utilization of means which are as culturally normative as possible, in order to establish and/or maintain personal behaviors and characteristics which are as culturally normative as possible." Its implementation through the 1970s generally involved a focus on the individual skills that would enable a person's participation in community life. Trent (264) argues that normalization was widely influential because it provided both an "intellectual rationale [and] a moral grounding" for community integration: normalization incorporated a vision of services that was sociological but also a vision of community defined by the capacity for inclusion rather than fear. Wolfensberger's vision was encompassing (1972, 27): he actually intended normalization to extend "beyond mental retardation to deviancy and human management in general."

However influential, the meaning and implementation of normalization have always been in contention. Many professionals endorsed the approach because of its compelling ideology but criticized its lack of practical, clinical, or administrative plans for service (Brown and Smith; E. Emerson; Wolfensberger 1995). Others criticized normalization's emphasis on assimilation and the enforcement of normative values rather than broader cultural change. Over time, these criticisms have reflected the changing political context and direction of services. Though normalization provided a justification in the 1970s for the development of smaller facilities, in practice the services often contradicted the basic principles of self-determination and integration (Ferguson, Hibbard, Leinen, and Schaff; Castellani).

Institutions persist today, but their nature and role in services for individuals with intellectual disability have changed. Castellani argues that in many states, but especially New York, the reliance on Medicaid funding programs accounts for the rapid expansion in the late 1970s through the 1980s of community services "systems." These systems, which are run largely by nonprofit agencies under the aegis of the Office of Mental Retardation and Developmental Disabilities (OMRDD), developed in relationship to new forms of funding and the changing role of large-scale facilities (which in New York are euphemistically dubbed "developmental centers").

Community services systems have been criticized in general as inattentive to individual needs, still effectively segregated, and burdened by complex regulatory and professional requirements, many of which were intended to correct and prevent a recurrence of the excesses of institutional practice (McKnight; Wolfensberger 1989; Castellani). There is still a small debate in the United States about the suitability of institutional over community services, especially for certain people. In the late 1990s, New York actually halted the scheduled closing of its remaining developmental centers and even built a new large-scale facility for the so-called criminally retarded (Castellani). Despite this, nationally the move toward smaller-scale settings has continued, however slowly and unevenly, and the vast majority of individuals with disabilities, family and parent associations, and professionals regard living and receiving services in the community not only as a more humane approach but as a fundamental right (Taylor 2001).

The persistent failure of systems-focused services has gone hand in hand with criticisms that individual difference has been eclipsed by the focus on normative standards of conduct in both the rhetoric of service and clinical practice. Normalization did grapple with the issue of individuality, but integration has taken shape in professionally oriented practices, largely at the expense of the active participation and particular needs of individuals with intellectual disability. Some critics suggest that even supporters of integration do not adequately question the current state of affairs. Researchers unwittingly affirm a narrow, service-oriented concept of integration when they measure it merely by the frequency of a person's activities (Myers, Ager, Kerr, and Myles). Such a methodological choice takes for granted the forms of segregation within the community as well as normalization's lingering assumption that conformity is desirable in itself. In the 1980s, the concern of critical researchers and professionals shifted toward the persistent institutional character and professional domination of services, which remains a major theme.[1] This research also reflects the related desire to capture the experience and point of view of individuals with disability, incorporating the criticism of professional perspectives in broader questions about identity and the ethics of social inquiry that have been central to the study of disability since the 1980s. Highlighting the perspective of individuals with disability has been one way of investigating the fact that professional approaches often cannot recognize certain kinds of knowledge and experience.[2]

Though "normalization" is a term no longer used, another early concept meant to individualize services remains central: "continuum of care." First advanced as a policy principle by President Kennedy's task force, it was integral to the legal strategy in *Wyatt v. Stickney*. This decision, finding a person's constitutional right to treatment in the "least restrictive environment," presumes the organization of services along a continuum, from the most restrictive (characterized by more intensive services) to the least restrictive (characterized by greater individual autonomy). Previously, only one form of service was on offer after a diagnosis: institutionalization. Now, the assessment of an individual's specific needs, in principle, determines where he or she is placed along the continuum of services. Steve Taylor (2001) argues that the continuum of care concept, though it is a cornerstone of deinstitutionalization and normalization, merely masks professional control as individualized services. Although "least restrictive environment" has provided a standard for more individualized services, it has never been clearly defined. Taylor (2001, 19–21) points out that although more restrictive environments ostensibly provide more services, historically they have provided far fewer, as with institutions. In practice, the standard is established on a professional basis that "confuses segregation, on the one hand, with intensity of services on the other." The continuum model sanctions the curtailment of basic rights in a way that makes the need for services analogous to the commitment of a crime: "The question implied by the least restrictive environment continuum is not *whether* the rights of people should be restricted, but *to what extent*." As a "readiness" model, Taylor argues, individuals must "earn" the right to move to a less restrictive environment, which establishes institutional "rhythms and routines" that are "fundamentally different than ordinary community life."

In the 1970s, the utter negligence of professionals was a primary complaint against institutions. This is reflected in key judicial findings

that one had the right to treatment and habilitation in the least restrictive environment (*Wyatt v. Stickney* [1972]) and that confinement was justifiable only for treatment and habilitation (*Halderman
v. Pennhurst State School* [1974]). However, increased professional
attention in community services has often come at the expense of self-
determination. With the continuum model, for example, access to less
restrictive settings is based on professional clinical assessment; it is
not a right itself.

Disability as a Social Category

The changing course of services prompted questions that have been
taken up since the 1980s by the emerging interdisciplinary field of
disability studies. The main contribution of this field, put simply, has
been demonstrating the significance of disability as a fundamental
category of social experience and analysis. More than that, the unique
questions raised by the study of disability have posed challenges across
other emerging fields that ostensibly share similar critical aims. African American, feminist, and queer studies have been forced to address
questions about the historical role disability has played in the production of normal life and experience, modes of social control and authority, and the embodied character of experience and knowledge.[3] Simi
Linton distinguishes disability studies from the disciplinary study of
disability by the guiding commitment of the former to a social model
that emphasizes not individual impairment but the cultural, economic,
and spatial determination or construction of experience. The origin
of the disability rights movement in the 1960s was also, in part, the
rejection of medical and clinical models that still view physical, mental, and cognitive difference largely out of context, as individual pathology.[4] Interestingly, the judicial finding of a right to treatment in the
legal action against Willowbrook (*ARC v. Rockefeller* [1972]) suggested a demedicalizing of disability in the acceptance of an expanded
notion of treatment. Rothman and Rothman argue that the plaintiff's
strategy was unusual and creative, claiming an expanded right to freedom from harm in order to encompass treatment. This strategy was
informed by the principles of normalization and the antiprofessional,
antimedical logic emerging within disabled peoples' movements.

    Debates about the social model of disability are beyond the scope
of this study, but it is worth noting that some writers have rejected the

traditional liberal opposition between social and individual explanations that presumes a narrow individualist concept of disability. Critics challenge the liberal assumptions of integration and rights-based
approaches, as they did normalization, for not addressing the social
and cultural contexts that define disability narrowly as an individual
matter. For example, the prevailing concepts of rights and the legal
focus on accommodation and discrimination in anglophone policy
and legislation reinforce a liberal individualist concept of disability
(Barnes and Oliver; Chadwick; Tremain). As a political strategy, some
have challenged the liberal notion of rights as too "negative" and individualist for effective organizing among people with intellectual
disability (Young and Quibell). Researchers have sought to define
autonomy for individuals with intellectual disability and ways it might
be measured in services that emphasize individuality, participation, and
choice (K. Barron; Jahoda and Cattermole; Treece, Gregory, Ayres,
and Mendis; Wehmeyer and Schwartz).

These arguments reflect the tension between authority and freedom
that is my empirical concern in the group home. For my purposes,
what limits attempts to think differently about rights and autonomy
is that professional authority and individual experience are still presumed to be contradictory. One of Trent's insights is that it is impossible historically to distinguish between care and control in any simple
sense. He argues not that claims of care mask practices of control but
that, at any given moment, the predominant forms of service, treatment, or care are inseparable from their social control functions, both
intended and unintended. Even criticisms of the juridical concept
of rights so crucial for deinstitutionalization and community integration do not adequately capture the fact that the supervision of individuals today occurs through the alignment of personal goals with the
professional goals of services; in other words, that governing individuals with intellectual disability necessarily involves—that is, requires—
their governing themselves.

The Group Home as a Technology of Government

Just as the modern state developed historically in relation to the range
of new problems and solutions that defined its purview, the nature
of individuals and individuality has been shaped in relation to specific problems of conduct and technologies of government. The term

"technology" emphasizes the systematic, rationalized approach to conduct that seeks specific individual outcomes in accordance with collective goals. It is through technologies of government that the interests of the individual can be linked to the interests of the whole. Attempts to shape conduct occur in relation to large-scale areas, such as the economy through the use of tax and investment incentives (Miller and Rose), and local ones, such as self-esteem-building programs as a form of welfare assistance to women (Cruikshank). As a research field, the empirical focus for governmentality is the technologies that shape the varied arenas (poverty, child welfare, public health, disability) and the local settings in which the problems and solutions of individual conduct are identified and acted on (charity associations, social service offices, clinics, group homes).[5] That government depends on the capacity for freedom does not necessarily preclude the use of constraint or coercion. Governing involves more than mechanisms of control, direct or indirect, and technologies of government effectively enable new kinds of conduct. Every technology, Rose writes, "inculcat[es] a form of life" (1999b, 52), and, in this way, individuals are "simultaneously capacitated and governed" (1998a, 27).

This book could be characterized as the investigation of the ongoing inculcation of a group home form of life at Driggs House through the government of both residents and counselors. Group homes emerged in the United States as the primary organizational solution to the legal, moral, and service failures of institutionalization. However, a new problem arose inevitably when individuals with intellectual disability were, in principle, free to choose for themselves and to live in the community. The defining dilemmas of liberalism took specific form in the tension between supervisory authority and the freedom of individual residents. This is not simply a tension between competing professional, moral, and individual values but a practical tension that must be managed in ongoing technical ways. In this sense, the group home itself is a technology, a setting organized by the clinical and administrative efforts that govern residents by cultivating the particular capacities that allow each resident to govern him- or herself. The question about "how to govern," as Dean puts it (1999, 34), is really a question about how we "should" govern most effectively. This question is at the same time both practical and ethical. This is why the regulations of the New York State OMRDD often describe group homes in ideal terms: "A community residence shall provide an environment that ensures client rights, promotes freedom of client movement, and increases opportunities for clients to make decisions and to participate in regular community activities consistent with their needs and capability. A community residence shall allow for the maximum level of independence consistent with a client's disability and functioning level" (14 N.Y.C.R.R. § 686.3). At other times, group homes are described in more concrete, if still general, terms: "A [community residence is a] facility providing housing, supplies and services for persons who are developmentally disabled and who, in addition to these basic requirements need supportive interpersonal relationships, supervision, and training assistance in the activities of daily living. Community residences are designed to accomplish two major goals: 1) provide a home environment; and 2) provide a setting where persons can acquire the skills necessary to live as independently as possible" (§ 686.99).

As a technical solution to the appalling violations of institutional life, what a community residence must do is translate the ideals of rights and integration into actual services that both supervise individuals and promote their independence. At Driggs House, effective supervisory authority depends on the freedom of residents to govern themselves. But freedom is also an ideal that must be realized in everyday life; for the residents, freedom is the ability to participate in their own supervision through their own specific pursuits of freedom. It is through the efforts to promote their own independence—the individual clinical plans and other activities that target specific aspects of conduct—that residents govern themselves. The group home must aim to cultivate in each resident the particular capacities for action that enable ongoing organizational function without impinging unduly on that resident's liberty. What Rose (1999b, 68) describes in order for "liberal government . . . to be possible" is true also for group home residents: they "must come to recognize and act upon themselves as both free and responsible, both beings of liberty and members of society."

In this way, providing services in the community has meant more than just extending formal rights to individuals with intellectual disability. It has also meant extending the practices of "well-regulated liberty" (Rose 1999b, 72) that enable them to know and act on themselves in specific ways as group home residents. This is illustrated nicely by a paper published in the *Journal of Applied Behavior Analysis* about the problems posed by "choice." For individuals with intellectual disability, the very obligation to choose can be a source of stress and confusion (Bannerman, Sheldon, Sherman, and Harchik). This often produces the contradictory result of compromising "personal liberties," because service providers often end up making decisions for others, if only for efficiency's sake (79). For this reason, teaching individuals "how to choose" must be a fundamental task of services (85). The goals of integration and liberty need not be in conflict, the authors argue, because people by their nature "strive for freedom in a broad sense . . . [and] enjoy making simple choices" (79).

The history of terms used to refer to the recipients of social services originates in a narrow concept of rights and the effort to demedicalize disability, but it has become ever more encompassing. In the 1970s, "client" was adopted (in place of "patient") to express the informed and consensual nature of a professional service relationship. Although "client" is still found in the regulations, in the 1990s OMRDD literature began using "participant" to imply the importance of active involvement in services beyond mere informed consent. Soon after, "consumer" became the favored term in policy and practice to express the ideal of the fully autonomous, choice-making individual. The OMRDD's use of "participant" and "consumer," it seems to me, is much like the public announcements on the New York City subway that now refer to "customers" rather than "passengers." Even the OMRDD (2006) uses "customer" in its planning materials. When these terms are used at Driggs House, however, they rarely invoke a particular ideology of service. Residents almost always refer to themselves as clients, and staff use this term too. The only exception, for counselors, occurs during the rare visits from clinicians, auditors, or agency administrators, when, for a brief time, residents become consumers.

The residents must learn how to govern themselves. The authors of the *Journal of Applied Behavior Analysis* article (87) recognize that "all people have the right to eat too many doughnuts and take a nap. But along with rights come responsibilities." This is why "teaching clients how to exercise their freedoms responsibly should be an integral part of the . . . process." But, just as all people have the right to eat too many doughnuts, all people must in some way learn how to exercise their freedoms responsibly. Freedom in this sense is not simply opposed to authority (in the group home and elsewhere). But in the group home, being a resident means learning to be a responsible resident. The responsible exercise of freedom necessary for effective government is produced *through* government. And the specific capacities that enable individuals to act on themselves as autonomous citizens define what we take freedom to be. This raises the general question at the heart of this book, but for which only specific answers will be found in the empirical analysis: at Driggs House, for individuals who are regarded (rightly or wrongly) as having a questionable capacity for freedom, what shape does freedom take?

The Ethical Authority of Expertise

Because I investigate the group home as a technology of government, I do not regard professional knowledge at Driggs House as posing a problem to be solved. My concern is not the typical sociological one, having to do with professional domination and social control, but concerns the role such knowledge plays in government at the group home. The authority to govern rests not only in its indirect character but also in the ostensibly disinterested and universal nature of scientific expertise. In contrast to the particularity of traditional authority, professional knowledge provides legitimacy to the attempts to mobilize individuals in systematic and rational ways to govern their own conduct in relation to specific problems of health, wealth, and happiness.

At Driggs House, psychological knowledge forms the ethical basis of staff authority. The dilemma inherent in providing services in the community was defined in the 1970s as a problem of individual psychology and framed by the clinical language of behavior, adjustment, coping, and skills. The ongoing tension between supervision and freedom is managed in everyday life by acting on conduct as a clinical problem. Residents are governed, and govern themselves, through their own clinical practice to "become more independent." The goal of community-based services encompasses all aspects of life as potential clinical matters. The goal, expressed in the 1975 Federal Development Disabilities Act, was "to promote and encourage independence, individuality, integration and productivity" in each resident, and OMRDD uses this phrase in its regulations and other written material (e.g., 14 N.Y.C.R.R. § 671.1). I use "independence" throughout the book because it is the term residents and counselors always use to describe their work at Driggs House. Perhaps "independence" is used most frequently to express the goals of group home work because it is at once encompassing and specifically measurable. The presumption of individuality is taken for granted, and the term "individuality" is not regularly used in relation to group home work. "Integration," however, which in group home work does not conjure a contrast to institutional life, refers only to defined activities that facilitate a resident's involvement with "the community." Similarly, "productivity" is almost always used to refer to the way vocational programs or activities are defined as providing the opportunity to pursue this goal. Independence not only is the most encompassing of these four goals, it is listed first in the regulations. Depending on how it is used in the group home, independence refers to specific goal work or, broadly, to the overall ideal of the work. As shorthand for the overall goal of community residential services, "independence" is also used widely in the professional rhetoric and regulations governing the group home.

Psy Knowledge and the Enhancement of Normality

In the nineteenth century, technologies of government established a new role for expertise that is ethical in yet another sense: as a guide to living. Bringing expertise into the realm of everyday life made it a basis for normative ideals of conduct. Rose (1994, 1998b) and Abram de Swaan both argue that theories of professionalization and medicalization (Freidson; Zola) are unable to account for the ethical consequences of the dissemination of expert knowledge, because of their emphasis on domination and imperial expansion. Rose and de Swaan argue, instead, that the diffusion of expertise cannot be understood separately from everyday experience. They do not take a normative position on either the substance or the dissemination of knowledge but pursue an analysis of how expert knowledge and techniques are available to and used by individuals to understand and act on themselves in particular ways. For de Swaan (105–6), a focus on professional power cannot recognize that, "in a society where so many and such serious troubles are entrusted to professionals," laypeople themselves become experts on expertise. What he calls "proto-professionalization" refers to not simply the imposition of a "cognitive orientation but also the acquisition of habits, of stances that correspond to the basic attitude[s]" and orientations of the relevant professions.

Explanations of the dissemination of psychology as a symptom of cultural degradation or the atomism of capitalist modernity (Lasch; Jacoby; Rieff) also do not provide an adequate account of how psychological knowledge shapes everyday life. Rose (1999a, 1998b) argues that through the twentieth century psychology has been central to the government of conduct in general. It is already as psychological selves that individuals in contemporary life are able and willing to govern themselves "therapeutically," not simply by the imperial exertions of a professional field that redefine natural experience but also in the many realms in which individuals are mobilized to act on their own conduct in particular, by social workers, teachers, therapists, parents, and, of course, themselves.

Rose uses Jacques Donzelot's term "psy" to refer to the range and proliferation of psychological concepts and practices too vast to attribute to a single professional field. In the nineteenth century, the field of psychology took form in the study of pathology and, in the process, developed knowledge about, and established standards of, "normal" conduct. Rose (1985) argues, for example, that the advent of mental testing transformed the nature and knowledge of both feeblemindedness and normal intelligence. An important aspect of this was that techniques of mental testing were easily adaptable to, and helped shape, other fields—such as education and workplace management—not through the treatment of pathology but in the assessment and enhancement of ordinary conduct.

Since the mid-twentieth century, behaviorism, like mental testing before it, has furnished many of the psy technologies central to the enhancement of normal life. The techniques developed in operant conditioning, token systems, and milieu therapy established that problems of conduct lay in the realm of overt behavior rather than in subjective meaning and experience. Behavioral techniques were easily used in many ordinary domains of life, including school, the workplace, and the social worker's office (Rose 1998b). Like mental testing, behaviorism was adaptable to fields with no clinical or rehabilitative aims but in which conduct nonetheless needed to be governed. What made the techniques of behavioral psychology especially adaptable was that they could function as ethical practices of government because they were able "to reconcile the requirement that human beings conduct themselves simultaneously as subjects of freedom and subjects of society" (Rose 1998b, 98).

Behaviorism is central to the history of intellectual disability. Although it had been used since the 1930s, it was not until the 1950s that behaviorism posed a significant challenge to the psychometric model that had earlier provided psychology a foothold in a field dominated for decades by medicine. Just as mental testing was central to disability and discipline formation in psychology in the early part of the twentieth century (Rose 1985; Trent), behaviorism was the basis of psychology's criticism in the 1950s of the dominance of mental testing in the diagnosis of mental deficiency. That behavioral techniques could be used easily in areas of life not regarded as pathological contributed to the expanding relevance of psychological knowledge in wealthy societies. In contrast to mental testing, the techniques of behaviorism were also actually adaptable to certain clinical problems, including mental deficiency, that were seen as intractable or unsuited to the esoteric practices of psychiatry and psychoanalysis. Moreover, nonprofessional staff in schools and institutions could easily be trained in their use. Psychology's dominance was established in the 1950s (Rose 1998b, 1999a), and this success helped revive the field's interest in intellectual disability (Simpson 1996a, 1996b). The victory of psychology (and related areas in education) was marked in 1959, by the replacement of "mental deficiency" with the diagnostic category "mental retardation," which included, for the first time, adaptive behavior alongside the IQ range (Trent).

The transition of intellectual disability from the institution to the community that was galvanized in the 1970s can be taken as an accelerated instance of how psychology has formed the ethical basis of normal living in liberal societies. It was the diagnostic expertise of psychology that once provided the justification for institutionalization but now must furnish technologies for governing free individuals in the community. The group home's goal "to promote and encourage independence, individualization, integration and productivity" is realized through the concepts and techniques of behavior modification. Normalization helped define integration as an individual problem of behavior and skill. Though Wolfensberger (1995) himself addressed the confusion about whether the point of normalization was to change individuals or to change the community, psychology claimed "the community" as its professional domain. As Murray Simpson (1996a) argues, this actually occurred in large part through the early influence of normalization and long after its consequences can be seen, for example, in the extensive debate about "social competence" as a category of assessment and an approach to service meant to encompass social, psychological, cognitive, and behavioral aspects of individual adaptation (Greenspan and Granfield; Siperstein). For Simpson (1996b, 94), such debates represent just the kind of professional preoccupation that reinforces psychology's grip: "life in the community" is reduced, as ever, to the technical enhancement of individual competence. At Driggs House, techniques of psy knowledge organize the relationships that residents can and should have to their own conduct as potentially independent and always amenable to change. Yet independence, in any conventional sense, cannot be achieved by the residents, which makes it an endless clinical pursuit toward an ever-receding goal.

Driggs House

A group home is a compelling example of the government of conduct, because it is a setting uniquely charged with the task of cultivating the capacity for freedom in individuals who are widely, if incorrectly, presumed incapable of the well-regulated liberty that is the responsibility of all citizens. There has, nonetheless, been almost no empirical research on intellectual disability using governmentality. When Foucault's ideas have been used, they have been his notions of carceral and disciplinary power (cf. Stanley Cohen; Kivett and Warren). Researchers have misconstrued these ideas both for (Danforth; Peter) and against (Gelb 2000) their utility for the study of intellectual disability. Only recently has a volume been published that represents the first worthy attempt to address the relevance of Foucault's ideas to disability theory (Tremain). In Chris Drinkwater's contribution, he draws on his experience as a direct-care worker to describe governmentality. What makes the group home a technology of government is also perhaps what accounts, at least in part, for why such a setting has rarely been studied this way. For some disability researchers, the approach is not pointedly critical enough. Steven Gelb (2000), for example, dismisses Foucault on this basis, as many have criticized so-called postmodernism for not being adequately political (or even anti-political). Though Scot Danforth (2000) acknowledges that Foucault's insights do not easily yield clear policy recommendations, he aims to demonstrate that the ideas are nonetheless worthy of study. For social researchers in general, the question of governmentality is hardly relevant, given the neglect of intellectual disability as a topic of inquiry. Perhaps the pervasive fear of stupidity Dexter described in the mid-1960s still makes intellectual disability appear to be a problem for social or clinical services but not for sociology. Perhaps it has been little studied because it is too difficult for social researchers to imagine that even citizens whose freedom is always potentially in question are nonetheless capable of systematically knowing and acting on themselves.

To suggest that group homes, in principle, are technologies of government, representative of rather than an exception to liberal authority, is not to deny the unique and tragic history of abuse suffered by individuals who have been considered intellectually disabled. Nor does it imply anything about the current state of services or deny the persistence of coercive control in the variety of community-based services increasingly available over the last three decades. And, of course, Driggs House cannot be regarded as representative of residential services. However, group homes do exist that reflect the principles of community integration, at least in the regulatory terms set forth by New York State's OMRDD. The larger question, whether the ideals of integration can be realized through the systems of accountability and regulation in place, is not one I ask. What I do ask is how these ideals are realized every day as practical matters of group home work.

Driggs House is a setting in which counselors and staff take seriously the basic commitments of the whole group home enterprise. A group home characterized by poor services, not to mention overt abuse and neglect, would have foiled my inquiry in two ways: first, I regarded it an ethical obligation to report any neglect and abuse I witnessed, and having to do so would have compromised my role as a field researcher; second, and more fundamentally, the very questions about freedom and authority I ask simply would not have made sense. In seeking a site for the research, I made inquiries at a number of private nonprofit agencies in New York City known for their generally good services. Three agencies expressed interest, but two wanted me to conduct research that would yield findings about specific issues of policy and programming. The remaining agency agreed to permit my access to a group home without making any claims on the nature of the inquiry. The administrators selected a facility based on the suitability of the residents, in terms of both their ability to consent to participate and the likelihood that they would be receptive to having a researcher in their home. Driggs House turned out just as I hoped. The rights of residents were observed in accordance with the regulatory requirements, and, well, the place was unremarkable in its day-to-day operations. Of course, my aim was not an evaluation of services. And, again, though the setting cannot be taken as a representative case, the ideal of autonomy that is now central to all social services means that the practical dilemmas of freedom and authority faced by the residents and counselors every day at Driggs House will no doubt be familiar beyond the arena of intellectual disability.

Conclusion

In one sense, governmentality's overarching concern is to understand how social regulation in liberal society depends fundamentally on the practices of self-regulation that align the aspirations of free individuals with the ideals of the whole. One purpose of this study is to show that governmentality is equally relevant to a setting that circumscribes the lives of its residents (and, in different ways, its staff).

Through the latter half of the twentieth century, techniques of the self became central to social regulation. Governmentality analysis focuses on the multiple strategies that aim to mobilize individuals to act on themselves "not just to control, subdue, discipline, normalize or reform them, but also to make them more intelligent, wise, happy, virtuous, healthy, productive, docile, enterprising, fulfilled, self-esteeming, empowered or whatever" (Rose 1998b, 12). From dietary regimes and exercise programs to advice-filled talk shows and psychotherapy, techniques for the ongoing enhancement of the ordinary organize life on the basis of the ethic of the autonomous self. Everyday psy practices to enhance the normal self have equated freedom with autonomy, as "the capacity to realize one's desires . . . [and] to fulfill one's potential through one's own endeavors, to determine the course of one's own existence through acts of choice" (Rose 1999b, 84). This can be seen widely in forms of disease prevention and health promotion, which presume individuals have control over their health. Individuals are recruited to take responsibility in multiple and mundane ways to prevent specific diseases through screening or changing behaviors associated with them. More than that, practicing risk reduction requires no pathological referent to be worthwhile. "Being healthy" is taken to mean one won't become ill (Kickbush; McQueen; Nettleton). But, in practice, being healthy is the ongoing use of expert techniques in the pursuit of an idealized state called health. Like independence in the group home, health is an ever-receding goal that individuals can achieve *only* in its pursuit. We do this by taking our own selves as projects of endless improvement and risk reduction. There is an ever-expanding repertoire of procedures and forms of conduct by which, with the encouragement and assistance of experts, we work on our bodies, emotions, and beliefs in order to achieve autonomous selfhood (Rose 1994, 1998b).

A central aspect of the development of psychology from the turn of the twentieth century onward was its broad relevance beyond pathology, to normal life. More than that, Rose argues that the pervasive influence of psy knowledge in wealthy liberal societies has offered ways of seeing, knowing, and acting on both individualized subjects and standardized populations. Through the second half of the century, behaviorism played a major role in the discipline's expanding authority over new clinical areas, among them what is now called intellectual disability, and the adoption of psy techniques in many areas of life. As behaviorism was emerging in the 1950s and 1960s as a vital way of knowing and seeing, both in the field of psychology and in a society of increasingly psychological individuals, it was also vilified as the emblem of repressive, totalitarian, and antihumanist control. Yet it offered a technical approach to being human that has turned out to define freedom as a kind of personal liberation achievable through the endless pursuit of autonomy that takes shape in our everyday work on the normal self (Baistow; Rose 1998b). This is no more the case for residents than for everyone else.

In light of this history, it would be useful to warn the reader of the unusual gerunds and other terms of art used at Driggs House. They are effectively the clinical expression of routine aspects of conduct and experience. Some reviewers have suggested that these sorts of terms require definition, especially for readers unfamiliar with group homes or similar services. Mostly, I use quotation marks in the remainder of the book to indicate that a word or phrase is said or written at Driggs House; occasionally, I do so to set off the word as "technical." In a few of the latter instances, I provide qualifying definitions, especially when familiar words are used in ways that depart from their common meaning. In any case, however technical a term may appear, what it means depends on the situated context of its use. But this point is secondary. I don't provide definitions as a general rule because the group home's technical language will already make sense to readers as aspects of our shared psy culture. Assigning technical-sounding terms to routine experience, as with the gerund "outbursting," is hardly unique to the group home. Readers who are "parenting" rather than "raising" children will understand. So will their child-free friends. In this same way, the group home's gerunds and terms of art may strike some readers as unusual, but they aren't esoteric or even specialized. Even inconsistencies of terminology within the group home—why Ruby's goal was called room cleaning and Paul's was called room maintenance, for example—have no clear professional basis and are accountable only as situated features of the work. So, although I cannot say when having a tantrum became "tantruming" or when tantrums became "outbursts," and so on, this issue encapsulates one of the book's basic themes: that using technical or clinical language to describe routine activities for which we already have perfectly good words is something that makes our life not so different from group home life.

3 THE WORK OF EVERYDAY LIFE

THE CLAIM THAT RESIDENTS ARE GOVERNED is plausible prima facie, given the mission of Driggs House and the indirect character of its authority. This study of everyday life there shows that the dilemmas of freedom are ongoing practical dilemmas that organize the social order of the group home. More than that, because of the common assumption, no doubt held by some readers, that a diagnosis of intellectual disability is equivalent to social incompetence, a description of how residents govern themselves will demonstrate that they actually do. The insights of ethnomethodology are particularly suitable to this task. It is a naturalistic inquiry that remains close to its phenomenological roots. Unlike philosophy and other sociological adaptations of phenomenology, however, ethnomethodology is concerned not with subjective meaning or with action as an effect of social structure but with the observable, accountable, and situated character of action.

By following Alfred Schutz—who argued that "paramount reality" (226) is the sphere of overt action, "the world of working" (212)—ethnomethodology allows me to make no distinction between formal work at Driggs House and the world of working that is everyday life. Neither deductive nor inductive, ethnomethodological analysis does not proceed from specific explanations and regards the situated, indeterminate character of action as incommensurable with theories of a fixed social order. Nor does it aim to develop such theories from observation, a common confusion given the painstaking detail that comprises much ethnomethodological writing. Instead of seeking "real" but hidden causes, the focus of ethnomethodology is ordinary action, which Eric Livingston (58) describes as observable "in the ways

an explanation or account or question is a feature of the organizational activity of which it is hopelessly a part." What makes description adequate is that it takes everyday life in its own terms and relies
on categories of analysis that are relevant in and for the action under
observation.

"Ethno" methods, as Harold Garfinkel (1984, 1) coined the term,
refer to the innumerable "situated practices of looking-and-telling,"
the practical methods individuals use routinely, without thinking,
that allow them to accomplish social orderliness. John Heritage (4)
describes the "commonsense knowledge and the range of procedures
and considerations by means of which ordinary members of society
make sense of, find their way about in, and act on the circumstances
in which they find themselves." A central concern for ethnomethodologists is the reflexive relationship between action and accounts of that
action as it occurs. "The description and describability of the world,"
as David Goode puts it (1994, 1), are integral and organizing features
of everyday activity. The production of social order is always reflexive, because it is an in situ, accountable, and self-organizing temporal
order. In other words, ethnomethodologists treat commonsense practical methods as observable accounting practices, and the action and
events they describe endlessly elaborate and modify each other. Setting
aside conventional assumptions of social science, ethnomethodologists
do not regard context as something describable independently of action.
Michael Lynch (1993, 30) explains that the language of ethnomethodological analysis implies the relevance of context for the same reasons
that individuals "commonly have no trouble with seeing, and seeing at
a glance, 'what's going on' in the situations in which they and others
act." Ethnomethodological inquiries "turn our attention to the reflexive
way in which the identities of persons, actions, things, and 'contexts'
become relevantly and recognizably part of an unfolding 'text' (or,
better, 'contexture') of practical details." In this way, social life can be
seen as an ongoing, concerted accomplishment of individuals whose
methods of practical reasoning organize their own routine action in
its course.

The Collection and Presentation of Data

Ethnomethodology has had an uneasy relationship to American social
science, and other writers have addressed this and the nature of ethno's

contributions (Lynch 1993; Maynard and Clayman; Rawls 2002, 2008). Though my thinking has been strongly influenced by the alternative perspectives on knowledge and social life that ethnomethodology offers, I do not use the naturalistic techniques of data collection and analysis that are its signature. My hope is that this study demonstrates in yet a new way the utility and power of ethnomethodology's insights.

Most fundamentally, I have aimed to describe and understand Driggs House in terms of its own relevant categories and routine rationalities. I did not observe group home practice in order to gather evidence for systematic theoretical explanations of authority, knowledge, or conduct. Nor did I proceed on the basis of any particular assumptions about the unequal distribution of power, the social construction of disability or clinical knowledge, or the general failure of community-based services. Many other researchers have addressed these concerns; furthermore, though I happen to agree with many of them, their theories are relevant in this study only insofar as they were observable and relevant at Driggs House. I do not deny that life there is shaped by its broader social and historical contexts, but, as Lynch puts it, the "specifications of such contexts are invariably bound to a local contexture of relevance" (1993, 125). Readers will discover these broader issues throughout the book as they are relevant to counselors and residents in their (the counselors' and residents') own ongoing analysis, itself an observable and reflexive feature of life at Driggs House.

Some of ethnomethodology's most extraordinary contributions have been in the study of work and organizations and of settings that are typically the province of the sociology of deviance and social control.[1] As a field researcher in a group home, my approach to everyday life as a local, contingent accomplishment—the everyday life of which I became a part—allowed me to draw on insights from both the study of deviance and the sociology of work and organizations without focusing only on questions of conflict and power. Ethnomethodology's insights provide one way of seeing group home work as much more than the counselors' remunerated activities. The competent participation of residents is organized by the ongoing clinical work they do to become more independent, and this makes Driggs House a workplace beyond the livelihood it provides counselors. Routine group home work, which includes the work of everyday life, involves the continuous and skillful activity of all those who work and live there.

For thirteen months, I spent an average of thirty hours per week at Driggs House. I conducted the research as a participant-observer in the sense that I became a competent regular member of the setting (this is apparently the "participant" part), but the residents and counselors knew that I was there only for a time and to accomplish a task that was ultimately unrelated to the group home (the "observer" part). In addition to being involved in the everyday routines, I attended weekly staff meetings, case conferences, residents' meetings, and other formally organized events—clinical, administrative, and social.

I never carried a notepad openly, because it would have been too cumbersome in the bustle of group home life. In my judgment, the constant reminder that I was a researcher would have made it difficult to develop the kind of easy rapport with residents and counselors that the research required. Such a rapport is necessary for most participant observation, but I think it was particularly crucial given the unique intimacy of this combined home and workplace. Because I had worked as a counselor myself in similar group homes, I had what Garfinkel called a "unique adequacy" as a researcher, which meant that I was already a more or less competent member of this specific setting when I arrived. My aim as a researcher was not just that residents and counselors feel comfortable with me but that I become familiar enough to be taken for granted. This happened, insofar as such a thing is possible, but in some unexpected ways that required multiple competencies. (These issues are discussed in chapter 4.)

It was generally difficult to take notes while I was at Driggs House. On weekends, when things were quieter there, I would occasionally have some time to begin writing a narrative about the visit, but most often I would use the hour-long subway ride home to begin writing. Once I caught the rhythm of the place, I learned how and in what circumstances I could jot things down. Sonia, the supervisor, was very pleased with the idea of having a researcher at Driggs House for a long term. Before I met the counselors, she told me they were very amenable to the idea as well, and she was confident that any unexpressed concerns they might have would be dispelled once they met me and learned about my project. Apparently, only one issue came up when she told them that a sociologist would be spending a lot of time in the residence for a research project. Two counselors were worried about whether I would be using a tape recorder. Sonia did not even ask whether I was planning to use one but suggested that it would be unwise. Given that the issue had been raised, she explained to me, and regardless of the legitimacy of the concern, using a tape recorder might make it more difficult to establish the counselors' trust. I agreed and was impressed by her pragmatic understanding of the kind of trust necessary to conduct field research in such a workplace.

The structure and style of the study may depart from the typical way data is displayed in ethnomethodology; it differs also from what is now so often expected of an ethnographic monograph. My aim has been not to craft an overarching narrative of life at the group home but to demonstrate some of the practices and ideals of practice that organize everyday life and work for residents and counselors. Although I use narrative description throughout, my choice of stories and the way I tell them were determined by their relevance to the observational analysis I offer. That is, I treat narrative and description as an embedded and organizing aspect of the analysis. The book is perhaps best characterized as the form of case study Max Gluckman (1956, 1957) called situational analysis, because its focus is less on ethnographic events as evidence of social structures or culture than on the observation of actors (rather than informants) in and as part of the group home's social order.[2]

This is not to suggest that selecting, writing, and organizing narrative and description was not a reconstructive process removed from the lived experience at Driggs House. Such retrospective reconstruction is inherent in observational analysis but does not require the confusion between readability and realism that often holds up fiction (that is, the *experience* of fiction) as a standard for judging ethnography. I have made no effort, justified by a claim about "context," to provide a complete description of the setting, individuals, and circumstances I observed at Driggs House. Such a descriptive narrative may be a worthy stylistic approach but cannot be the sole measure of ethnographic writing. It happens also not to be what Clifford Geertz meant by "thick description." Geertz's phenomenological perspective of the complex, layered character of meaning implies an ideal of ethnographic writing that has nothing to do with the way the phrase he made famous is used so glibly, so indiscriminately, to mean "reads like a novel." When I have described the tone or feeling of a situation or attributed assumptions to an individual, I have been careful to refrain from explanations that would not also have been available to the people involved, given my knowledge of them and the circumstances.

Though I regard the reconstruction of observation in writing as unavoidable, it is a methodological liberty that can be exercised in circumscribed ways to keep in view the always vexed relationship between observation (especially that done by a lone individual who, to start with, *observes* rather than simply *sees*) and reports of observation that inevitably refashion it in one or another way. I draw on concepts from elsewhere but have made every effort not to obscure the concepts discoverable to me in the everyday life of the specific place in which I spent more than a year.

Ethnomethodology and Governmentality

For Garfinkel and Cicourel, the preoccupation in social science with "method and measurement" reflects an epistemological confusion about the relationship between the practice and topics of inquiry. Unquestioned assumptions not only shape what can be seen and known in research but also render invisible social life's already accountable organization. In the strictest sense, governmentality commits this theoretical error, and no doubt many regard the approaches as incompatible. Nonetheless, as Lynch (1993, 131) has recognized, some Foucauldian analysis is compatible with ethnomethodology; they share certain fundamental criticisms of conventional social science. The connections I make between them allow me to take a unique approach to the group home, one which lends itself to similar questions in other settings.

Like ethnomethodology, governmentality analysis seeks to explain not *why* action occurs, but *how*. Each approach emphasizes the reflexive and practical relationship between its own concerns and empirical inquiry. Though the concerns of governmentality may shape inquiry in ways that are untenable in ethnomethodology, both share the assumption that a priori theories cannot explain much about social life and, in different ways, that adequate analytic categories become available only in empirical study of specific domains.

Both approaches identify similar drawbacks in the study of interaction, which seeks to identify the hidden causes of action in meaning, culture, or social structure. Studies of interaction treat the social world as equivalent to the interactional production of meaning, something that is often expressed as a methodological matter but that takes particular theoretical assumptions for granted. Similarly, when interaction is presumed to be the observable micro level reproduction of macro structure, a theoretical assumption about social order is expressed as a methodological issue. Ethnomethodology and governmentality both reject the conventional distinction between macro and micro levels of social order and analysis. From an ethnomethodological perspective, the absence of observable causes requires sociologists to posit an order of macro causes that can be represented only by abstract methodological forms, which are external to and distort the social experience under study. In governmentality, the opposition between micro and macro orders of experience is collapsed in the analysis of the technical basis of conduct. That is, the difference between the government of large or small spaces and processes is understood only as a matter of scale, "not ontological but technological" (Rose 1999b, 5).

For my purposes, one of the most important convergences is governmentality's focus on technology to specify its empirical object and ethnomethodology's focus on practical methods of everyday reasoning. I treat psy techniques at Driggs House as methods of practical reasoning, because, in their routine and often unwitting use by counselors and residents, they are organizing features of the setting. Many techniques of psy conduct are the specification of already available practical methods of ordinary action, particular ways of seeing, knowing, and acting. A good deal of governmentality research refrains from making epistemological claims. This is a basic principle of ethnomethodology: knowledge that is relevant to an analysis of action is, by definition, not external to that action. This is what Garfinkel and Sacks meant when they said they were "indifferent" to questions, epistemological and otherwise, that presume causal social factors or any other external criteria of judgment. For this reason, no explicit claim of "skepticism" is necessary (Lynch 1993, 17). I do not pursue questions about the legitimate basis or socially constructed character of professional knowledge, for the simple reason that diagnostic classifications of disability, clinical assumptions, techniques of intervention, and so on, were relevant to everyday life at Driggs House when they were observably relevant to residents and counselors.

That I do not treat knowledge in the group home as a problem to be solved is related to the criticism ethnomethodology and governmentality together offer of the wide-ranging analyses encompassed by the phrase "social construction." In much of that research, knowledge is treated largely as a force external to and greater than everyday action and, as in labeling theory, presumes causal relationships between structures and processes of power. Another common focus in social construction analyses is the question of agency. Demonstrating that research subjects are active agents and arguing that this is important for understanding social life have dominated a good deal of social research, including research on intellectual disability. This effort sometimes reflects a confusion of intellectual and political aims. I take for granted that the residents at Driggs House are active agents, because they must be if what the phrase means is the individual capacity for action in relation to the social order of which actors are a part. That residents are active agents is demonstrated throughout the book but does not reflect a particular theoretical aim, and, apart from this instance, residents will not be addressed as such. I do so here only because it has become a watchword in social analysis, and again because of the belief probably held by at least some readers, that individual agency and a diagnosis of intellectual disability are mutually exclusive. It is a truism that all socially competent people are active agents, and people with intellectual disability are no exception. Only a few researchers share this assumption. Goode (1994) offers an excellent example in the innovative use of ethnomethodology with nonverbal children who are severely disabled, observing capacities for communication that are presumed by professional carers not to exist. For both governmentality and ethnomethodology, the question of capacity is always a situated and practical one. Empirical claims about agency (if it is useful to make them at all) should not be evaluative, nor, by affirming personal expression or experience, should they equate agency with "resistance" in some political sense.

Social scientists are also preoccupied with the concept and political significance of identity, which poses similar problems. Though one of my aims at Driggs House was to understand the nature of group home persons, this is not a study of identity in the sociological or subjective sense. Some research emphasizes the perspectives of individuals with disability and seeks to provide a venue for their subjective expression. This is a worthwhile undertaking and has yielded some excellent scholarship (Bogdan and Taylor 1982, 1989a; Ferguson, Ferguson, and Taylor; Goode 1983; Langness and Levine), but this approach presumes the theoretical conceptions of agency and power that I have chosen to set aside. In both ethnomethodology and governmentality, persons are treated neither as passive social constructions nor as determined by structures of power.

Following Ian Hacking, Rose (1998b, 53) suggests that the primacy of language and meaning, as well as identity, indicates a misunderstanding of the construction metaphor in "social construction." What the phrase actually implies is the practical and technical character of knowing and being. Governmentality is oriented not to the processes and structures by which identity or subjectivity is "asserted" or "determined" but to the technical ways in which certain kinds of persons are "elicited, fostered, and promoted" (Dean 1999, 32). Hacking (1986, 1995, 1999) characterizes this simply as the processes involved in "making up people" and calls for an analysis of kinds (or "kind-making") concerned with how kinds of persons are "made up" through the techniques of knowing and being that furnish the practical conditions of conduct in specific settings and fields. I treat counselors and residents as kinds of persons in that I ask how they are made visible and knowable in the group home work they organize, the ongoing work that makes being a certain kind of person possible. Residents and counselors are organizationally "incarnate," to borrow a term from Garfinkel (1967a), and I understand their conduct as a reflexive feature of everyday life at Driggs House, not as an aspect of individual character, skill, judgment, or presumed disability. This is a study of group home kinds and the ways they are able to see, know, and act on themselves and each other as certain kinds of persons.

Back to Work

Garfinkel and Wieder (202) describe the empirical object of ethnomethodology in customary phenomenological style: "the lived, concerted, unavoidably embodied, smoothly achieved work in content-specific detail that makes up the accomplishment of the most ordinary organizational things in the world." Everyday life is a concerted accomplishment, a kind of work itself, and ethnomethodologists long ago turned to the work of everyday life in actual workplaces in order to understand how even formally structured settings depend on distinct and local orders of mundane activity (Garfinkel 1986, 2002; Rawls 2008). Even "the most ordinary organizational things" are the basis of what is presumably the most esoteric work—scientific research—which is approached in terms of the "work-specific competencies" that constitute the local order of biology laboratories and astronomy observatories (Lynch 1993, 114).

The work-specific competencies that organize and define Driggs House are not only the province of counselors. Residents are workers, too, not simply in the ethnomethodological sense, in that they are competent participants in the accomplishment of everyday order, but because their competent participation also (and inseparably) requires that residents take up the endless work to become more independent. The work residents do on themselves is the work of self-government, and their skillful, ongoing pursuit of independence is the very work that defines residents as certain kinds of Driggs House persons. In sociology, of course, resident work would not be regarded as work at all; it is neither productive, in the conventional sense, nor paid. To suggest that the self-government of residents is work only highlights how pervasively the notion of work shapes contemporary life despite the categorical limitations of sociology. In fact, many areas of social services increasingly reflect a "contractual ethos." People are required increasingly to participate in activities meant to demonstrate their capacity to take responsibility for themselves. In some cases, such activities are seen as a form of "earning" services and support, even state entitlements (Cruikshank; Dean 1995; Dordick; Yeatman). But working on oneself is hardly limited to those who receive social services. All individuals are "incited to live as if making a *project* of themselves," as Rose puts it. "They are to *work*," and this self-work is taken for granted in the same way our "quotidian affairs . . . have become the occasion for introspection, confession and management by expertise" (1998b, 157–59, emphasis in original). At Driggs House, of course, the very organization of the place enables residents to be presented endlessly with the opportunities afforded by their own ordinary experience. But setting the group home apart this way misses the point. Residents are not unusual because they take their own selves as objects of clinical work: the never-ending pursuit of self-enhancement is the mundane work we all must do. What do set the residents apart are not their questionable capacities for independence, autonomy, freedom, or personal responsibility but the organizational and documentary practices that make *their* work *group home* work.

II. How the Group Home Works

4 ALL IN A DAY'S WORK

ON WEEKDAYS, I TRIED TO ARRIVE AT DRIGGS HOUSE around noon, to take advantage of the relative quiet before the evening shift, when the house was full. Most of the residents were not at home during the day, because residents of community-based facilities in New York State must be provided services (or be employed) outside their group homes for at least five hours per day during the week. This requirement is meant to prevent group homes from turning into institutions, if only on a smaller scale. Along with residential facilities, day treatment programs and sheltered workshops since the late 1970s have marked out what Rose (1998b, 179) describes as the "complex institutional topography" referred to as "the community."

Diane, Evelyn, Johnny, Marty, Paul, and Theresa attended day treatment (sometimes called day habilitation) programs. These programs "may vary widely" but must include "activities that provide a combination of diagnostic, active therapeutic treatment and habilitative services" (14 N.Y.C.R.R. § 635.99-1). Diane, Evelyn, and Marty attended the same facility but were in different "rooms," based on the way their needs were assessed. Many of the activities resemble the kind of curricula found in preschool, in that they emphasize creative expression and interpersonal relationships. In addition, there is "prevocational" training, which emphasizes specific skills or kinds of work. Diane's program included more of this than Marty's or Evelyn's. Johnny's was largely prevocational, and Paul and Theresa were in a program that catered to older people. "Program," as it is called at Driggs House, resembles school, and some residents, such as Diane and Evelyn, referred to it that way. But Johnny called it work, because, according to the counselors, it eased the sting he felt in being an adult who goes to school.

The other daytime service was provided by the sheltered workshop, which OMRDD regulations describe as "a facility providing remunerative employment designed to provide a controlled and protective working environment and employment activities, with individualized goals to assist the individual to progress toward normal living and productive vocational status. The objective is competitive employment if the potential exists" (14 N.Y.C.R.R. § 635.99-1). Unlike those who attend program, who get picked up and returned by van or school bus, those attending workshops take public transportation. Remuneration is nominal, but a workshop is yet another setting, as Linkow and Moriearty (169) point out, in which "the framing of activity as work" defines its main purpose. Although the regulations use the same rhetoric about the goals of individualization and productivity as that for group homes, workshops do not appear to be held to quite the stringent level of programming that group homes are. Sheltered workshops usually arrange to bring in piecework from private-sector firms of the sort that involves sorting and bagging small items such as screws. On many days there was no work at all, which for some of the residents made the workshop boring, if not frustrating. Watching movies was one solution at Jennifer's workshop, but there really was no argument with her complaint that "I can always watch movies at home." Chris, David, and Kenneth also went to workshops.

Still other residents had actual jobs, in these cases secured through supervised training and placement programs. Ruby was a stock person in a neighborhood food shop, but after some months she found the physical work taxing and a bit lonely, always being on her own in the back. She returned to the training program in hopes of acquiring a preferable job. Evan worked in a similar arrangement, bagging groceries at a large supermarket. James attended an employment training program that placed him in temporary, supervised jobs in both public-sector and not-for-profit settings.

The staffing schedule at Driggs House essentially follows the basic schedule of the residents. On weekdays there is a morning shift of three counselors (from roughly 7 a.m. to 3 p.m.) and an evening shift of five counselors (from roughly 3 p.m. to 11 p.m.). Between the hours of 11 p.m. and 6 a.m., only one counselor is required to be on duty, and he or she must remain awake. The morning and evening counselors are the staff primarily responsible for the work with residents and the bulk of paperwork. Almost all these counselors work four weekday shifts as well as one on the weekend. This provides continuity across the different weekend shift schedules and staffing patterns. Weekend counselors work twelve-hour shifts (for some the job is a part-time second position). Though all residents are potentially at home on the weekends, fewer counselors are required in the group home because there are many fewer formal tasks of work and the days are generally unstructured. Weekend counselors do not have the additional responsibility of a caseload or paperwork beyond the required daily reporting. They also do not attend the weekly staff meeting; and though it is their responsibility to review the daily log entries for the week, in practice the weekday counselors keep them up to speed on changes or problems.

Quiet Mornings

On weekday mornings, most of the residents are gone by 8:00. The morning counselors arrive between 6:30 and 7:30, in time to assist the residents with breakfast, give meds, and keep after the stragglers—especially Chris and David—who are always in danger of missing their program bus or being late for work. Sonia may arrive anytime after 9:00, although she sometimes spends whole days out of the residence, usually at the agency's administrative office for meetings and training. As the main morning counselors, Angela, Maria, and Monica are chiefly responsible for coordinating the residents' medical services. Like the evening counselors, morning counselors also have a caseload, but the main focus of their work is the residents' medical and health issues and services. This requires a substantial amount of administrative work in addition to assisting residents at the house and attending appointments. The administrative burdens of a morning counselor's work are substantial even for residents who have no health issues, because New York State mandates a variety of annual medical and psychological assessments for everyone. A large calendar in the staff office functions as a master schedule. The current month is on display and indicates, in the counselors' varied hands, the many appointments residents have with professional service providers of all sorts. The morning counselors not only ensure that the group home is in compliance with the monitoring of residents' health, they also function as advocates and health educators in doctors' offices and at home. The nurse, Beth, comes weekly. Though she has contact with the evening counselors, the morning counselors regularly consult with her about all the residents. On a day when a resident has an appointment, he or she stays home from work or program. That it is usually quiet during the morning shift means the counselors spend a great deal of time with residents who are home. Traveling to and from appointments also affords opportunities for residents and counselors to spend time together out in the community, often going shopping or out to lunch, in breaks from routine that most residents relish.

Irving was the only resident always at home during the day, because he also happened to be a group home employee, paid to do light cleaning in the kitchen three hours per day during the week. (This unusual arrangement is discussed in more detail in chapter 6.) He was aloof but for a willing listener always had a story. Often while he was cleaning the kitchen, I would sit on the radiator below the window and we'd chat. Irving had occasionally been involved in self-advocacy, the movement that emerged in the early 1970s that urges people who are labeled intellectually disabled to represent themselves in professional and political contexts. Self-advocacy has now also extended into services. Many agencies have ongoing groups that meet weekly at night, and day programs have incorporated self-advocacy as a regular activity. Irving appreciated that I was familiar with the issues, largely, it seems, because he saw it as my acceptance of his frustrations in living at Driggs House, which were often interpreted by the counselors as psychological matters.

Theresa was home more often now that she attended day treatment only three days a week, sitting quietly in the living room or with the morning counselors in the staff office. A five-day schedule became too difficult with her arthritic knee, but this semiretirement at age sixty-eight in no way diminished her active vigilance over domestic order. Theresa kept an eye on things: stopping to return stray items to their proper place; attending to someone who seemed upset; dispensing orders to residents and counselors about unfinished chores and other matters. Daniel once remarked to me with great affection, "C'mon, she's like my grandmother!" This in no way implied that Theresa is just a sweet old lady, however. Her infamous temper was occasionally provoked by Angela's insistence that Theresa do her knee exercises. On many days, I arrived to find a grumbling Theresa, perched on the edge of a chair in the middle of the staff office, Angela cheerily instructing her movements and counting out loud. Theresa was given

to running her fingers through her thick, whitish gray hair and uttering the occasional curse (in English or Italian), which was usually met
with a peal of laughter and a wink from Angela, who all the while was
doing other work as well: moving back and forth to the shelves and
drawers for filing; working at an open treatment book on the desk; or
carrying the telephone in the crook of her neck as she waited to speak
to a doctor, day program teacher, or psychologist.

Paul also attended program only three days a week. For him, semiretirement meant more time out in the community. About two weeks
after I started the research, he invited me to join him one afternoon to
return a video to the library. His arthritic knees made his walking
slow and gave him something of a shuffle. His obvious pleasure being
out and about on his own seemed to compensate for his pace. That the
five-block walk to the library took a half hour, however, had nothing
to do with his gait. As a twenty-three-year denizen of the neighborhood, Paul had a good deal of local business to conduct. He is a
sparkling character, his captain's hat covered with pins and buttons,
and he occasionally brandished a toy six-shooter or other accoutre-
ments. The shopkeepers, waitresses, and newsstand clerks we visited
along the way largely welcomed us. When we were shooed out of one
shop as soon as we crossed the threshold, Paul explained it with a dismissive wave of his hand. We had a different reception up the street,
at a discount store that carried toys, videos, CDs, and assorted gift and
novelty items. Speakers in the doorway were pumping merengue inside
and out, and Paul treated us to his version of the dance. The two
clerks standing inside laughed with us and greeted us with shouts
of "You go!" and "Huepa!" Noticing my delighted amusement at his
Caribbean Spanish cheer of excitement and appreciation, one of the
clerks affectionately explained, "Oh, yeah, we know him for years and
years. Yeah, he's been coming here forever."

After 3:00

After 3:00, the weekday-morning calm gives way to the buzzing activity of evening. The office begins to brim with counselors changing shifts
and residents coming home from program and work, mostly by 4:00
unless they have another activity elsewhere that evening. Around 3:30,
Marty, Evelyn, and Diane usually came directly into the office from
the front door across the hall. They produced their own fanfare upon

arrival, full of backslapping, handshakes, and hugs. Pictures and other projects they had made were often passed around to accompany their enthusiastic stories about the day. Diane was shy but in these moments could be very expressive and friendly. After the excitement of arrival, she settled into her more solitary pleasures. Diane moved from her mother's house only three years earlier. Her mother was eighty-five and had significant health problems, and though Diane visited often, she could never be persuaded to sleep there, always returning to the residence for the night. Evelyn had been living in the group home for five years, when she moved from the home of her long-widowed father. He became too frail to provide the regular support and attention she requires and died shortly after she moved. Evelyn, the opposite of shy with an easy and generous laugh, was comfortable and even coquettish.

Marty was also extremely sociable and always eager for conversation. Our relationship had an opportunity to develop right away, because he was home for medical appointments during the very first week of my research. Marty was delighted to have a new companion for conversation, especially someone who responded to him with equal delight. For me, having just arrived as a researcher in a workplace of busy people, his enthusiasm was both exciting and a relief. We often sat together in the living room, looking at magazines he had purchased. I was puzzled by his diverse and unlikely choices, which often included *Entertainment Weekly, Black Hair,* and *Soap Opera Digest,* but soon figured out that his pleasure was in looking at the photos of the women featured in the advertisements and articles. Those first days also established a practice we continued on and off throughout my thirteen months there: sitting together and going through the daily paper. Marty did not read well enough to make the paper an interesting activity on his own, but our collaboration made reading and discussing the tabloids interesting for us both.

Into Evening

When residents return in the late afternoon having fulfilled their outside responsibilities, like all people home from work, they pursue routine personal pleasures and take care of household chores. However, they must also participate in the formal activities that relate to becoming independent. Evening counselors spend time with residents in the bustle of group home life: giving meds, supervising dinner, chores, and most goals. It should be noted that all the core counselors have worked both morning and evening shifts, sometimes swapping or covering for each other when there are schedule changes. Counselors take for granted the difference in kind of work and tone between shifts, which I emphasize here only to convey the overall rhythm of the Driggs House day.

Meds at 5:00 and 9:00 were central organizing features of the evening schedule. The counselor giving meds might walk through the residence to announce that he or she was starting, though this was hardly necessary, given how attuned most residents were to the schedule. Given that meds took at least an hour to dispense, some residents hung out in the living room until the counselor came through or a resident returning from the med office told them it was their turn. David, Diane, Donna, and Jennifer, paper cups of water in hand, often assembled in the staff office around 9:00. Although these four did not converse with each other much, the staff office could be a lively spot at that hour, and it's just next door to the med room. Meds could sometimes shape the course of an evening by disrupting other plans. They must be given on schedule (at 7:00 in the morning, and at 5:00 and 9:00 in the evening) and only by staff members who have received state training and certification (14 N.Y.C.R.R. § 633.17). So when Daniel became ill and went home early one night when he was planning to do 9:00 meds, Susan happened to be the only other certified counselor working that shift, which meant she wasn't able to do Evelyn's hair as planned. This situation points to the changeable course of things at Driggs House, an issue I discuss in a number of ways in the remainder of the book.

On weekday afternoons, it wasn't long after the residents got home that some gathered in the living room to hang out, chat, and watch TV while they waited for dinner. Individuals used the living room in their own ways. Although the television was on, it never prevented conversation, and often people just sat quietly or as Diane did, in the middle of the action with her own soundtrack. The living room is pleasantly furnished, with three couches and two large armchairs, all in burgundy or brown. Wallpaper, some framed still lifes in the same color scheme, and two end tables with lamps give the room a comfortable glow. Only the two armchairs and one couch face the television, but this provides ample seats for viewers. (The 2000 World Series was the one exception, resulting in a temporary rearrangement of the furniture, but as a Subway Series between the two New York teams, it was an exception in itself.) Dinner was usually served between 6:00 and 7:00, depending on the skills and schedules of the counselor and residents at work in the kitchen. People were always passing through, and the traffic between the living room and the rest of the house brought regular news about the projected time of dinner. That dinnertime varied from day to day was a frequent source of annoyance for Kenneth; he watched impatiently for Ruby to set the table, which she waited to do until the last few minutes. This was not a new problem, so he himself told me, and on many occasions he stopped himself in the middle of complaining to say, "Really, I shouldn't be so upset about dinner. It's not something to be upset about. I worry too much."

Aside from talk about what was being served up and when, there was an ongoing conversation in the living room among certain residents about group home operations. Chris, Irving, Jennifer, Kenneth, Marty, Ruby, and Theresa were always engaged in shoptalk and knew everyone's schedules: who attended evening recreational programs on which nights, and what time they came home; who had medical appointments when, whether a counselor was going along and, if so, which one; who was visiting family, where, and for how long. These residents also understood the general medication procedures and knew which counselors were certified to give meds. They followed staffing issues with a keenness and accuracy one might expect of a traditional worker. The practical ramifications of a counselor out for illness or vacation were an endless source of discussion and analysis. There were animated debates about the distribution of counselor tasks, staffing patterns, and schedules. When counselors wandered through the living room, also waiting for dinner to be served, they were often consulted for missing pieces of information: "When is Cheryl getting back from her vacation?" "Why is Sally away again? She just went on vacation!" "How many days will Sonia be at her meetings?" Counselors passing through were also informed of the discussion's findings. Carlos came in one day at about 5:00 to announce he was giving meds, and Kenneth asked, "So what happens if Daniel's sick again tomorrow?" Carlos replied matter-of-factly, "He *is* gonna be sick again tomorrow. He has the flu." Kenneth was incredulous: "But that's not fair! That'll mean you have to do meds three days in a row!"

Which counselor cooks dinner was decided during the "shift meeting," the brief, informal huddle that occurred around 3:00 when the evening counselors arrived. There were several routine responsibilities that must be assigned on each shift, including giving meds. Cooking was unpopular with some counselors, because being tied to the kitchen could be an impediment in work that is largely characterized by contingency and the juggling of multiple tasks. Most of the residents had a cooking goal, and any given one of them was supposed to be working on it with the counselor who was preparing dinner, but on most evenings residents did not want to participate. Counselors were also not terribly concerned about the cooking goals for practical reasons: they were too busy keeping their eye on activities occurring elsewhere. At one point, Sonia announced at a staff meeting that residents were not participating enough in cooking and chided counselors that it was their responsibility to encourage residents to do their cooking goals, but this had little effect.

Nevertheless, cooking provided me an opportunity to spend time with certain residents or to ease a bit the workload of an evening counselor. Cooking goals organize meal preparation in terms of the specific techniques that teach residents how to do it. There is an analogy between recipes for cooking and goals as recipes for conduct. The systematic approach to cooking that recipes represent easily exacerbates counselors' routine workload conflicts, and counselors often did not use written recipes. This did not pose a problem for me. I found that even though residents had little interest, someone who was scheduled to do his or her cooking goal might help out a little with the meal preparation or just hang around the kitchen more than usual. Just as with recipes, the precision with which all goals are written does not determine how they are actually followed or how they shape conduct.

When it was time to eat, it took only a holler or a casual mention to a nearby resident to marshal everyone. From all over the house, residents and counselors responded to the welcome cry: "Dinner! Wash your hands! Dinner's ready!" People took a plate from one of the four round tables in the dining room, already set by Ruby, and filed through the kitchen to be served. As each resident finished eating, he or she got up and deposited dish, silverware, and cup in the kitchen sink, where they piled up until Diane loaded them into the dishwasher. This was her chore, one of many that were carried out in a slow swell of activity following the meal that continued into the evening. In addition to cleaning up the kitchen and dining room, chores included cleaning the bathrooms, emptying all the garbage cans in the residence, and vacuuming the offices and living room. Some people disappeared into their rooms or hung out in the staff office when they finished their chores. Others settled in the living room, where a typical scene might include Diane and Marty watching TV; Kenneth, Ruby, and Theresa talking about which counselors were working on the weekend; Johnny doing one of his word-find puzzles; and Donna snoozing. Irving spent most evenings in his room watching television. Ruby was sometimes there too. She was his one regular friend and occasional lover. The counselors suspected so, but apparently neither would acknowledge it to them. Irving once implied to me in passing that he and Ruby were involved sexually, and I asked outright. He replied incredulously, "What'd you think I meant?" On another occasion, Ruby also implied to me that their relationship was romantic or sexual, but I was not comfortable asking her directly. I often stopped in to Irving's room in the evenings to hang out, and Ruby was often there. With the TV tuned to the news, we would chat about current events taking place in the house and elsewhere.

To say that people settled down after they had finished their chores is really to say that the evening settled into its regular rhythm. In the group home there is always movement. In the course of routine evening activities, residents and counselors were always passing between the staff office at one end of the house and the living room at the other. In addition to specific goals and other tasks that residents and counselors did and demanded of each other, weekday evenings included various scheduled activities. The residents' meeting on Mondays at 8:00 was the only event that included everybody. On other nights, there were activities involving only individuals or specific groups of residents, and sometimes additional people were even added to the mix. On Tuesdays, the speech therapist came for a few hours to work one-on-one with four residents, and used the med office or supervisor's office for privacy. On Thursdays, Cynthia, the behavior specialist, and Miles, an evening counselor, ran a peer support group with four or five residents in the supervisor's office at 8:00. For three months, Christina, a master's student in psychology, came on Wednesdays as an intern.

Some Quiet

Despite the relatively predictable pace of weekdays—the quiet morning giving way to the bustle of evening—the group home is characterized by contingencies of all kinds, which in the main are treated as routine. There were fewer surprises on weekends. Then, the house was typically tranquil all day. Residents came and went on their own or in small groups. Some preferred to hang around the house and relax. Others went to the movies or the park. There was usually one rec trip, a scheduled outing organized by residents and staff, usually at the residents' meeting. A rec trip might involve taking a large group in the van to the beach, to Daniel's mother's house for a barbecue, or bowling. It might involve a few residents getting on the subway with Sally and going to a department store or just out to lunch in the neighborhood. The easy feel of weekends always kept me around the residence, hanging out and talking, listening to music and watching TV; or out in the community for lunch, shopping, a walk around the neighborhood, or, with Marty, for haircuts.

On weeknights, it was just before 11:00 that Theresa usually returned to the residence from her nightly excursion to a neighborhood twenty-four-hour coffee shop. She presided over "going down for coffee," though David went with her every evening and more often than not they were joined by any combination of others, who might include James, Kenneth, Ruby, Donna, Chris, Johnny, or me. When we arrived, around 9:30 or 10:00, and took our places at the counter of the coffee shop, it was never especially busy. Even so, we were not the only regulars. There were the familiar faces of a few hospital workers, cabbies, and others having a meal or coffee at the beginning or end of their own workdays. Some acknowledged us warmly. Others took no notice at all. The hour or so we spent at the counter each evening provided an alternative to the bustling group home, but the topics of conversation were the same: the logistics of scheduling and appointments, rec trip plans, disputes or trouble in the house, and so on. The waitresses knew us by name and, as they wiped down the stainless, filled creamers, and cut pies, would inquire about the group home pleasures and problems they followed nightly. Often we would just sit and sip our coffee, watching them work.

Although on weekdays I usually arrived before the evening counselors, I rarely stayed after 11:00, because by the time their shift was over, the house was quiet for the night. There might be a few residents in the living room and staff office, but most were in their rooms. When the house was truly still, Theresa did her rounds. In powder blue felt slippers and a housecoat over her nightgown, she put away any pots left to dry after dinner; woke Paul or Donna, who might have fallen asleep in the living room in front of the TV; and checked on the overnight counselor in the staff office before heading to bed herself.

Research Work, Group Home Work

My first day at Driggs House started with a staff meeting in which I made a presentation to the counselors about the research. I emphasized that my approach was "social" and focused on the residents—on what they do every day and on their ideas about group home life. I did this largely because I knew from my own experience as a counselor that the nature of group home work and the personal investment counselors have can make them suspicious of outsiders. When Sonia and I met privately before the staff meeting, she indicated that she understood this also. It wasn't long into the research that I was able to imagine how individual staff members had reacted to her announcement that a sociologist would be in the house regularly doing a long-term project. Sonia's sensitivity to these issues influenced how I presented the research to the counselors at that first staff meeting. Besides emphasizing my interest in the residents, I omitted the degree to which the counselors' own work was also of interest to me. At first sight, the ethics of this strategy may appear questionable. Because of my unstructured approach to participant observation, however, I do not think this omission raised the ethical question in the way it would have if I had used formal techniques with the staff (such as interviews or questionnaires).

What I knew with certainty from my own work experience was that the trust of the counselors was utterly crucial to the research. I emphasized that I was not there to conduct an evaluation of group home services and assured them that, apart from obvious violations that I was obliged to report, anything they discussed with me would be confidential and discussed with neither Sonia nor anyone else at the agency. I carefully attempted to distinguish the group home's clinical perspective from my social one. The counselors were largely receptive and appreciated that I was "trying to understand the residents in a different way." Only one counselor in the meeting was openly skeptical. For Lisa, mental retardation plus residents' specific psychological or physical issues made the whole enterprise at Driggs House self-evident: "What more is there to know about the residents' perspectives? I mean, how is it relevant?" Though most of the counselors found the project interesting and seemed pleased about it, it was less easy than I expected to define a social perspective in a setting where the matters at hand are patently not social at all. One way that I illustrated this distinction was by explaining my decision not to read the residents' records right away. I didn't want my initial perceptions and developing relationships with them to be colored by official diagnostic and other information. It was important to get to know them first as they interacted with each other and the staff, and as they participated in group home routine. The counselors found this very compelling. What I did not explain was that I regarded the records also as records of counselor work, and I did not want their formal clinical accounts to color my initial observations of either the residents in their work or the counselors in theirs.

In fact, the counselors did not appear either suspicious or threatened, and there is no question that from the outset my credibility was enhanced by having also been a counselor in similar group homes. Even so, it was in the course of the work itself that they were convinced I wouldn't just be getting in the way and that I had the interest of the residents—as well as the counselors' own interests—at heart. From the first, counselors saw that my past work experience meant I was comfortable with the rhythms of group home life, and they realized immediately that my regular presence at Driggs House eased the demands residents made on the counselors' time. The counselors may have had to be convinced in this practical way, but Sonia was frank with me before things even got started that, whatever my research interests, she presumed my presence alone would be a benefit to residents and counselors alike. There were many routine activities in which I could participate right away, because they required no assistance or explanation from a counselor: preparing dinner, running errands with residents, helping with their laundry, helping to clean their rooms, packing for a weekend visit to their families, and many other things. After a few weeks, counselors confessed that they had assumed I would simply "do nothing but hang around and get in the way," as visiting clinicians and interns are usually seen to do. It was my willingness to "really get involved with the guys," the counselors said, that allayed their worries as they anticipated my arrival on the scene.

The counselors regarded my return to a group home as a researcher as recognition of the importance of the work they do. For a few weeks they treated me as a kind of expert, which made me wonder whether they really were at ease with me being there all the time. My presence seemed to oblige spontaneous explanations of every aspect of group home life. This no doubt reflected the counselors' adjustment—and mine, as I was aiming to craft just the right personal identity as a non-staff group home worker—but it also reflected their engagement in the work. They were attentive to me in part because Sonia had told them to be of assistance, but they were always eager to talk about their work, especially their clinical work with residents, and not just with me but also with each other. My status as counselor-cum-researcher seemed to offer them an opportunity to exercise their interest and skill in the clinical issues that are, for them, the professional and most meaningful aspect of the job. After a few weeks, when I got the hang of the routines and was developing relationships with both staff and residents, my presence no longer seemed to oblige special attention or instruction. It would be naive to suggest that my presence went unnoticed, but it wasn't long before my being there was in no way unusual. One indication of this was the counselors' willingness in my presence to complain about Sonia, the agency, and each other in their routine shoptalk. Throughout my thirteen months there, however, I continued to ask counselors for explanations of what they were doing. On occasion I elicited a laugh or raised eyebrow with questions that were "so obvious," but this never seemed to affect the perception of my group home competence, precisely because counselors were always engaged in shoptalk. In chapter 6, I describe their shoptalk as a central feature of their work and as a kind of work itself. It was not long before my questions simply became a routine part of that work.

It was after my first staff meeting that I met the residents, informally, in the course of a normal Thursday afternoon. I explained that I was not a counselor and did not work for the agency. I was a researcher doing a project for school about "what happens at a place like Driggs House" and "what they do there every day," and I hoped they would be willing to tell me about life in the group home. No one was particularly surprised by my being there, because Sonia had announced at a residents' meeting when I was coming and what I would be doing (though I was never able to get a detailed description of what she said). I had assumed it would be necessary to obtain a signed consent from each resident and had prepared my own forms. However, though it was a community residence (CR), the residents were not regarded as competent; their consent was provided in loco parentis by the agency.

Nevertheless, over the first week I made a point of discussing with each resident individually not only the nature of the research but also the meaning of confidentiality and the voluntary nature of his or her participation. These two issues seemed to be of little concern to the residents as a rule, because, I realized in time, they were quite used to people passing through—for an evening or for months—who were seen to have the privileges, interests, knowledge, and authority of staff. This was doubtless the case with me, especially at first, but even more relevant was the fact that I was a novelty: a new person who was going to be around (and for some time). The real issues for them included my schedule, how long I'd be there on any given day, and whether I would have time to spend with them.

Most of the residents understood I was there "to learn about the group home" and "for the clients to teach me things." There were three—Donna, Evelyn, and Diane—who appeared to know only that I was "not staff." For everyone (just as for the counselors), it was in practical ways that my distinct nonstaff personal identity came into focus: I did not have keys. I did not have access to the spending money, which for most residents was kept in a metal lockbox in the staff office. I did not do meds. The residents realized immediately that I was not burdened by the demands of counselor work and had time to spend. Most were comfortable with me from the very beginning. A few were more reticent. With Jennifer, who was frankly suspicious, it took more than a week before I felt I could approach her comfortably and ask her to sit and talk so I could explain what I was doing. She assured me quite decisively that she wouldn't be talking to me about much, but even she soon warmed up as she watched my unique role at Driggs House take shape. During my months of research, I was both a pal to the residents and a source of assistance and support. They frequently asked me to help with goals and innumerable other mundane matters for which they usually turned to counselors. But often I just hung around the living room, chatting and watching television; going for walks, coffee, or errands with them; or spending time with them in their rooms talking, listening to music, or viewing their personal collections and memorabilia, such as photographs, magazines, books, puzzles, mugs, stuffed animals, and cassette tapes.

Although what confusion there was about the nature of my nonstaff role diminished pretty quickly, it did raise sticky problems throughout my time at Driggs House. The counselors had more difficulty than the residents in recognizing that I was not there to "work" with the residents. As much as the counselors found my research generally interesting (or at least harmless and unobtrusive), I do not know whether it ever made sense to them outside the perspective of their own work. There is no doubt they came to see me as a relatively trustworthy colleague, but occasionally their expectations of me in relationship to clinical issues produced confusion. Lisa remained skeptical and for a few weeks took the occasional opportunity to remind me that I was not an insider and to imply, as I perceived it, that she regarded me as nothing more than a voyeur. In several instances when residents were upset about something or there was conflict in a staff meeting, she made snide remarks: "Oh, *that* will be interesting for your research." Lisa left the job four months into my research so she could attend a master's program in psychology full-time. Her skepticism, though short-lived and unique, proved to be an early indication that it would be impossible to undo the assumption shared by most of the counselors that their work and my work had the same goals. Whatever else this assumption reflected, it was an indication of the kind of commitment counselors have to their sense of the group home's clinical mission. It occurred to me that this assumption may have been an unintended result of how strongly I emphasized my interest in the residents during the presentation at my first staff meeting. Yet during my first month or two at Driggs House, the counselors and I discussed the research frequently. The nature of my role and the residents' reactions to me were frequent topics of shoptalk, because my presence furnished novel occasions for the counselors' ongoing clinical analysis. Early on, when counselors asked questions or offered examples they thought would interest me especially, I would take care to distinguish my perspective from theirs. These discussions, however, were always part of counselor shoptalk and though their specific interest in whether I saw things differently never disappeared, it was soon hard to separate out from the general ongoing conversation about the residents and life at Driggs House.

I began a systematic examination of the records after about two months. I read them only when residents were not around, in the early afternoons or on weekends when the house was relatively quiet. Although they had access to their own records, in a formal legal sense, the content was largely inaccessible even for those who were able to read. It didn't seem to occur to residents that I wouldn't have access to the records in the office, and some were well aware when I began reading them. In fact, there were few places where I could look at these materials in private. Sometimes the med room or Sonia's office was empty, but after 3:00 on weekdays there was always somebody eager to use the room for assistance or companionship. I could have read the records in view in the staff office, as the counselors did, or I could have closed the med room door and said I was busy with paperwork, which counselors sometimes must do to get their work done. But claiming that reading the records was work that had to get done and that warranted privacy would have come into conflict with my unique not-a-counselor personal identity. And, given that the residents always wanted to spend time with me, I thought that spending time with their treatment and goal books rather than with them would have been simply inconsiderate.

I was also very conscious from the outset about how and when I would take field notes. After a while, I was comfortable doing this in the staff office, because "doing paperwork" was not out of place there. But I would not do more than jot down something quickly in the presence of residents or counselors. If Sonia's office was free in the evenings or on weekends, I might sit in there with the door open and write for the short time I could be alone, usually not more than ten or fifteen minutes. When she was not at the residence, her office served as a refuge for everyone. On weekends, when the house was quieter, I spent a good deal of time there with residents, and it came to be a place where everyone knew I might be found. They understood the purpose of my writing, so when they discovered me taking notes, if they commented on it at all it was in the unremarkable declarative manner of Jennifer's question one Saturday afternoon as she walked in and greeted me: "Are you writing about the clients."

Passing Work

To preserve the trust of both counselors and residents, I had to demonstrate different kinds of competence in ways that can be described only as "passing." Following Goffman (1963), the concept has remained a cornerstone of writing about stigma in many areas, and it was Edgerton who used it first and most famously in the study of intellectual disability. Even though the management of personal information is a central aspect of field research, I am not aware of any writing that has used passing to describe the experience. Ivan Karp and Martha Kendall

discuss the analogies that have been used to describe fieldworkers—
the stranger, the second-language learner, the developing child—and
emphasize the inherent paradoxes that in my experience at Driggs
House were best captured as passing. "Field workers," they wrote,
"are persons who both affirm and deny the validity of native conceptions . . . know less than natives, but claim to know more . . . [and] . . .
must of necessity experience their mode of existence as profoundly
alienated" (269). This process of affirmation and denial was particularly sticky for me at Driggs House.

I had no choice with counselors but to pass as a kind of colleague.
There was never a moment when I was unaware of having to avoid
appearing to be an "advocate," a role they claimed for themselves and
used antagonistically to describe others. The counselors were quick
at times to peg outsiders as naive about "the reality of the house" and
"what's really going on" with a resident—the things that families,
upper-level supervisors, agency and outside clinicians, and others "just
don't see." The sticky part was that, at the same time, I had to avoid
appearing to be a counselor, both to counselors and residents. Because
there is no clear distinction between work and other activities at Driggs
House, passing in public involved maintaining an appearance that
the counselors could see as tacit agreement and acceptance of their
authority but that residents could see as nonstaff.

Given that counselors were always intervening in residents' conduct, being in the presence of both required maintaining what often
felt like an uneasy neutrality. For example, when a counselor shut
down the casual conversation of a resident because the topic was, for
whatever reason, inappropriate, I would say nothing even if I disagreed. I let the resident determine how to handle the situation and
would never intervene. Mandell described managing analogous dilemmas in ethnographic research on children by assuming what she called
the "least-adult role." When I was alone with residents, passing as a
nonstaff "normal," to borrow Goffman's (1963) ironic use of the term,
involved little work. I did not pursue or enforce the clinical concerns
of counselors, which released me from the tension I experienced in varying degrees whenever I was with counselors or, especially, both counselors and residents. Residents caught on quickly to my indifference
to many of the issues that were central to counselor work, and their
expectations did not produce conflicts with the not-a-counselor personal identity at Driggs House that I crafted and worked to maintain.

The phrase "personal identity" is perhaps not necessary for under-standing how I had to pass in the group home. I have borrowed it, again from Goffman, to emphasize that in order to observe the social order of the group home, I had to be a taken-for-granted part of it. This was more difficult than I expected and required the ongoing work of passing in different ways. Maintaining the trust and ease of both counselors and residents was obviously necessary for my research work, but passing had implications beyond the interpersonal work it involved. The kind of group home person I was perceived to be had everything to do with how group home work was observable to me. Goffman's explanation of personal identity in *Stigma* (1963, 57) cap-tures something I came to learn at Driggs House about organizational life and field research:

> Personal identity . . . has to do with the assumption that the individual can be differentiated from all others and that around this means of differentia-tion a single continuous record of social facts can be attached, entangled like candy floss, becoming then the sticky substance to which still other biograph-ical facts can be attached. What is difficult to appreciate is that personal identity can and does play a structured, routine, standardized role in social organization just because of its one-of-a-kind quality.

Some of the tasks I was not permitted to perform at Driggs House involved specific issues of liability, such as administering medication. There were many other kinds of tasks that I might have been permit-ted to do but that the counselors judged to be clinically inappropriate for a nonstaff person or simply a potential source of confusion about my role. Occasionally counselors addressed such a question explicitly. The clearest example occurred during a period when staff were observ-ing Marty in the shower to ensure that he washed properly. In a shift meeting, the counselors were figuring out who would observe him that night. Sally, a South Asian American woman in her early twenties, said that she did not want to do it. She reminded us that a month or so before, she had knocked and announced herself at Marty's bedroom door, and he invited her in even though he was masturbating openly on the bed. Sally had been upset when it happened but said she did not feel threatened by Marty in general. Such experiences are not un-familiar in services; researchers have examined how men with intel-lectual disabilities use sexual provocation to challenge the authority of women staff (Thompson, Clare, and Brown). As far as I know,

however, this was the only such instance with Marty. The only similar
instances between a resident and counselor at Driggs House were
Paul's requests to Angie and Maria on different occasions to describe
the bathing suits they had worn to the beach. This was treated un-
equivocally as inappropriate but not described by the counselors as
unmanageable or threatening. When Sally reminded us of her experience with Marty, they all agreed that the women counselors should
not observe Marty in the shower. Miles suggested that perhaps I could
do it along with the other men, because I had a good relationship with
Marty. This idea was dismissed immediately by the other counselors
(including Sally, the only woman working that night) as "inappropriate" and "too intrusive." I said that I would be perfectly comfortable doing it if they felt it appropriate, but the decision had already
been made.

Counselors did expect me, however, to address the routine clinical
concerns they regarded as necessary work with the residents. It was
in these ongoing, everyday ways that the tensions of passing in public
were most acute. I could not always predict when a counselor would
question why I had refrained from intervening in what they viewed as
a resident's problem. (This happened only rarely, because I learned
early that I had to be careful.) One lesson occurred in the first month
of my research. Around 9:00 in the evening, David came to find me in
the living room, where I was watching TV with a bunch of residents.
He was wearing his bathrobe and asked if I would help him regulate the water temperature for his shower. I obliged him happily. That
he seemed to have sought me out specifically made me suspect that his
request was not random. Later that evening, in the staff office, I mentioned it to Lisa as "interesting." This was the kind of little story that
for the counselors could generate a rich and sustained discussion, but
Lisa frowned with displeasure: "Well, he's supposed to ask his peers
for assistance and then, if they won't help him, he can come to staff."
I acted contrite about having assisted him. Lisa emphasized that the
responsibility was David's—"He knows what he's supposed to do"—
but chastised me for not having already known about the issue. She
suggested I read the goal plans right away so I would "know how
to deal with the guys." I immediately regretted mentioning David's
request to Lisa, because I worried she'd discuss it with him and he'd
presume I reported to staff that he had not followed the plan. That
never happened, as far as I know. But I took the conversation with

Lisa as an early indication of the kind of expectations counselors might have of me. It was also a lesson that, for counselors, coordinating their action, at least in principle, represented an important affirmation of their work as clinical work. And it was soon clear to me that disputes about how to deal with residents in one or another respect were flashpoints in the group home that often caused conflict among counselors.

In theory, there were many tasks that presented general concerns about liability, and my participation when they arose depended on the residents involved and the degree to which Sonia considered me capable of handling certain problems. But only one issue raised this question repeatedly: Marty's falls. For some time, Marty had been experiencing episodes when he was suddenly unable to remain standing. On a few occasions, he hit his arm or head falling down and sustained cuts and bruises (though in the vast majority of his falls, Marty was not injured). He had been taken to several specialist physicians, but no physiological cause could be found. A few months before I started the research, a psychiatrist had provided psychosomatic diagnoses (factitious disorder and conversion disorder) and referred to the falls as "pseudoseizures." In the group home, the falls were seen as symptoms of Marty's anxiety. Staff saw them at times as "beyond his control" or "resembl[ing] panic attacks," and at other times as "attempts to seek attention" and "escape." Marty found these falls very upsetting and would often cry and call out to counselors and other residents when they occurred. He himself did not require neurological evidence to regard them as troublesome and involuntary. He described them as "nervous moments," though I do not know whether it was Marty or the staff who first suggested the connection between his falls and anxiety ("being nervous").

For staff, the psychological basis of Marty's falls meant that the behavior was amenable to change and he could learn how to manage or even stop falling through the systematic technical approach of a behavior plan. The aim of a behavior plan is to reduce or stop some kind of negative conduct. A plan identifies the "target" conduct and provides specific techniques for both counselors and the resident to use when it occurs. When I started the research, counselors were very frustrated by Marty, because various plans had failed to eliminate or even reduce his falls. Early on the Thursday afternoon one week after I started my fieldwork, Sonia described to me the more rigorous behavior plan that had been implemented just two weeks earlier. The plan defined falling as inappropriate attention seeking behavior that should not be reinforced. For counselors, the plan provided techniques that would not reinforce Marty: counselors must "interact in a neutral manner" until he "regains control." In effect, Marty was to be ignored (if he did not injure himself) until he was able to stand up and walk on his own. As Sonia explained, Marty would learn that his falling was related to the way he managed (or didn't manage) his own feelings. When he fell, staff members were not supposed to talk with him about "his issues" until he "calms down and is able to get up on his own." This apparently frustrated him and "for the moment" had even increased his agitation, which for Sonia was evidence that the plan was "having some effect" and "actually working."

When I was alone with residents, I did not follow the clinical interventions, formal or informal, that counselors expected of me and each other. I would intervene, however, in instances when I judged that not responding or responding differently could potentially harm or confuse residents or pose work problems for counselors. Marty's situation illustrates this conflict most clearly, because it posed the possibility of real physical harm. Because Marty was home a good deal when I started the research, we had the opportunity to spend time together, and he never had a fall when we were alone. When he fell during the evenings and lay in the middle of the hallway or in the dining room calling out to people for help, it was painful to me to ignore him as the plan prescribed. But these episodes were very public, and counselors were required to document them in a special log. I knew that dealing with him in any unusual way would inevitably be known to staff. This would have put me in conflict with the staff consensus about a problem that was a source of great frustration to them not only because of the potentially serious consequences but also because their work seemed never to make much difference.

When the falls became a problem, Marty was prohibited from going out in the community without a staff member, for fear that he would fall in the street or injure himself and not be able to get home. If he did fall, the plan called for counselors to move Marty to safety, if necessary, and return him to the residence immediately. Furthermore, unlike Diane, Donna, and Evelyn, Marty was not allowed out with other residents. Marty was also not allowed out alone with me at first.

Less than two weeks after I arrived, however, he began asking Sonia and the counselors whether we could go out together. I approached Sonia privately to let her know that I would also like very much to be able to go out in the community with him and was comfortable doing so. I had not expressed this to the counselors, I told her, because they generally opposed the idea, and I did not want to appear to be challenging their judgment. Sonia had the authority to make such a decision, and at my third staff meeting she announced that she had given me permission to go out with Marty. She said that she felt I could handle any problem that might come up, given how smoothly my transition to Driggs House had gone and my prior work experience. In addition, Marty had been pestering her about it and seemed to like me so much that she thought it was worth reinforcing the positive relationship. She portrayed the decision as clear-cut and motivated by Marty's interest alone. Some counselors who had opposed the idea before were perfectly comfortable. A few opposed the decision, not on the grounds that I couldn't handle it but simply because I was non-staff or because it "sent the wrong message" to Marty.

This situation points to the particular discretion I was able to exercise at Driggs House, which was both part of and concealed by my work of passing. Marty and I took many neighborhood excursions on our own: for coffee and doughnuts, for errands, for walks, and for haircuts. The first time we went out, I was slightly worried that Marty would fall. It was actually many months before he had an experience out with me that warranted returning him to the residence; and in all the times we were out in the community by ourselves, there were only two such occasions. Both times, Marty suddenly said he was unsteady but not actually falling. I was out in a group with Marty, other residents, and a counselor a number of times when the same kind of thing happened. Even the suggestion that Marty might fall resulted in the counselor immediately returning with him. By the time such a thing occurred when we were alone, Marty and I knew each other well and I was long over my worry about the kind of risk he posed to himself. In both cases, when Marty said he felt unsteady on his feet, I suggested that just we sit and relax for awhile. The first time, we sat down on a conveniently located stoop, where we chatted for about ten minutes before he announced that he felt fine and we were on our way. The second time, we plopped ourselves right down on the sidewalk in front of the regular doughnut shop, where, over coffee, we chatted and watched the passersby before heading home. I never reported these incidents as required, because as far as I was concerned they were not incidents at all. And, of course, I would have had to justify not returning with Marty immediately. I had made a judgment in these instances that not following the plan would risk neither Marty's safety nor the staff's discovery of what I had or hadn't done.

5 ENDLESS, UNCERTAIN WORK

DRIGGS HOUSE is very much like the kind of workplace Michael Lipsky calls a "street-level bureaucracy." Counselors face many of the dilemmas that characterize the public service work of "people processing" in a range of settings—welfare offices, public schools, free medical clinics, and police stations, to name a few—in which there is an inherent conflict between always-limited resources and potentially limitless work. The climate of regulation and accountability that dominates social services, both public and private, is also always at odds with an ideology of care. That is, bureaucratic rationalization and the prevailing emphasis on client autonomy and individuality are always in tension and must be made compatible in the work itself. Lipsky argues, in a phenomenological vein, that in order to cope with these conflicts, individual workers develop informal patterns of practice that are at times unwittingly opposed to official principles of service. These practices nonetheless manage the ongoing clash between professional ideals and organizational demands, because they enable workers to get the job done and in relatively satisfying ways. It is in these informal yet routine practices, rather than in policy meetings and legislative chambers, Lipsky argues, that service outcomes are actually determined.

Lipsky argues that street-level bureaucracies are fundamental to contemporary social order in a way that is strikingly similar to other researchers' historical argument about technologies of government (Dean 1996, 1999; Miller and Rose; Rose 1998b, 1994). Street-level bureaucracies are "organizational embodiments of contradictory tendencies" in the welfare state (Lipsky, 183–84), because they must always be both normative and coercive. Across multiple areas, street-level bureaucracies "delimit people's lives and opportunities . . . provid[ing] the social (and political) contexts in which people act." For Lipsky, such settings "hold the keys to a dimension of citizenship," because, in addition to providing specific services, they also "socialize" individuals "to expectations of government services . . . [and] a place in the political community . . . [by] mediat[ing] aspects of the constitutional relationship of citizens to the state."

I observed these inherent conflicts in the work at Driggs House less as a criticism of the welfare state than as the embodiment of the problem of liberal rule. Lipsky's phenomenological focus on work practice and service outcomes sets his analysis apart from most research on social service workplaces, but he is also concerned with power and control as questions for policy. His argument about street-level bureaucracies provides a useful point of departure away from the familiar approach to settings like the group home as "forcing houses for changing persons" (Goffman 1961, 12), which focuses on the coerced nature of identity and experience. I approach Driggs House as a workplace precisely because it allows organizational participation and commitment to be seen not simply as a problem of power but also as a dilemma of freedom.

Autonomy and Professional Work

Like all street-level bureaucrats, group home counselors have a good deal of autonomy. This has a practical basis: much of their work is done individually with residents and out of view of supervisors and often colleagues, and requires the constant exercise of individual judgment. The need to exercise discretion reflects, in part, the very nature of their material—human conduct—work on which cannot be accomplished with standardized procedures. For counselors, having a good deal of discretion is an indication of the importance of the job, and they often emphasize the "human dimensions" that make their work serious professional work (Lipsky, 50). Everett Hughes (44) recognized that "profession" "is not so much a descriptive term as one of value and prestige," functioning as "a symbol for a desired conception of one's work and, hence, of one's self." Paperwork, by contrast, is regarded largely as a burden, but it is not "dirty work," in Hughes's sense (70). Counselors recognize paperwork as necessary, if at times burdensome, especially because it is imposed by those who appear most out of touch with the everyday demands of their work: supervisors, the agency, state regulators, auditors, and the like. Clinical work is the "real" work, both meaningful and interesting; counselors often refer to their low pay and unusual hours as proof of the job's moral value and the personal sacrifices they make for it.

Whatever the tensions at Driggs House between bureaucratic accountability and clinical ideals, work on human conduct is complex, ambiguous, and indeterminate. Outcomes are difficult to define and measure, which makes the very work that is most meaningful to counselors the most prone to personal disappointment and the greatest source of conflict with colleagues. The counselors make sense of their daily successes and failures through ideas about their work that have emerged in that work: the mission of the group home, the characteristics and needs of residents, and clinical and moral beliefs about their own role. At times, counselors are strongly committed to their ideas about the clinical function of Driggs House. At other times, they consider their work too clinical. Sometimes their commitment to the rights and autonomy of residents accounts for choices or outcomes in the work. At other times, these ideals are obstacles to what a resident "really needs." That counselors account for their work in varied, even contradictory, ways is not an indication of poor training or limited capacity. It indicates how they must make sense of the ambiguous and indeterminate work they do. Treating it as meaningful professional work is one way counselors get a handle on work that is characterized by such inherent conflict. Lipsky (xiii) observed this of street-level bureaucrats generally, who "believe themselves to be doing the best they can under adverse circumstances." They "salvage service and decision-making values," in part, through the ideas they develop about themselves and their clients, which "narrow the gap between their personal and work limitations and the service ideal."

Counselors at times portrayed Driggs House as a buzzing and chaotic place: demanding but exhilarating, thankless but satisfying. Especially when they understand their unpredictable, even failure-prone, work as clinical work, it can be enjoyed for the discretion and knowledgeable judgment it involves. When they embrace the clinical mission, counselors align themselves with the overall message promoted in training by the agency and in the group home by Sonia. In a staff meeting, Sonia once addressed counselors, much to their pleasure, "as translators for people with mental retardation. They have feelings but don't always know what to do with them or how to express them, and . . . you partly are there to assist with this." Daniel favored analogies to parenting and attributed his understanding of, and even ease with, residents to his experience having teenage daughters. The general assumption that both teens and residents are characterized by their questionable autonomy meant, for Daniel, that they similarly require guidance and leadership but also encouragement to be as independent as they can and to have the confidence to take risks. He described the group home ideally "as a cushion for [residents] to fall back on," a notion he qualified with one aspect of group home work that makes it endless work: "Of course, there are guys here who can't go beyond where they are, which is fine."

Daniel's analogy illustrates how the dilemmas of freedom that define Driggs House are framed in clinical terms. What seemed to make Daniel's analogy plausible in the group home was not the historic equation of intellectual disability and childhood but the increasing assumption that raising children itself is understood increasingly as a technical practice—parenting—that depends on the knowledge of experts (Wrigley; cf. Brockley 2004). As with teenagers, presumably, the clinical orientation at Driggs House frames but does not necessarily solve the problems related to exercising authority over citizens considered incapable of living freely. Sally expressed her frustration with Diane in a staff meeting in this way: "She's so hard to motivate— refusing rec trips, requiring lots of prompts for ADLs, you know?" ("ADL" refers to activities of daily living, which include basic hygiene, personal care, and other routine matters.) Sally paused before expressing her exasperation in a rhetorical question that presumed her sentiments were shared: "I mean, where do we draw the line? They're adults, I know, but we're providing a service."

Counselors can be ambivalent at times about the clinical work that is so meaningful to them. Sally told me that the counselors' initial training with the agency "creates the idea that [Driggs House is] more clinical and not just a house where people live." Miles described how clinical work determines who people are: "Really, you get to know people in terms of their goals and not fully at all. The other day I hung out with Chris for, like, an hour, which, you know, is very unusual, and I realize that I didn't know him at all." In one conversation, Daniel described a tendency he saw in younger counselors to take the clinical work too far: "The training is good, but it contributes to the idea that it's sort of, you know, like a hospital. I mean, I love staff meetings; we talk about everything from the most complex clinical stuff to toothbrushing. It's fascinating. But some staff, young staff, come in and think it's like a hospital." Sonia once complained to me in a conversation about Irving that "all" the counselors sometimes let their clinical expectations get in the way: "They can't see who Irving really is. They don't treat him like an adult, they get frustrated with him and his complaining. But sometimes despair sets in. Can someone be in therapy for life? I'm not saying they shouldn't work with him, but [they should] accept him."

Though the counselors' commitment to the clinical orientation might reflect their acceptance of the agency's expressed mission, it also provided accountable grounds for criticisms of the agency, Sonia, and each other in disputes over "what needs to be done" with a resident. Sometimes counselors invoked the clinical orientation as an obstacle to their work, as "making too much of things," a claim that was often used in disputes about how to define a resident's conduct as a problem and how to intervene. When counselors expressed frustration that Driggs House was "too clinical," it was often a criticism directed toward "the agency." Claims that "nothing is being done" and references to "the group home" or "the agency" were familiar grammatical abstractions that avoided directly naming Sonia or Mike. They allowed counselors to identify obstacles in their work and to challenge prevailing approaches by assigning responsibility indirectly. Cynthia was also a focus of this frustration. As the behavior specialist, she worked two days per week at Driggs House (and the rest of the time in two other agency residences). She is a white, Protestant woman in her early thirties, with a master's degree in psychology, whose primary task is to develop and write the goal and behavior plans. Although Cynthia had some authority to determine the course of this work, it was largely collaborative, and counselors perceived Cynthia as more of a peer. Still, counselors perceived her at times as representing the agency in general and clinical authority in particular. When this happened, Cynthia could be a target of criticism, frustration, or ridicule. Once, when she arrived late to a weekly staff meeting, Carlos whispered sarcastically to Miles and me, "Cynthia's here. Oh, goody! Now we can talk bullshit."

By the same token, as Sonia's comment about the counselors' expectations of Irving indicates, their strong commitment to the clinical work often inclined them toward intervention, sometimes more than Sonia believed was necessary or even permissible. This was especially clear when an "obvious" clinical solution was perhaps not so simple to implement because of larger principles of service, such as a resident's rights. Daniel expressed frustration with this in one staff meeting by drawing on his familiar analogy between residents and teenagers. In this instance, the parenting function of the group home was not guidance and support but teaching responsibility. "I mean," he exclaimed, "we talk all about their rights, but if they are going to learn to be more independent, then they also have responsibilities!"

The therapeutic model that counselors value as complex and skilled defines group home work in specifically manageable ways. Both Lipsky and Rose (1998b, 1999b) challenge the typical argument that clinical approaches manage work simply by controlling behavior. The pervasive use of therapeutic and medical models in many settings can be explained less by professional power than by the way these models clarify and simplify goals. As Lipsky puts it (15), a clinical approach also "provides a defense against personal responsibility . . . by resting responsibility for clients in their physical or psychological development. . . . It provides a theory of client behavior" that helps explain the complex indeterminacy of the work.

Rose's more encompassing argument about the broad ethical role that psy knowledge has come to play in contemporary society is especially helpful for understanding Driggs House. Psy knowledge provides more than goal clarification and a theory of client behavior; it defines what actually counts as clinical and organizes the nature of consensual participation. Clinical assumptions, jargon, modes of intervention, and so on, are practical techniques that enable ideal outcomes to be defined and acted on as everyday work for both counselors and residents. With human conduct, the conflict and ambiguity of work goals "can never be eliminated and even the accepted definitions of . . . tasks call for sensitive observation and judgment . . . [because they] are not reducible to programmed formats" (Lipsky, 15). Psy knowledge and techniques are an organizing feature of Driggs House, serving as resources for group home workers that, in their use, shape the contours of counselor discretion. In other words, psy techniques shape the ways in which the uncertain work at Driggs House is managed *as* clinical work.

Endless Demand

As in all street-level bureaucracies, the demand for services at Driggs House always exceeds supply. Services must be rationed in settings that typically have limited resources, so, apart from official procedure, rationing occurs informally and determines how the work actually gets done. Lipsky (34) rightly criticizes a narrow economic concept of demand in these contexts. Demand is more than "a mere transaction"; it is always situated and negotiated in relation to changes in actual resources and the perceptions workers and recipients have of services and their availability. The qualitative as well as quantitative dimensions of demand are unique at Driggs House, because all of everyday life is a potentially clinical domain, and even the most mundane interaction shapes the perceptions of and demand for services. Counselors ration supply in practical ways to cope with multiple demands: for example, making residents wait in order to finish paperwork, or claiming to have a meeting in the staff office in order to shut the door for a few moments of quiet.

But counselors also understand their practical techniques of managing the residents' demands (which are often necessary to accomplish their work) as interventions in problem conduct (which they regard as an essential responsibility of the work). When residents are "forced to wait," as Lipsky (95) puts it, "they are implicitly asked to accept the assumptions of rationing," which are that the resources of counselors—time and attention—are limited and must be allocated somehow among the obligations to others (residents and staff) and to other kinds of work (paperwork, meetings, and so forth). For example, Johnny was upset one evening because he wanted an additional dollar from the lockbox where residents' spending money is kept. Carlos was at work in the office, and he explained that Johnny did not have another dollar budgeted for that night. Johnny entered the office several times asking for another dollar; he was persistent. Carlos grew annoyed and finally lost his patience: "Why are you doing this? You know, we did your budget and you don't have another dollar today." Johnny just stood there, glowering. After a pause, Carlos continued impatiently: "Don't you have anything else to do? Well, *I* have to do paperwork." He turned back to the desk. Johnny looked deflated and left the office. One could easily see Carlos's impatient response as simply dismissive, reflecting his frustration at Johnny's persistence. But this interpretation doesn't take into account their developed personal relationship, which was inherent in Carlos's question ("Why are you doing this?") and in the answer he himself provided ("You know, we did your budget and you don't have a dollar today"). The exchange oriented Johnny to his own conduct—repeatedly asking a question in the hope of the desired answer—and to his understanding of what a budget is and how it functions. Whether Johnny shared Carlos's assumptions about budgeting and whether this was the reason he gave up asking for another dollar are questions that it is not possible to answer. Regardless, the way Carlos acted was accountable as an intervention in Johnny's conduct as a clinical problem.

In a similar example, which also took place in the office, Kenneth had been preoccupied by the difficulty his brother was having getting a job, and he talked about it at great length with anyone in his vicinity. I was in the office, helping Paul with something. Kenneth was sitting next to us but facing away from the desk. Sally came in and said, "Hi, everybody." She went straight to the shelf and took down the data book. As she was sitting down at a desk across the room, Kenneth said, "I'm upset about my brother." Sally presumed he was addressing her, and she replied without affect, "I know you are, Kenneth, you already told me . . . several times." She then turned to the open binder, her back to the room. In what seemed a reply to her tone, Kenneth made an apologetic defense: "But I can't help it. I worry about my family, my mom, all the time." Sally turned halfway around as he spoke and looked at him, but said nothing before turning back to the data book. After a minute or so, Kenneth pleaded to the room, "I am just worried about my brother." Sally took this as an opportunity to address his inability to manage his own conduct: "Will you please stop telling me about it. I know that you're upset, but you can't talk about it over and over. You get more upset. And you're bothering everybody else. I have to finish this before I leave—" Kenneth interrupted her last sentence with an embarrassed apology: "I know I worry too much." Sally turned back to her work.

Scheduling

The overall rhythms of the day at Driggs House are set by the residents' work and program schedules, the staff shifts, and regular mandated procedures such as doing meds. Scheduling the multiple other activities that constitute group home life involves ongoing negotiation over time and resources and provides another way of seeing the inherent conflict between work ideals and resources that must be managed. That the course of everyday activities is full of contingencies is usually taken for granted, but on occasion it does cause tension. Whether an activity is regular, with a fixed time (Daniel and Marty always did his budgeting goal on Friday evenings), or just occasional (such as Sally taking Evelyn to the store to buy batteries), when it actually occurs is often the result of ongoing negotiations that themselves are a reflexive part of the day's work.

> Daniel found Theresa watching TV in the living room. He said, "I can't help you with your trip plans at eight. Wanna do it now?" Theresa suggested, "What about before I go down for coffee?" Daniel hesitated. "Well, okay, we'll see if that works."

> James came into the office with Donna and said to Sally, "We're going down for coffee. Donna needs her dollar. Wanna come?" Then, to the rest of us (Paul, Miles, and me) he asked, "You guys wanna come?" As she was getting Donna's money, Sally asked James, "What about working on your clothes?" James thought and said, "Oh, yeah. Let's do it tomorrow," and she agreed.

> Carlos said to Johnny one afternoon, "I can't go with you to Barnes and Noble, because Nicky called in sick and I have to do meds." Johnny asked, "Tomorrow?"

Though both residents and counselors initiate the scheduling and rescheduling of activities, ultimately counselors have the authority to determine when things actually get done. In some circumstances, they end negotiations that seem unresolvable or are taking too long by setting a specific time. This is an intervention that aims to orient a resident to his or her own conduct—making unreasonable demands—as problem conduct. Residents who are "too demanding" may be required to "wait their turn," which counselors see as both deterring residents' pursuits and directing them to conduct themselves in a way that indicates an awareness of the constraints of group home work. They must come to terms with what counselors call "the reality of the house."

One evening, I was sitting in the living room with Marty, who was extremely eager to meet with Sally to fill out forms and arrange his payment for a weekend trip organized by a private holiday agency for people with intellectual disability. He explained to me that there was nearly a week before the deadline arrived, but he was keen to do it that night, and Sally had promised to do it with him after dinner. Now, as the time neared 9:00, he was upset because it turned out Sally had to do meds and did not know whether she would have time after all. At one point, when Sally came into the living room to fetch Evelyn, Marty asked, "Can we do my budgeting now?" Sally was clearly frustrated with him, but in an even tone said, "I already told you five times. We'll try to do it if we have time. You know, I have other things to do, and you're not the only person here. It doesn't matter if we get it done tonight anyway." Marty said, "I'm sorry, Sally." When she left the room, he was contrite: "She's very busy. I won't bother her."

Endless and Uncertain Work

Work at Driggs House is not endless only because demand is endless. Counselors and residents are always at work because nothing happens that is not potentially work. For ethnomethodologists, the fact that everyday life is a concerted accomplishment makes it a kind of work, and, of course, it is a kind of work from which there is no relief. This can be said also of life at Driggs House because of the relationship between its spatial-organizational character and its clinical mission. In the simplest sense, there is no "back region" (Goffman 1961, 106) where counselors and residents are permitted to remove themselves, at least not for more than a few minutes at a time. The constant visibility of counselors and residents, like that of flight attendants, dining room staff, and certain other service workers, means that work encompasses far more than their formal tasks. Just the presence of counselors is understood to have clinical value (as "role models"), they are always at work not only managing their own conduct but also maintaining surveillance over the ordinary course of life at Driggs House and the opportunities for work it presents. All of life is a potentially clinical domain, and its contours take shape in the counselors' ceaseless intervention in the conduct of residents as problem conduct. This is how residents are also kept always at work: they are oriented again and again to the way they conduct themselves and to the project of becoming more independent—the endless work that defines them as residents.

Lipsky (78) recognizes that people processing is endless because the problems addressed by street-level bureaucracies are "not subject to closure," and "people do not stay fixed." His criticism, in large part, is that social issues are perceived ultimately as individual problems, so the solutions on offer are fundamentally inadequate. This criticism doesn't quite apply to Driggs House or its services. More important, however, there is a fundamental reason why group home work is not subject to closure. The very formulation of the goal of residential services in the state regulations indicates that it is a goal without end. It is a *process,* ambiguous by definition: "to promote and encourage the independence, individuality, integration and productivity" of residents. The goal is not independence per se but its pursuit, and for individuals unable to achieve independence in any conventional sense, this pursuit is endless. The group home's fundamental goal is expressed in the broadest terms because it must be. Given the nature of the work, defining and measuring outcomes is complex and indeterminate. How the promotion and encouragement of independence gets realized in actual tasks depends on the specific practical conditions in any given group home. These inherent aspects of group home work must be managed, made sense of, in ways that enable the work to get done and to get done with some sense of personal satisfaction.

The fact that work is never done when the goal is a clinical process such as independence does not mean the work is destined to fail, though it often does. Group home work is organized by a temporality of progress that enables the perpetual deferral of final assessment. It is a race with no finish line. But the importance of the individuality of residents makes this a race that is not run against others. Within limits, residents set their own pace. In this way, there can always be progress in the pursuit of goals that are ever receding from reach.

Doing the Log

Given that there is little distinction between work and other activity in a group home, one way the uncertainty and endlessness of work at Driggs House takes specific shape is in the daily log's record of everyday life. Although counselors, much like sociologists of work and organizations, often regard paperwork as posing conflicts with professional ideals, the very possibility of progress depends on the group home's documentary practices. It is in and through them that progress gets defined and measured and that abstract needs and problems are realized in actual tasks of work. The multiple demands for documentation, which are a large part of the counselors' responsibilities, make the monitoring and assessment of group home work a central aspect of that work. The daily log is the most basic example of a monitoring technology, because "doing the log," which refers specifically to writing notes, is a responsibility of counselors at the end of each shift and because the log itself is not designed with any specific clinical outcomes in mind. A daily face sheet provides for the documentation of emergencies, changes in medical orders, unusual events, and any information that must be communicated across shifts (even, for example, when to expect the plumber). The face sheet serves as a cover page for two other pages of notes: one for the day shift and one for evening, photocopied forms with each resident's name in its own box for writing notes about that resident.

The daily log certainly functions as intended, as a simple instrument of communication that also generates a record of events. It functions in another way, too. In addition to the communication and documentation of information vital for regulatory compliance—from changes in medical orders to behavioral issues to maintenance and repair—the daily log encompasses all of everyday life within its documentary purview. And it is a technology of perpetual monitoring because it functions around the clock. The log is sometimes used to render a given troublesome aspect of resident conduct, or the possibility of trouble, an observable problem. In one example, the evening log notes contained a description of a dinnertime flare-up of the long-standing occasional conflict between Evelyn and Johnny as a harbinger of possible trouble for morning staff. In another instance, staff at David's day services program contacted the group home because they believed he was shaving too infrequently and not combing his hair. The counselors decided to press David each night to shower and shave. This meant, for a time, that evening log notes frequently indicated when this occurred and how much reminding David required.

That the daily log is not designed to include any specific clinical outcomes makes this technology of perpetual monitoring "endless" in the sense that the innumerable mundane aspects of residents' lives must ostensibly be kept in view. Counselors organize the endlessness of work through the basic documentary techniques that doing the log involves. Of course, very few aspects of everyday life actually get documented as knowable and seeable matters of counselor work. The following is a sampling of representative notes from relatively uneventful shifts.

From morning log notes:

Chris: *Fine mood, left early to work*

David: *A little agitated. Very slow to motivate—went to work*

Diane: *Fine, no issues*

Donna: *Good morning, went to program*

Evan: *ok*

Evelyn: *Please observe for having too many clothes on, i.e. t-shirt and two sweaters and a jacket*

Irving: *quiet but ate in dining room, did his work*

James: *Great mood, went to work early*

Jennifer: *appearance looked good, showered last night/attitude was pleasant, went to work*

Johnny: *out for coffee-psych appt and work*

Kenneth: *Upset re: funeral @ work. Counseled by staff. Perseverated all morning about the [party on the] 17th*

Marty: *A little shaky this am, went to program*

Paul: *in better form this am, out for appt*

Ruby: *cool and quiet, no problems*

Theresa: *Good mood, did exercises without complaining*

From evening log notes:

Chris: *Great help. Out in the community for smokes*

David: *Pretty quiet after getting home from program, down for coffee*

Diane: *got her hair done by Susan, good mood, listened to walkman*

Donna: *out in the community with staff. Good evening, showed interest in cooking a lot.*

Evan: *Got in late but okay mood*

Evelyn: *good mood, no probs*

Irving: *Isolated, except from Ruby*

James: *fine, no issues*

Jennifer: *very friendly to staff, good evening*

Johnny: *got upset when he thought Evelyn was mad at him. Redirected and was great*

Kenneth: *Whining about laundry, wanted to be first, and counselor not being present*

Marty: *out in the community with staff, a little unsteady when asked to do room maintenance*

Paul: *Was caught by counselor eating Ritz crackers in bed. Spoke to Nurse about his test next week*

Ruby: *hung out in Irving's room a lot. No issues*

Theresa: *Good mood, down for coffee*

Counselor Shoptalk

Whereas the daily log is formal, there is an informal kind of monitoring in the ceaseless conversation among counselors throughout their shift. I call this shoptalk to distinguish it from the usual chatter and small talk that occurs among colleagues in most workplaces. Shoptalk is the ongoing conversation about matters of work sustained throughout and across shifts as counselors are called to assist in the laundry room, to administer medications, to cook dinner, and so on. A topic may be interrupted in the dining room and picked up again later in the staff office. Or maybe not. There is no shortage of topics, and seemingly no topic is too small.

Shoptalk is both talk *about* the work and, as Michael Lynch (1985) describes it, talk *in* the work. Shoptalk is a kind of work itself, a fundamental and reflexive aspect of the very work that the talk continuously monitors. The ongoing, situated selection of topics shapes what is knowable and seeable in relation to the group home's formal technologies of documentation (of which the log is one example). These technologies, which are a large part of the counselors' responsibilities, clarify goals and organize the course of work in specific ways and over various durations, from the daily log all the way to annual reviews of each resident's progress. (The group home's documentary technologies are the focus of chapters 8 and 9.) These technologies alone, however, do not adequately manage the ambiguity, endlessness, and uncertainty of the work. Counselors rely also on the close and continuous monitoring of work with the situated selection of topics in shoptalk to keep a handle on complex situations and make sense of their successes and failures. Shoptalk makes observable the counselors' moral and professional commitments, especially to that aspect of the job which is most satisfying but also the most prone to failure and frustration: helping residents work on their independence.

What may appear to be casual conversation among colleagues is, as shoptalk, actually an aspect of the ongoing, situated process of defining and acting on resident conduct that constantly transforms the field of intervention. Here is an example:

> *"Don't you think Diane has been really quiet tonight?"* Sally asked one
> evening in the staff office, during a lull after 9:00 meds when no residents
> were around. Miles hadn't noticed: *"D'ya think so?"* Sally was tentative:
> *"I dunno. She went straight to her room when she came home from program.*

I think maybe something happened at program." Miles asked, "Oh, did you hear something?" When Sally shook her head no, Miles was reassuring: "You know what she's like. Sometimes she just sort of retreats. I mean, she's shy anyway." Sally agreed. As Miles was talking, Daniel came in and sat across from them on the file cabinet. He heard Miles's main point but asked, "Who are you talking about?" Sally posed the question anew to him: "Diane. Do you think something's up with her? I think she's quieter than usual." Miles chuckled, apparently at himself for failing to convince her, and Daniel answered in Miles's jocular, reassuring spirit: "No! She's the same as always." Daniel indicated Miles and said to Sally, "He's right. You know she sort of has periods. Who knows? Remember she was really obnoxious for a while, wouldn't brush her teeth or anything without hundreds of prompts? You had to remind her a hundred times?" Both Sally and Miles indicated they remembered and agreed. Daniel added, "Then at one point, she just started being more independent with her hygiene again." This settled the issue for Sally: "Oh, you're right."

At this moment, Theresa came in and faced Daniel, who joked, "And what do you want, Miss?" "My dollar," she replied, holding out her hand. "Gimme my dollar. We're going down for coffee." She turned back to the door and called, "C'mon David. Let's go!" Miles asked her whether David had showered and shaved, but before she could answer David appeared in the doorway, freshly shaved, his wet hair neatly combed. Daniel was retrieving money from the lockbox. Theresa looked at Sally and said in an offhand way, "Marty's on the floor." Sally reacted with good-humored exasperation: "Oh, you're kidding?" She rose from her chair. "Where? In the living room?" she asked. Theresa said, "Yes," and after a pause added, to no one in particular, "He's a pain." Sally headed toward the living room, and then Theresa and David crossed the hall and left the residence.

Daniel gestured out the door of the office, indicating the direction Sally had gone, and both Miles and I knew that Daniel was referring to Marty when he asked, "What's up with him? It's like he doesn't need anyone around anymore, you know, it just happens." Miles agreed: "It used to be only with the counselors that he'd fall. Well, I haven't gone in there [the living room] since dinner. Who's around?" I said, "I saw him before in the living room, talking to Christina [a psychology intern who came once a week for three months]. Miles laughed: "Well, that should have prevented a fall— all that attention." Daniel joined in the joke: "Yeah, talking to her? You mean he wouldn't let her talk to anybody else?" Then he asked, "What the hell does she do here, anyway? It's ridiculous." Miles returned to the topic of Marty: "I just don't understand what's up with him, really. He had such a good week last week. He even went to [a party at] Jemma House on Saturday night." Daniel shook his head skeptically. Miles added, "I think Angie took him to the doctor on the subway. I mean—" Daniel interrupted sternly: "He's only getting worse. He fell last week, a few times, I think."

Miles shrugged. Daniel appeared increasingly frustrated as he continued: "We have done everything for him, you know. I mean, how much can he be restricted here? He really needs to be at Jemma [House, an intermediate-care facility (ICF)]. It's not fair to him!" Miles was noncommittal and did not encourage the topic: "Oh, I don't know. I guess you're right." Daniel continued: "They [the supervisors] are just not listening to us. It's not fair to us, either. I mean, it's really stressful. You never know when you come in what's gonna happen with him [Marty]." Sally returned and we all looked at her as she sat down, which she took as a request for a report. "He's fine," she said, waving her hand to indicate that the incident was nothing out of the ordinary. "He was on the floor in the doorway of the living room, and he just got up when I asked him to. Who knows?" I asked, "What was Christina doing? Is she in there?" Daniel's eyes widened as he seconded the question eagerly: "Yeah?"

There is no way to present an excerpt of shoptalk without losing the sense of its embeddedness in the ongoing course of counselor work. Thus, where this selection begins and ends is determined somewhat arbitrarily by the details I have chosen to feature. One important aspect illustrated here is the constant monitoring of residents' affect, mood, and conduct in Sally's tentative queries about Diane and in Daniel and Miles's joking about Marty's interaction with Christina. Despite the two different topics, both display the microscopic scale of attention to residents' conduct that commonly characterizes shoptalk. Even the most subtle changes are noted, discussed, and theorized by counselors, and unexpected occurrences, both large and small, are continuously puzzled over and analyzed.

Marty is one resident who embodied the unpredictable and failure-prone character of group home work. Setting aside the always-possible divergence of opinion about "how he's doing," counselors assigned responsibility for their ongoing problems with him elsewhere by defining them in terms of the agency's failure to act on the counselors' knowledge and experience or in terms of Marty's personal failure to respond to the group home's interventions. It would be a mistake to understand this as anything but a practical way of making accountable work that is not subject to closure. When Daniel said, "They are just not listening to us," he was referring to what a few counselors perceived as Sonia's refusal to consider seriously their persistent claims that Marty required a more restrictive residential setting (such as an ICF). They knew that such decisions are made neither quickly (for reasons both of clinical assessment and residential availability) nor

solely on the basis of their recommendation, but counselors often manage unsolvable problems by hashing over them in ways that extend
beyond their sphere of authority and discretion. For this reason, Marty
was a frequent topic of shoptalk ("We have done everything for him";
"They're not listening to us"; "He should be in a lower house [an
ICF]"; "We don't have the staff here"; "It's not fair to him"; "It's not
fair to us"), and repeated discussions enabled counselors to keep hold
of an upsetting problem that had no apparent solution. Daniel's frustration about the situation with Marty and Sally's hunch that "something's going on with Diane" both indicate how shoptalk itself often
can function as an intervention not in the conduct of residents but in
the counselors' problems with their own work.

Given that, as Lipsky (49) puts it, "there are too many variables
to take into account to make evaluation realistic," uncertainty in the
group home is often managed in shoptalk by acknowledging it in clinical analysis. The discussions about Diane and Marty, although abbreviated and general here, demonstrate the counselors' use of clinical
reasoning to make sense of uncertainty. In shoptalk, the counselors'
commitment to their clinical work is observable in the practice of
analytic skill, the use of psy language, and the recounting of previous
problems and solutions. Counselors often demonstrate their clinical
skill by analyzing the impossibility of knowledge in certain situations,
sometimes using the issue of complexity just to express exasperation
in the assertion that "nothing can be done."

The strategy of managing uncertainty by acknowledging it not only
demonstrates the general value placed on psychological knowledge
and skill but also is a situated account of what counselors believe they
know and do. Counselors often imply that the esoteric nature of the
knowledge they possess is analogous to claims of superior skill based
on uncertainty and complexity in a field such as medicine (Attewell
1990, 1992; Hughes). Virtuosity can also be a feature of uncertain work,
as when new, risky, or highly technical medical interventions are associated with particular members of the profession (Attewell 1990, 438).
A parallel emphasis on the virtuosity of skill in the group home can be
seen in the identification of certain counselors who are "good with"
certain residents. Skill is located here, however, in counselors' individual attributes and personalities as predictors or accounts of positive
clinical outcomes: Drew, who is "consistent," "firm," and a "male role
model," works well with Kenneth, who is "needy"; Susan is also "firm"

and "no-nonsense," and she is good with Ruby, who is "shy"; Miles is "gentle" and "keeps a low profile," which makes him compatible with Irving, who is "obsessed with his privacy."

It is in shoptalk that counselors engage those aspects of the work that generate personal satisfaction. Although they work individually with residents, counselors do spend a lot of time together and, when on duty, share responsibility for everyone's welfare and the smooth operation of the facility. Shoptalk makes observable the personal and organizational identification that brings counselors together in work perceived as stressful and demanding mutual support. For example, Daniel and Sally, in the shoptalk excerpted earlier, both indicated, though in different ways, the personal toll counselors pay in their work. Counselors frequently share tips about how best to approach clinical as well as administrative situations. They often complain about residents and supervisory problems, but they also remind each other that the work is morally and professionally important and that they face particular challenges in a job that rarely yields clear, and only ever modest, results.

Even the vernacular term routinely used to refer collectively to the residents—"the guys"—reflects the personal dimension of counselor work that is at once satisfying and confusing. Counselors commonly referred to the residents as "the guys" and, in reference to their own caseload, "my guys." The term functioned to manage the ambiguity inherent in work that is seen as professional but for which intimate personal relationships are necessary for success. "The guys" acknowledges informally, without invoking clinical categories, that the residents are, after all, objects of work. There was an inherent confusion for counselors, because they work in a setting based ostensibly on the rights and choice of individuals who, for all practical purposes, are defined by an asymmetry of knowledge and authority. Although "the guys" functioned in effect as a term of art in the group home, it always had the ring of familiarity and often affection.

Resident Shoptalk

The monitoring practices that organize everyday life are not exercised only by counselors. Residents do their own monitoring work in addition to the work they must do to become more independent. Routine group home operation provides residents a practical opportunity for participation that involves monitoring each other and staff and that is observable in the residents' own informal and ongoing shoptalk.

There was a group of residents who worked regularly on routine group home operations and served as resources for others (including counselors) who had questions about scheduling, rec trips, appointments, and so on. Chris, Irving, Jennifer, Kenneth, Marty, Ruby, and Theresa most actively paid continuous attention to the staff schedule and the coordination of residents' many medical and other appointments and activities. In their shoptalk, they demonstrated an adequate practical knowledge of staffing patterns; medication procedures and certification; residents who had appointments, the days and times those appointments would take place, the residents' mode of transport, the question of whether they would be accompanied, and by which counselor; residents who attended evening leisure programs during the week, the times when they were expected home; and more.

Resident shoptalk occurred often in the living room when people were gathered to relax or just to wait—for dinner, for meds, for work on goal plans with counselors, or for other residents to go with them out in the community. On a typical evening after dinner, Kenneth and I were sitting together on the living room couch facing the door to the dining room, and he was telling me something that happened at his workshop that day. Theresa was on the kitty-corner couch facing the back of the living room, and across from us Ruby was watching TV. Ruby turned toward Theresa and asked, "How are we getting to bowling on Sunday?" Theresa replied, "Cheryl's gonna drive us." Kenneth stopped talking to me in order to add, "She can't drive the van. No." (Counselors must be certified to drive agency vehicles.) Ruby agreed, still looking at Theresa: "Yeah." Theresa speculated: "What about . . . Is Daniel working?" "No," Ruby chided. "He'll be on vacation. I don't think anybody can drive us. We have to take the subway. I'm not going." "Me neither," Kenneth agreed. Theresa shrugged, Ruby turned back to the television, and Kenneth resumed our discussion. When Jennifer came into the living room a few minutes later, Theresa greeted her by asking which counselor would drive to bowling on Sunday. Jennifer answered tentatively, "Cheryl?" Kenneth, Ruby, and Theresa responded with a disappointed "no" or a dismissive wave. Jennifer sat down next to Ruby. After a while, Daniel came in and Theresa greeted him with a question about whether he'd be driving on Sunday. He answered, "I'm not gonna be here, remember?"

"Oh, right," she said. Daniel added, "What's the difference who drives anyway? What do you care, if you want to go bowling?" Ruby explained that without a counselor to drive, it would mean taking the subway and she would not bother to go.

Administering medications was a familiar topic of residents' shoptalk. One evening at dinner, during a casual discussion about what activities people were planning for the approaching weekend, Jennifer mentioned in an offhand way that Angie would not be working on Sunday. From another table across the dining room, Ruby asked, "She's not? Who's going to do meds?" On another occasion, I was sitting with Ruby and Kenneth in the living room on a Sunday afternoon, which was even quieter than usual because a large group of residents had gone on a rec trip to a shopping mall some distance away. Kenneth noted that it was just after 4:30, and he was worried that the group would not return by 5:00. Ruby asked, "Oh, because of meds?" Kenneth assented: "Miles shouldn't have gone with them. Now there's no one to do meds." Kenneth and Ruby went through the counselors on shift and determined that Miles was, in fact, the only one who was med certified. This confirmation increased Kenneth's annoyance and agitation, and he repeated his criticism of Miles's decision to join the group. I said, "It's only twenty to five or so; they could still get home in time." Kenneth was not convinced: "That place is too far away and . . . Linda should have gone instead." Ruby rolled her eyes: "It doesn't concern you, so why are you worried?" Kenneth retorted, "It's not right." Ruby ended the conversation by saying, "Gimme a break. You don't even get 5:00 meds." Kenneth stood abruptly and, as he left the living room, announced, "I'm gonna see where they are!" Ruby looked puzzled and laughed, calling after him, "How're you gonna do that?"

Though shoptalk was used by all group home workers as a continuous and informal practice of managing work, uncertainty did not pose the same obstacle for residents as it did for counselors. For residents, the work of involvement in group home operations is unremarkable, in the sense that it reflects the pleasures and frustrations most people experience in the quotidian detail of domestic life. For counselors, however, this routine resident work also has clinical meaning. Counselors constantly encourage residents to be involved in the group home as a measure of their healthy investment and participation ("It's your house, after all"). Minding day-to-day operations is one form that participation can take for those who live in a setting that aims both to be a personal domestic environment and a workplace for becoming more independent. Yet the very activities that often demonstrate residents' investment may be seen, for whatever situated reason, as outside their "appropriate" sphere of concern. It is when counselors see and act on residents' failure to recognize the boundaries of legitimate involvement that routine resident work becomes a clinical problem of conduct.

This is a paradox of conduct in the group home that often reflects the need to ration services. One aspect of the residents' work involved gathering and analyzing information, and counselors were continually called upon to answer questions and give advice. Certain counselors were particularly annoyed at one point about residents' information-gathering activities in the office. The problem was discussed at a weekly staff meeting, prompted by a counselor who saw Chris "openly" reading the log. Residents were constantly looking at the staff schedule, the large appointment calendar on the wall, and now even at the daily log often left open on one of the desks. Residents also talked openly about other people's business, especially medical appointments. At the staff meeting, Angie suggested that residents' access to the staff office be limited in some way. Daniel agreed: "There has to be a shared responsibility if they want access. Looking at the calendar is a violation of others' privacy." Susan was incredulous: "I can't believe the guys are reading the log notes! That is interoffice communication only." Cynthia reminded everyone, "They have a right to know who's working with them, and that's why they can [are permitted to] look at the [staff] schedule." Angie, as a morning counselor responsible for coordinating outside medical services, was particularly concerned about the posted appointment calendar, which generated many of the residents' questions: "They go on about things that don't pertain to them. It's a source of anxiety." Daniel suggested posting the staff schedule outside the office because of the residents' right to have access to it and "maybe on the calendar, [writing] doctors' names instead of specialties as a way of concealing the nature of the appointment." After a pause, Daniel laughed and added, "But they don't know what the specialties mean anyway." The fact that access to the staff office was never addressed again; that residents' access was never limited; and that the calendar and log continued to be displayed in the same way indicated, in retrospect, that what was raised as an issue of confidentiality and privacy was really an attempt by frustrated coun-selors to ration their time and to exert more control over their work space.

Although the group home poses different kinds of problems for res-idents than for counselors, they are still taken-for-granted, routine problems that must be managed. The uncertainty that residents face is the kind of uncertainty that characterizes everyday life and is man-aged in one way or another by virtually everyone everywhere in the rhythm and detail of domestic routine. Of course, this universal expe-rience takes specific shape only in the settings and mundane practices in which it is defined and managed. My schedule at Driggs House was fairly predictable, but there might be changes in any given week: switching my usual days, coming in later or leaving earlier, and so forth. But because I was nonstaff, my schedule was not posted, and in order to carry on with their work, residents needed to obtain this information from me directly: when was I coming, how long would I stay, why was I coming next week on Tuesday instead of Monday, why I was coming on the weekend as usual but leaving early on Saturday. This continuous intelligence gathering was not limited to questions about when I would or would not be there but encompassed changes in my teaching schedule, my mother's surgery and recovery, the pro-gress of a chronically ill friend, and other ongoing concerns that might or might not be relevant to the time I spent at Driggs House. This work was evident in the way I was greeted by some residents almost every time I arrived: "How long are you staying?" The counselors saw this as pestering, anxious, and indicative of an inability to appreciate things in the moment rather than as the mundane work it really was. They would sometimes answer with a question of their own, such as, "What does it matter? He's here *now*." As a practice of participation, monitoring group home operations was a kind of resident work. Yet it was a kind of work that could generate conflict, because it placed demands on counselors and sometimes put residents plainly in the way. This is a paradox inherent in the group home, and when such conflicts occur, routine resident work becomes yet another aspect of the work counselors must endlessly manage.

6 THE CLINICAL PROBLEM OF EVERYDAY LIFE

ANOTHER WAY I APPROACHED WORK was in group home know-how, the practical, often tacit knowledge individuals have about their work that they develop in doing the work itself. Know-how is a kind of knowledge posed in contrast to what counselors learn in their formal training and have available in written materials such as procedure manuals and the goal and behavior plans of residents. Because the domain of clinical work extends to all of everyday life at Driggs House, any aspect of a resident's conduct can at any time be defined and acted on by counselors as a problem. This ongoing intervention in routine resident conduct as problem conduct shapes the clinical contours of everyday life. And because it encompasses more than counselors' formal specified tasks, they must be able to account for what they do in the group home's terms.

I offer too stark a contrast, however, between know-how and what might be called formal knowledge in the group home. There is a parallel in early research on formal and informal organization and the unintended consequences of bureaucracy (Blau; Gouldner; Merton; Selznick). Wolfensberger (1989) adopted this to demonstrate the difference between the "rhetoric and reality" of human-service organizations. In fact, there is an ongoing reflexive relationship between these kinds of knowledge (Garfinkel 1984b; Lynch 1993; Suchman). Jeff Coulter makes a distinction between psychiatric knowledge and clinical work to demonstrate that diagnoses themselves make sense only as situated practice. At Driggs House, formal knowledge and practice can be distinguished in the observation of the counselors' situated interventions, which make everyday life a clinical problem.

Workplace Know-How

Workplace know-how has been the subject of research on technology change and its consequences. Researchers have challenged arguments about "deskilling" by showing that automation actually demands new kinds of skill and that even so-called unskilled work depends on a wealth of tacit knowledge (Attewell 1990, 1992). Zuboff describes how paper mill workers developed a new and fundamental kind of "craft know-how" when computer systems replaced the manual management of equipment. In an automated textile factory, Juravich shows how "craft knowledge" is integral to production because workers rely on it to solve frequent equipment crises. For Juravich (305), craft knowledge does not refer to an artisanal notion of production. Here the idea of craft is a recognition of the role of "knowledge that cannot be rigidly systematized to procedural rules but is developed through years of experience." This type of knowledge not only develops in unskilled work but is fundamental to it. Deskilling arguments also hold that automation erodes the historic basis for collective organizing. However, Kusterer's research of various low- and unskilled occupations demonstrates that workers are not as alienated as deskilling predicts. Know-how, a fundamental component of what Kusterer calls "working knowledge," is actually a source of pride, meaning, personal investment, and worker control in the larger process. Given that know-how is integral to production yet largely hidden from management, Kusterer suggests that it actually provides a new basis for organizing that is compatible with technological change.

In challenging deskilling arguments, Juravich, Kusterer, and Zuboff all seek to reveal the unrecognized but essential role of know-how that makes even low- and unskilled workers integral and active participants in the work process. Although my analysis of tacit knowledge is not meant to address how workers adapt to technology change (a question that does not apply to the group home workplace), I share the basic assumptions of this research about the relationship between the process of work and the practical, unspecified knowledge of workers.

What do counselors and residents know, and how does it relate to the accomplishment and organization of their work? The answer is in an analysis of know-how not simply as an integral (yet hidden) component of work but as the work itself. Textile plant and mill workers' craft knowledge can ultimately be assessed by production output, whereas the nature of group home work precludes this kind of reliable measure. This fact in itself indicates the role played by know-how in the group home, especially in relation to the discretion required by counselor work. Even so, much like that of plant and mill workers, counselor know-how is observable only in the production process itself and in the way workers account for what and how they do what they do. Given the difficulty of measuring and defining group home work, know-how provides a particularly suitable way of observing work. The situated use of counselor know-how is integral even to what counts as work in the routine course of life at Driggs House.

My descriptions of all the bustle and energy at Driggs House do not preclude the fact that group home workers were often to be found hanging out in the living room and staff office, watching TV, or looking at the paper or a magazine. These were times that were not taken up with what in any obvious sense was "work," but it was in these times that nonwork might suddenly become work. That is, the clinical significance of everyday life took specific shape in and through the counselors' ongoing interventions, which might at any time transform routine resident conduct into problem clinical conduct. One Sunday afternoon, for example, I was sitting in the living room talking with Cheryl about her college and career issues. The usual level of house activity was at an ebb, because most of the residents were on a rec trip. Paul was adjacent to us on the couch watching TV. He turned to Cheryl and asked, "When will dinner be ready tonight?" Cheryl said, "You know, Paul, we're having a conversation and you didn't even say excuse me." Paul responded with rote frankness: "Excuse me." Then, after only a second or two, he asked again, "When will dinner be ready?" Cheryl answered simply, "Six thirty," and resumed our conversation without further comment. This brief exchange may seem trite, but it is as good an example as any of the kind of ongoing work that gives shape to everyday life as a clinical problem.

Everyday Life, a Clinical Problem

A staff meeting discussion that occurred in my second month at Driggs House further illustrates the clinical significance of everyday life there. Mike, the regional supervisor, was present at this particular meeting and, at one point, took the floor to say that he heard the residents' meetings were not being held weekly as they should be. That

Mike "heard" about it this presumably meant that Sonia had asked him to address it and to underscore the importance of this weekly event. He asked the counselors to describe their understanding of the purpose of residents' meetings. Daniel described them as the venue for assigning house chores, deciding on weekend recreation trips, and general house business if there was any. He continued without pause, "But there's a problem with the meetings now," as though answering the question Mike was *really* asking: why had counselors shirked their responsibility to call these meetings weekly? Daniel explained that some months earlier, the residents had voted to change the chore system from the weekly swapping of chores each Monday night to more or less indefinite assignments. Residents were now less interested in attending residents' meetings. Miles added that "the meetings need a sense of urgency to get everyone there."

Not only did swapping chores no longer have any relevance to the residents' meeting, but this fact pointed to a problem larger than the counselors' failure to ensure that meetings were held every Monday night. The discussion shifted to what was really the problem all along: the new chore system. I had never heard the counselors express concern about the way the chores were assigned, but, in this meeting at least, there was a consensus that it was a problem. (In fact, it was only in this staff meeting that I learned the chores had formerly been swapped every week.) Miles said that the new system was a "catch-22," because, despite the end of weekly chore rotation, "everything works": the kitchen and dining room were cleaned after dinner, the bathrooms and hallways were cleaned, and the garbage was collected from all the rooms and offices. The problem was that it had become "routine," and the counselors said that the residents "take it for granted." As far as I knew, there had also been no complaints from the residents. They seemed satisfied with the arrangement, and even an individual's occasional desire to swap chores was easy to address by negotiating here and there without reorganizing the whole system.

Nonetheless, the chore system provided both a clinically warrantable aspect of everyday life and a solution. Miles identified the problem as "complacency," and Susan agreed: "Residents just do their chores without thinking about them." The complacency of counselors was a problem, too. Perhaps the reflective character of this acknowledgment in the context of raising the broader problem is what made it forgivable. Mike and Sonia were in agreement with the counselors' assessment of the problem. The counselors appeared to realize in the meeting that permitting the residents to take their chores for granted had encouraged "dependency," which was used here essentially as a synonym for "complacency," as "getting too comfortable with things." The counselors had failed to take advantage of the opportunity inherent in daily chores for the residents to work on being more independent. Housecleaning and kitchen chores were discussed as ways to "stimulate" the residents' capacity to be "proactive." Daniel said it would be good "to shake things up for the sake of it" and "to stoke a fire"; the residents should be "less dependent and more proactive." These claims were formulated as clinical imperatives that reflected the counselors' sense of their own professional authority, if not obligation, to disrupt a perfectly functional system that apparently had garnered no complaints.

Nevertheless, the way chores were assigned to the residents turned out not to pose enough of a clinical concern for the counselors to warrant any action. In the eleven months that followed this staff meeting, the chore system was neither changed nor raised as an issue again. It may be that the problem was a situated feature of this specific discussion—plausible and compelling as it took shape in and organized the staff meeting talk—but not a warrantable matter of group home work in any ongoing, practical way. Be that as it may, the conversation illustrates how everyday life is the clinical arena of group home work and takes shape in situated accounts of specific problems and solutions.

The Flexibility of Psy Knowledge

There is no aspect of everyday life at Driggs House that does not have potential clinical significance. In *Asylums* (1961, 156), Goffman notes a similar "license": given the "legitimate claim to deal with the 'whole' person, [staff] need officially recognize no limits to what they consider relevant." That there is much clinical work to be done in the routine course of group home life may appear to be a familiar aspect of "total institutions," in which all spheres of activity are conducted in a single setting. In Goffman's ideal type, however, work is defined largely in terms of organizational control. Even the underlife that develops in the cracks, as it were, he describes as a form of "adaptation" to the demands of the institution. The spatial organization of work is also different in the two kinds of places. In Goffman's total institution, spatial arrangements enable the control of "collective blocks of people" and help preserve the integrity of professional service by separating it in certain ways from the imperatives of administration. In the group home, the clinical significance of everyday life takes its practical shape in the constant close proximity of counselors and residents. The spatial arrangement of the asylum provides some relief from the demands of the institution; Goffman illustrates this by describing its underlife. Although the organizational demands of the group home are of a very different sort, there is little relief from the work. The relationship between the spatial organization and psy knowledge in the group home is not quite like the historical relationship between the architecture of hospitals and medical discourse (Prior). However, there is no equivalent architectural or spatial template for group homes as there is for hospitals. It is more that psy knowledge in the group home organizes that space as *workspace*. Although the particular spatial organization of Driggs House is an important factor in the way its work gets done, what all group homes share, perhaps, is a collective life that takes shape through the flexibility that psy knowledge requires in the community. Outside the rigid structures of the institution, psy knowledge has adapted by becoming relevant to all aspects of life.

Clinical know-how enables counselors to make intelligible the contingent and indeterminate course of their work. The group home's overall goal to enhance the independence of individuals shapes the work in terms of endless overlapping processes that are subject to and defined by continual reassessment and modification. The flexibility of psy can be observed in the way that counselors act on their individual clinical objects of work not as fixed objects but as open and adaptable ones (cf. Coulter; Ingleby). The flexibility of clinical knowledge derives from its regulatory and relative function, which does not depend on the arbitrary standards of tradition (as in theology) or on the ostensibly unambiguous standards of professional authority (as in medicine).

For Hughes (53), that even presumably unambiguous technical fields require explanation reflected "the social drama of work": the role of relationships and organizational interaction that constitute workplaces. For Garfinkel and Coulter, roles and organizational structure are sociological concerns that become a conceptual barrier to understanding the way work is accomplished and the character of knowledge. Donzelot argued, in compatible ways, that it is the regulatory function of psy that has enabled it to cross the technical thresholds of other fields without undermining them as legitimate and autonomous professional domains. In the nineteenth and early twentieth centuries, psy knowledge fundamentally shaped the problems and practices that defined juvenile justice, child protection, and public hygiene. Psy knowledge enabled the normalization of any and all individual conduct by treating it in an indeterminate, "floating" relationship to norms and providing techniques of "automatic readjustment" when necessary (Donzelot, 217). In the example of juvenile justice, Donzelot describes how psy made it possible to assess the criminal conduct of adolescents not in terms of rigid moral standards but in relation to a child's unique psychology and family experience. In this way, social workers' expert assessments about the causes of criminality and the prospect of rehabilitation became central to the management of adolescent offenders, as well as to the legal process it reshaped. Group home counselors keep a hold on the frequent contingencies in their work by defining and acting on them not in terms of rigid principles but in terms of the always adjustable, relative meaning that counselors' clinical know-how makes available. It is in relation to specific concerns about individuals—both residents and counselors— and their conduct that the flexibility of psy knowledge is necessary to the group home work it organizes. For Rose (1998b, 97), this is the link between psy and the practice of governmentality: "A psychological ethics is intimately tied to the liberal aspirations of freedom, choice, and identity. . . . [It] promises a system of values freed from the moral judgment of social authorities. Its norms answer not to an arbitrary moral or political code but only to the demands of our nature and our truth as human beings."

Conducting Oneself Politely

That all of everyday life is a domain of potential clinical work is one way counselors make their ongoing intervention in routine conduct accountable. What, in effect, defines interaction as an intervention is that it is meant to furnish for residents the know-how that makes visible and knowable their problem conduct in specific and specifically manageable ways. Psy know-how, in this sense, can be understood not in terms of ideas or values but as technique. It is always "bound into ways of seeing and acting" (Rose 1998b, 83). Clinical assumptions, clichés, vocabulary, and modes of monitoring, assessment, and intervention are available only as specific methods that in the situated occasions of their use translate professional knowledge in everyday life.

The earlier example of Cheryl chiding Paul for interrupting points to an issue that was commonly addressed by counselors: politeness. The problem of politeness illustrates well how the clinical contours of everyday life took shape reflexively in and through the situated intervention in residents' conduct. There is no way for me to know why Cheryl responded to Paul as she did. Paul may have been genuinely rude. Cheryl may have been particularly sensitive to interruption or perhaps sensitive to Paul. The point is that chiding him as she did was observably accountable as a clinical intervention.

Counselors frequently demanded that residents fulfill their conversational obligations by uttering social formalities such as "Thank you," "Please," and "Excuse me." Residents often dispensed with the routine "Hello" and "How are you" and launched immediately into their own concerns: appointments, special events, their goals, or what was being served for dinner and when. These routine requests and questions might be answered as such, but they might instead be met with joking, sarcastic, and annoyed responses from counselors. A response such as, "Can't you even say hello?" or a friendly, if exaggerated, "Hello, Donna, how are you?" demonstrated to residents that a slew of questions is not an acceptable form of greeting. For residents, it appears that the proximity of counselors and the comfortable intimacy that generally characterizes group home relations did not always require formal greetings. Although this situated judgment was affirmed more often than not, counselors might transform these mundane exchanges into clinical opportunities that urged residents to manage their conduct in "socially appropriate" ways.

Counselors sometimes defined conduct as impolite by trying to correct an "absence," attempting to elicit a specific utterance from residents. For example, one evening, Susan was doing Diane's hair in the staff office. Diane was seated in a chair and Susan was perched over her, sitting on the desk. There were several counselors and residents hanging around, and the mood was jovial. When she finished, announcing, "Okay, I'm done," Diane simply stood up and left the office. Susan called after her jokingly, "Don't you say thank you?" She received no answer and, again with a laugh, called out, "Excuse me, Miss D, don't you say thank you?" Sally, who was sitting next to

Susan at the computer, smiled. There was still no reply from the hall-way. Susan suddenly got down from the desk and exclaimed with exasperation, "I can't believe her! I do her hair all the time!" and raced out of the office after Diane. Sally looked over at me with an incredulous and disapproving roll of her eyes.

Sally's expression indicated that counselors might understand Susan and Diane's interaction in different ways. It was also Sally's situated use of know-how that assumed I shared, or could share, her understanding. I was not able to ask Sally what she meant, because there were residents with us in the office. I understood it as a criticism of Susan's conduct: she had been too serious about such a minor issue and had taken herself too seriously. Susan's conduct could be understood plausibly as excessive. Then again, Diane's conduct could be understood plausibly as rude. What *was* observable was Susan's commitment to intervene in rude conduct, which was a practically available way of knowing and acting on residents. Regardless of how Susan's conduct might be evaluated, it reflected her specific capacity as a counselor to act in a spontaneous and accountable way, and her situated and reflexive use of know-how made observable to me one way of being a counselor.

In an ongoing, practical sense, politeness is a matter within the clinical purview of counselors, although they do not act on it uniformly. Some counselors regard it as central to their clinical work, as Susan did; others regard it generally as a matter of "personal style" and therefore not clinically warrantable conduct. The identification of conduct as impolite, when it occurs, is always situated and practical but always available to counselors as a method of clinical intervention. There is an instructive analogy to group home work on politeness in the responsibility adults often assume to teach manners to children. Goffman (1961, 115) uses this analogy to explain the treatment of asylum inmates, who are considered to have failed to achieve personhood or adulthood—that is, autonomy. Children and inmates de facto share the same limited status: "Only children can be openly sanctioned . . . for showing improper deference; this is one sign that we hold children to be not-yet-persons." Therefore, "to the degree that the inmates are defined as not-fully-adults, staff need not feel a loss of self-respect by coercing deference from their charges." Goffman notes that within total institutions, the display of deference is more formal than elsewhere. This is not so in the group home. Impolite conduct is not a self-evident violation, partly because group home authority is less rigid and partly because manners in general are far less formal than they were in the middle 1950s.

Goffman's analogy between children and inmates does not obtain in the group home for a more fundamental reason, furthermore. In *Asylums,* Goffman identifies the tension in liberal societies between the freedom of individuals and the demands of organizational life, and even anticipates some of the ways this tension later emerges in various theoretical and political movements. However, he assumes a binary conception of personhood as autonomy that ipso facto defines children, inmates, group home residents, and others as "not-yet-persons" or "nonpersons." This binary concept was necessarily abandoned in the rights-based movement that started to bring inmates into the community in the 1960s and 1970s. Tensions posed by liberty, which had been insignificant (especially in the institutional treatment of individuals with mental retardation and mental illness), have transformed the professional practices of managing certain kinds of persons. Although deemed incapable of fully managing themselves, individuals in community settings are citizens and as such are managed in terms of their rights. For this reason, the analogy between the treatment of children and that of group home residents reflects more complex conceptions of status and the conferral of rights that have been extended to both as new kinds of persons (cf. Hawes; Postman). The professional consensus regarding adults with intellectual disability is that they should, as a legal and clinical matter, be treated in "age-appropriate" ways. Thus, in the community, residents must be governed, which presumes their capacity for freedom and, by extension, their adulthood. In the group home, however, impolite conduct is a clinical concern that makes it possible to cast residents as childlike in specific and situated ways but not in the thoroughgoing way of Goffman's analogy. His analogy is instructive in a more precise formulation: what children and residents share is that they can both be acted on in ways that presume their capacity to act on themselves; that is, both are expected to demonstrate their responsibility to general notions of propriety by at least attempting to govern themselves.

Just as adults may feel entitled, even obliged, to teach children manners by insisting on "please" and "thank you," counselors' occasional use of a patronizing tone—though it risks offending others—presumes a capacity in residents to learn how to conduct themselves in specifically polite ways. In the field of intellectual disability, the emphasis on the "self-determination" of individuals as "consumers" of services no longer sanctions staff attitudes that reflect older but resilient cultural assumptions about disability. In the group home, although it was clear in staff training that condescension is unacceptable, it remained available as a practical method of counselor know-how. For example, one Thursday afternoon as the weekly staff meeting broke up, a few residents came crowding into the office where the meeting had been held. The usual bustle ensued, with people carrying the extra chairs back to the dining room, gathering up their materials, chatting, and greeting each other. Some residents were keen to be around when the meeting broke up, as it was conventional that they might eat the leftover snacks. On this day, Donna strategically squeezed her way through the crowd to a bowl on the desk that contained a modest amount of popcorn. As she was eating, Nicky noticed her over the hubbub and asked, in a patronizing tone, "Donna, have you had enough popcorn?" The question was patronizing because it indicated the "preferred" answer (Sacks 1987), which Donna provided: "Yes." She paused briefly before taking another handful. Nicky: "Donna, I thought you had enough?" Donna said nothing, and Nicky attempted to elicit a response: "You're going to have dinner soon." Donna remained silent, arms at her side. Nicky persisted because questions, as a practical method of talk, usually oblige an answer, even (or especially) rhetorical, "leading" questions: "What about leaving some for other people?" Donna mumbled, "Yes," and finally resigned herself to forgo the little remaining popcorn. Nicky asked again, "Don't you think you should leave some for other people?" Donna nodded in agreement as she left the office. Nicky's condescension, especially in front of so many others, was a method of intervention that was not a direct disciplinary prohibition but oriented Donna to her own conduct—eating too much popcorn before dinner and not leaving any for others. Nicky's questions indicated the preferred answers, but they functioned also as "invitation-correction devices," which Sacks described in his observation of police interrogations (Silverman, 95). "From a police point of view," as David Silverman explains, such devices are used because their "aggressive character is not so obvious" as direct accusations; invitation-correction devices are invitations to correct an assumption, often through the hypothetical answers offered.

Another day, also in the staff office, Angela and Irving were sitting together, and she was on the telephone making medical appointments; Daniel was retrieving money for Johnny at the open lockbox on the file cabinet; and I was sitting with Paul, looking through the *Daily News* for coupons. Diane, Evelyn, and Marty burst through the front door, and Diane and Evelyn came directly across the hall into the office, full of happy hellos. I put my finger to my lips and pointed to Angela on the telephone, and Daniel said, "Ssshhh!" They quieted immediately and disappeared from the office, presumably heading to their rooms to dispose of their coats and bags. Marty came into the office, said hello to the room, and then stood next to Johnny facing Daniel, who quickly glanced up and down again to the little manila money envelopes in his hands. Marty spoke: "We went out in the community today. I had Chinese lunch." Daniel remained silent, looking down at the envelopes he was shuffling. After about ten seconds, Marty asked, "Can I go to the party at Jemma House on Saturday?" Daniel's immediate response was incredulous but friendly. Looking at Marty, the envelopes now still, he said, "Don't you know how to say hello?" "Oh, hello, Daniel," Marty said with a laugh. "I'm sorry . . . so can I go?" Daniel resumed his work and, without smiling, answered, "I'm serious. It's totally rude of you to barge in like that with questions—and you don't even say hello. Anyway, can't you see that I'm busy?" Marty looked sheepish, uttering a quiet, contrite "Sorry," which Daniel acknowledged immediately by smiling and adopting a sympathetic, even forgiving tone: "Why don't you go relax; you just got home. Then we can talk about Jemma House later, when I'm not in the middle of doing things." Daniel's advice and promise accounted for Marty's impolite conduct as an honest and understandable result of the excitement of having just arrived. No matter what Marty specifically understood, he heard Daniel's remarks as a sympathetic acknowledgment of his request for attention, which was deferred only until "later," and thanked him happily as he left the office.

Counselors disagree about the clinical warrant of precisely this kind of conduct. That they occasionally treat residents like children, or at least act in patronizing ways, does not reflect a standard of group home practice. Nor do counselors necessarily regard such an exchange as contradictory to their ongoing work to enhance the independence of residents qua adults. As a technical matter, counselor work is always work on and with adults, but adulthood is itself a situated and practical matter in the group home. This is true elsewhere as well, as Martha Copp (1998a) shows in the interactional distinction between adolescence and adulthood in a workshop for individuals with intellectual disability.

Reinforcement and Job Satisfaction

Everyday life gets organized clinically through intervention not only in problem conduct but in conduct as appropriate, desired, or normal. Counselors intervene spontaneously to "reinforce" what they regard as a resident's acceptable self-management. When this occurs, it is accountable by the assumption that a resident might well have conducted him- or herself otherwise. When Evelyn got upset, for example, she often cried and complained in ways that counselors regarded as "dramatic," and they referred to her among themselves, with a certain affection, as a "diva." Evelyn had a behavior plan that targeted her "outbursting"; it instructed staff to "redirect" her until she was "calm" and able to "seek staff assistance appropriately." The specified technique of Evelyn's self-management was to find a "private space" and "relax" before she approached a counselor for "support." At dinner one evening, Evelyn was sitting at the back of the dining room with Theresa, Chris, and Johnny, when an argument sparked between her and Johnny. Her loud and tearful remark, "I hate you!" drew the room's attention. We turned our heads all at once toward the back to see Evelyn rise from her chair, yell at Johnny, and make for the opposite end of the dining room, with the apparent intention of leaving. Linda happened to be sitting at a table near the door and stood up to block Evelyn's passage. Linda took her arm and asked earnestly, "Are you going to your room?" Evelyn, who had been barreling through with her head down, looked up and sobbed, "Yes." Linda smiled and said, "That's good!" She released Evelyn's arm, and Evelyn disappeared from the dining room.

There was nothing in the question itself—"Are you going to your room?"—that indicated whether Linda saw Evelyn's conduct as the target behavior (outbursting) or as appropriate self-management of it. That is, the question could have functioned either as Linda's "redirection" of Evelyn or as reinforcement that Evelyn was conducting herself in accordance with her plan (going to her room rather than remaining upset in the dining room). Only in retrospect did Linda's intervention reflexively constitute Evelyn's conduct as "appropriate." Some goal and behavior plans specify techniques for counselors to reinforce successful conduct. These may involve material reinforcers (such as money or special privileges) or a kind of response such as "verbal praise." The only reinforcement Evelyn's plan identified was the permission to seek staff attention when she could do it appropriately. Regardless of what goal plans specify, counselors are always using practical methods of reinforcement such as simple encouragement or praise. Often counselors reinforce positive conduct in ways that organize their work in terms of its moral and professional satisfaction. By using a smile and encouraging tone, Linda's intervention constituted, before the fact, Evelyn's specific capacity for self-management as a personal triumph. This was not only Evelyn's triumph, however, because it was also a situated opportunity for Linda to act on her own work as a practical reflection of that work's success.

Reinforcement work is also a practical method of counselors' satisfaction on occasions when problems of conduct are constituted by acting on their absence. For example, counselors praised residents for things that were unremarkable to the residents themselves, such as cooperatively negotiating TV channels or making arrangements for someone to cover the chores of residents who happened not to be home that evening. When a resident's conduct did not accord (either positively or negatively) with counselors' expectations, work satisfaction was a topic of shoptalk. Johnny had planned a week's vacation long in advance that was canceled about a month beforehand, because too few people signed up. On the afternoon the holiday agency phoned to inform the group home, the counselors' concern about how Johnny would "take it" was a primary topic of shoptalk that day. When Johnny arrived from his program, Carlos earnestly broke the news to him in the staff office. He responded with a shrug, saying, "Oh, okay, that's too bad," and then routinely asked for his afternoon dollar for coffee. There was no indication through the afternoon and evening that Johnny was upset about the canceled trip. The counselors treated his unremarkable conduct as a reflection of "how well he is handling it." They were astonished that Johnny was in a "good" mood (a situated distinction for counselors that usually meant he was not in a "bad" mood). In their talk, the counselors, without any demonstrable basis, equated Johnny's good mood with his handling of the disappointment he must be feeling. In the living room at one point, I observed Daniel reinforcing Johnny with the offhand remark, "It's great you're not upset about the trip." Johnny acknowledged this praise with a nod, which for Daniel simply confirmed the assumption that Johnny's conduct was evidence that he was managing his feelings effectively. It was only at the very end of the evening that an alternative account of Johnny's conduct was suggested, when the counselors were in the staff office completing their documentary work for the shift. Even then it was a joke. Sally laughingly mused that Johnny might actually be pleased the trip was canceled. Whatever the case, the counselors' pleasure in Johnny's conduct that evening was enshrined in the daily log. Their intervention to reinforce the residents' appropriately managed conduct defined such conduct as a reflection of their own work's success. Counselors use their know-how in this way to organize, as part of the work, its caring aspects, which are the most satisfying and meaningful and also the most prone to failure.

Copp (1998b) describes this latter point, in the context of a sheltered workshop, as a kind of emotion work that is "doomed to fail." In the group home, when disappointment or frustration in the work is too much, it becomes clear that residents are not the only focus of clinical work. For example, in a staff meeting discussion about Marty, counselors worked on themselves; the disturbing nature of Marty's behavior led to a discussion about how counselors should manage their own feelings. They encouraged each other not to "take him personally," because "he can't help himself." There appeared to be an increase in problems with Marty in the morning, and the counselors were discouraged about what to do. Monica speculated, "Maybe I need info from the evening about incidents the night before, so that I can understand when he's bad in the morning. I mean, Marty's really capable but doesn't want help." Miles responded sympathetically, "It's never clear what precipitates his falls and stuff." Daniel agreed: "We have to remember how hard it is not to personalize it and feel frustrated." Miles continued, "Marty can't help how he behaves. . . . We shouldn't be expecting to cure him." The counselors accounted for the unchanging nature of Marty's problems, in this discussion, as not their failure but his. What may seem to be a contradiction between the claims that, on the one hand, Marty "can't help himself" and, on the other, he "doesn't want help" is reconciled in accounts of the vexing emotional nature of counselor work, rather than accounts of Marty's persistent problems. Comforting each other takes shape in the psy techniques of clinical know-how, already available as an organizational feature of the group home setting. The knowledge one must have and knowing how to use it to be a counselor are themselves a demanding aspect of counselor work. One must know Marty and his disability, but one must also know oneself—one's own feelings and how to manage them—and must remember not to be unrealistic or to personalize relationships with the residents.

Residents' Methods

Just as counselors are not the only objects of clinical work, they are not the only ones whose know-how is an organizing feature of group home life. Resident know-how reflects their own local knowledge of Driggs House and is observable in the methods of practical reasoning they use in their group home work. For Harvey Sacks, the principles of everyday social order can be observed in the temporal, situated accomplishment of ordinary talk. Like most people, the residents all use talk to negotiate everyday life. Their methods of everyday talk, however, illustrate how they accomplish group home competence *as* residents.

If communicational competency is generally measured by the efficacy of talk across a range of occasions and settings, then one thing the residents' use of ordinary methods of talk indicates is how their lives are circumscribed by the group home and by a "complex institutional topography" (Rose 1998a, 179) comprising day programs, workshops, and supervised recreational activities that constitute "the community." This explains in part why the topics of resident talk are relatively narrow. Researchers have shown the highly contextual and practical character of social knowledge among adults with intellectual disability (Soodak; Oetting and Rice). Of course, the residents all have their unique concerns and pleasures, which are topics of their talk. However, my focus here is on certain methods of talk that all the residents use, to a greater or lesser degree, and that demonstrate some ways in which they accomplish social competence in the specific local order of Driggs House.

To suggest that there are methods of talk that the residents share, more or less, and that distinguish them in the group home as residents does not provide an explanation of who they are or what ostensibly warrants their living at Driggs House. I must emphasize that, as individuals, their characteristics and capacities make them far more different than alike. My aim is not to address the diagnostic classifications that ostensibly allow all the residents to be regarded as somehow the same. Likewise, I do not address the category of intellectual disability or whether it is adequate to the residents' capacities or experience. Whether this and prior classifications are adequate to the claims made for them is an important question, but it is an evaluative one that I do not ask. Also, if it need be said, though I focus on how ordinary talk makes certain kinds of group home competence observable, I do not mean to suggest that methods of practical reasoning be considered as an alternative basis for establishing general classifications. Sabsay and Platt used ethnomethodology in this vein to study the context-specific natural language use of people with intellectual disability. The issue of diagnostic classification aside, it is worth noting how little ethnomethodology has been used to capture the lived experience of disability. In addition to Goode's research (1994) on the situated communication practices of nonverbal disabled children, the other compelling recent example is Robillard's analysis (1999) of his own progressive paralysis to demonstrate the embodied nature of talk.

The Moral Order of Talk

The practical methods that individuals use unwittingly to construct everyday talk make morality observable as a local order (Sacks 1975; Sacks, Schegloff, and Jefferson 1974; Schegloff and Sacks). Sacks (1992a, 1972) provides another instructive parallel with children. Children's rights in conversation are limited, and they know at a young age how to use questions as a practical method to gain adults' attention. In a similar way, group home residents know how to make claims on counselors' time and attention: to generate conversation as an activity in itself, to show off new purchases, to seek comfort, to share news, and so on. They are aware that direct questions usually oblige a response and that refusal is an accountable failure. Silverman (20) describes this as a "trading off" of conversational rights that are not equitably distributed. Residents oblige counselors with questions so that they assume the role of hearers. They know that just a first name can function this way. In the staff office, even when hunched over her paperwork, Kenneth's question obliged a response: "Sally?" She might fulfill her obligation by saying, "Not now, Kenneth, can't you see I'm busy?" Her more likely response, "What?" permitted him to raise any topic he chose.

That residents competently use questions to oblige counselors to become hearers shows that the distribution of authority in the group home is not a zero-sum game. Authority can be exercised "at all points," to borrow Sacks's phrase about where social order is observable in talk. Questions come in handy as a method when residents want attention. By the same token, counselors may exercise their authority to refuse the obligation to respond or to intervene in ways that define residents' conduct as impolite. Once residents have secured their right to speak, they continually make their talk tellable, as all competent speakers do, through methods that preempt or resist counselors' attempts to close the conversation. By asking questions of the hearer and pointing out details, residents continually indicate their talk in the course of that talk. Like all participants in talk, when a counselor is in the role of hearer, he or she uses what Sacks calls "response tokens" as methods of giving permission to the speaker to continue and to indicate that he or she (the counselor) is not poised to claim a turn to speak. Such response tokens include questions, "Mm-hmm," "Uh-huh," nods, and other gestures (Sacks 1992b, 410–12).

Residents sometimes use talk that is conventionally incompetent to accomplish group home competence. For example, in the routine failure to attend to hearers in the usually expected ways, residents may continue speaking even when counselors refuse their methods to retain the right to speak. Residents persist despite the absence of regular response tokens, often ignoring counselors' demonstrated impatience or boredom. How individuals initiate and close conversations can reflect the differential rights of individuals in particular settings. Counselors, for example, move conversations to an end; they "open up closings" (Schegloff and Sacks) in ways that determine whether a resident has ultimately demonstrated competent participation. There are situations of talk in which a resident's competence as a speaker breaks down and he or she becomes repetitive or confused. On the one hand, counselors may act on these situations as mere incompetence, by claiming the role of speaker in order to close the conversation or withdrawing abruptly, or by claiming an exemption from the general obligation of hearers to secure from a speaker the practical permission to close a situation of talk. On the other hand, counselors often participate in ways that result in a resident's social competence, hearing and acting on incompetent talk not as incompetence but as intellectual disability. In this way, they do not claim the role of speaker so that residents may retain it far longer than conventionally competent talk requires, regardless of persistence, confusion, or repetition.

Paul's extensive knowledge of the neighborhood and the city, a function of both his age and his twenty-odd years in the group home, was always a useful method to initiate conversation. One afternoon, he was reading the paper in the staff office when he secured Angela's attention and then switched the topic after only one turn.

> PAUL: I'm going to visit Robert Moses Pool on Friday. Have you ever been
> there?
> ANGELA: Oh, yeah. That's been there forever. When I was a kid we used to
> go there.
> PAUL: I am going to buy another airplane.
> ANGELA: What kind?

Just Angela's question, "What kind?" accepted Paul's switch in topics. Despite what in other circumstances would have been a strangely abrupt shift, Angela acted on and permitted Paul's talk to be competent simply by asking a question. In fact, I heard a topical relevance in this switch for Paul—being out in the community meant that there were places to visit as well as things to buy—and maybe Angela did, too.

An example of a counselor's refusal to maintain a resident's competence in the face of his or her conventional incompetence occurred with Kenneth. He was discussing one of his regular concerns, his mother's age and health, in the office with Sonia. When he appeared to begin the conversation again, she ended it abruptly.

> KENNETH: She's getting old, and my brother doesn't live here anymore.
> Maybe I should move home and take care of her?
> SONIA: Do you think she would want you to do that?
> KENNETH: Yes, I can live in my old room.
> SONIA: But, Kenneth, do you really think that you would be able to take
> care of her?
> KENNETH: Yes.
> SONIA: Like how?
> KENNETH: Well, I could cook and, um, you know, go to the store and—
> SONIA (laughing): But you don't even like to do your cooking goal here.
> Or help with the shopping or anything.
> KENNETH: But she's old.

SONIA: Well, I know. But she is happy that you're here.
KENNETH: But my brother is not here and—
SONIA: Okay, I've got some things to do. We can talk about this later. (As she spoke, she rose and left the office.)

Residents also demonstrate competence as hearers in *their* use of response tokens. The inexhaustible variety of available response tokens not only provide ongoing and practical permission for a speaker to continue, they also display attention to and understanding of a speaker's talk. Schegloff (1982) shows that, in their competent placement, response tokens are markers of attention, comprehension, and sometimes agreement. They are ambiguous, however, because the demonstration of attention or agreement does not necessarily require comprehension. As with the familiar method of nonfluent second-language speakers, response tokens enable the ongoing display of competent attention regardless of actual comprehension.

However limited the scope of the residents' topics, their knowledge of group home work nonetheless provides for effective methods in talk. Residents' shoptalk is a practical method of managing everyday uncertainty, but it is also an effective method of making claims on counselors and each other. By initiating discussion about staff schedules, chores, goal and behavior plans, and so forth, residents demonstrate their competent membership, which especially obliges counselors because it demonstrates the very initiative and self-knowledge constantly urged of them. When Kenneth was helping with dinner or assisting other residents with their chores or laundry, he frequently attempted to corral passing counselors: "Look what I'm doing. I'm helping with dinner," or, "I'm helping Donna with her laundry." Kenneth's "announcements" attempted to engage counselors by indicating what he was doing and, in effect, his reflexive awareness that doing it was a good thing. In a similar way, Marty repeatedly posed questions for which answers were already known: "Do you know Sally is my new counselor?" or "Didn't I have a good night?" He also routinely came into the office in his bathrobe, clean-shaven and with wet hair, and announced to the staff that he had showered and shaved.

In demonstrating self-knowledge and commitment to their own work, residents demonstrate also their understanding of counselors and the work they do. However effective these strategies are, residents are nonetheless aware that counselors may act on them not as the situated expression of the residents' competence and commitment to becoming more independent, but as a failure of self-management. Counselors may refuse the obligation in various ways to orient residents to their talk as problem conduct. Often impatient or sarcastic with Kenneth, for example, counselors heard the announcements of his routine work as attention-seeking and needy. Similarly, Marty was considered to be merely "asking for praise" and seeking acknowledgment for routine tasks that "he should already be independent with." They saw Marty as confused about what it means to "be independent"; it's not just the ability to accomplish something on his own without prompting or supervision from counselors. Counselors "knew" that Marty was capable of proper personal hygiene, so, in this instance, they defined being independent not only as being able to do things but also as not seeking attention for doing the things one can do.

The counselors were not wrong to see the residents in these examples as merely currying favor. But Kenneth and Marty's use of talk makes observable the reflexive relationship they had to their group home work. The work itself furnished practical methods of knowing and acting on themselves and others as certain kinds of group home persons. Marty and Kenneth demonstrated a commitment to their work and what they took it to be. This exhibits a practical knowledge about being a resident and also about counselors as a kind of person. To make oneself available as a resident, in this practical sense, is to make oneself available as an object of the group home work that one understands quite well as the work of perpetual monitoring, assessment, and intervention in one's own life.

Confusing Identifications: "Acting like Staff" and the Paradox of Peer Support

At Driggs House, attempts to shape the way residents conducted themselves with each other could produce paradoxical results. Counselors were always attempting to shape residents' conduct toward each other as "peers" by encouraging mutual assistance in various ways both out in the community and at home. Counselors believed that resident relationships of mutual support promoted independence by tempering the hierarchy of group home authority. In the counselors' formulation, decreased reliance on staff was ipso facto increased independence. Peer support figured even in formal attempts to shape the interaction of residents. The story about David seeking my help to regulate the shower temperature is a perfect example. Though it happens that at one point the services of the building superintendent were required to fix the knobs, David's nightly requests for staff assistance were regarded as a sign of dependence, which is why his behavior was addressed with a goal plan that required him to seek assistance from his peers *before* asking a counselor.

The informal, everyday work residents do with each other draws partly on practical methods that are made available by the counselors' own observable work of "helping." Yet the counselors' expectations about how residents should conduct themselves with each other are not entirely available to residents. The distinction between mere assistance and "acting like staff" is a situated one, and counselors often intervene in conduct as a problem of "acting like" or "identifying with" staff, as "bossy," "not minding your own business," "controlling," "acting superior," or "undermining other people's independence," and so forth.

Theresa's unusual level of involvement in life at Driggs House makes her the clearest example of these issues. When chores were being done during the evening, she assumed a supervisory role, actively monitoring the other residents' performance of their duties and offering criticism and encouragement as she coordinated the work. After dinner, she circulated from the living room through the dining room and kitchen and back again, dispensing compliments, orders, and criticism as she went. Theresa frequently returned from her rounds to alert residents watching TV that "it's time for your chore," and usually they responded by getting up and going to do it. Kenneth was particularly upset one evening, sitting in the living room with his head in his hands. Theresa tapped his shoulder and said, "Diane is finished. You can sweep now." He looked up at her with an expression that indicated he did not appreciate her interruption and looked down again. She said, "C'mon it's time for your chore." Kenneth remained still without looking up. After a minute or two, Theresa said emphatically, "C'mon, Kenneth, it's time for your chore now." He responded angrily, "Shut up, Theresa! You're not my counselor. You're always telling me what to do." Miles, from the other side of the room, asked, "What's the matter?" Kenneth replied in an upset tone, "Theresa's telling me what to do. I'll do my chore! Tell her to mind her own business." Miles looked at her blandly and said, "Theresa, leave him alone," and then, to Kenneth, "But you don't have to get so upset about it.

She's only trying to help." In other situations, counselors were not as accepting of Theresa's informal role. Just as the dining room had emptied out after dinner one evening, Theresa was sweeping and supervising others as she worked. Daniel was walking through to the living room just as she said to Ruby, "C'mon, clean the tables so I can sweep. Hurry up!" Ruby replied half in amusement, half in anger, "Shut up! I'm working as fast as I can." Daniel stopped and stared at Theresa. She asked, with mock indignation, "What?" He replied, "Why are you bossing everybody around? It's not your job; you're not staff." Theresa dismissed him by saying, "G'wan, get outta here," and carried on with her sweeping.

"Acting like staff" was a situational designation. Conduct that might sometimes be seen as acting like staff in some contexts was not a problem when it was useful to a counselor's immediate work. One evening, people were assembled in the office getting their money to go down for coffee. Miles told Paul he had already spent his dollar for that day. Paul protested, demanding the next day's dollar. The other residents vigorously discouraged him. Theresa said, "You don't have the money, and that's that. Okay?" She then consoled him: "You can come down tomorrow night." James seconded the practical choice: "You don't want to spend tomorrow's money. You have a budget." Miles gently agreed, and Paul relented. Counselors may not intervene in residents' "minding other people's business" if it serves their work. When residents use their know-how to shape each other's conduct and it turns out to assist their peers, counselors' work is notable by its absence. Not intervening allows residents' know-how to be a practical method in the situated accomplishment of counselor work. Miles's refusal to give Paul another dollar may well be considered an instance of rationing, but the story shows how residents' methods also function to limit demand, as Lipsky (95) describes: "[Clients] are also controlled by the social pressures exerted by others who wait . . . [who] share the burden of waiting for services."

These issues beg comparison with what Goffman, in *Asylums* (1961, 65), called the "lines of adaptation" that "represent a way of managing the tension between the home world and the institutional world." The group home does not function in such stark opposition to "the outside." Of course, there are instances when residents' conduct seems like adaptation to the inescapable demands of the group home in the way Goffman described. What he called "conversion" (61–63) might very well describe Theresa and others who enjoy doing the group home's work and embrace its smooth operation and routine order. There is no empirical basis, however, for understanding residents' conduct as adaptation in any special sense. That the walls of the group home may not be as transparent as they are claimed to be does not mean that it is a total institution:

> Walled-in organizations have a characteristic they share with few other social entities: part of the individual's obligation is to be *visibly* engaged at appropriate times in the activity of the organization, which entails a mobilization of attention and muscular effort, a bending of oneself to the activity at hand. This obligatory engrossment in the activity of the organization tends to be taken as a symbol both of one's commitment and attachment, and, behind this, of one's acceptance of the implications of participation for a definition of one's nature. (Goffman 1961, 176–77)

At Driggs House, "confusing identifications" refers to several processes at once. The counselor's situated designation of a resident's conduct as acting like staff presumes a generic sense of identification: that the resident identifies him- or herself with the counselor's role. Of course, most do identify with (even *as*) counselors in a number of ways. If this is merely a personal adaptation, in Goffman's sense, and not also the effective nature of government in general, then unremarkable conduct would also have to be explained as strategic, perhaps as "keeping cool." Acting toward each other in ways that at times are observable as "thinking one's actually a counselor" is the unintended consequence of the residents' use of their own know-how. This seems quite different from the strenuous adaptation Goffman implies by the "muscular effort" and "bending of oneself" to the demands of a total institution.

Whether the situated distinction between support and control is made by counselors or by residents among themselves, it often reflects a practical confusion inherent in the work. Counselors unwittingly furnish residents with know-how about advice giving that enables precisely the conduct that may be defined as acting like staff. Counselor authority is a routine, practical method residents use to undermine the right of other residents to offer advice or assistance: "Hey, you're not my counselor, you know!" Irving was frequently confused by the way counselors responded to his attempts at peer support. Acting like staff was a known problem of Irving's conduct that had become more visible because of his paid job in the house, cleaning the kitchen and dining room for three hours per day during the week.

This was an unusual arrangement, because, to prevent the exploitation that was characteristic of institutionalization and the long history of institutional peonage, regulations bar residents from being employed in group homes, just as residents are required to have services or employment at another site each weekday (14 N.Y.C.R.R. § 633.7). Employing Irving required obtaining approval from the agency, and Sonia had to argue for its contribution to his self-work in the group home.

For some time, Irving had simply refused to attend a sheltered workshop. He was critical of the frequent lack of jobs and the nominal wage, and, though he was physically capable of commuting by subway, his leg braces made this somewhat onerous. At Driggs House, there was a housekeeper on weekdays, responsible for heavy cleaning and ordering and stocking supplies. A month after I began my research, the housekeeper quit, and Irving asked Sonia whether he could have the position. Sonia and Mike decided to offer him a part-time job by carving out a small number of the housekeeper's tasks in maintaining the kitchen, which encompassed his regular chore. They argued this would benefit the house until the position was filled, and then the new housekeeper could serve as his supervisor. It was an opportunity, they argued, to reinforce his willingness to work and his independence despite his refusal to participate in employment and training at a workshop. A number of counselors were adamantly opposed to this arrangement, not on any historical or legal basis—they were unaware that Sonia had to seek the agency's approval before offering Irving the job—but because it rewarded his systematic refusal of the programs that other residents attended willingly. Most importantly, these counselors believed that being employed in the group home would just increase Irving's already inflated sense of authority. It "puts him above his peers" and "reinforces" his tendency to identify with staff, the counselors argued. They accounted for Irving's sense of "superiority" over other residents as "denial." Irving's explicit resentment about having to live in the group home was evidence for these counselors that his tendency to identify with staff was not occasional bossiness but a "deeper" psychological issue. They regarded his refusal to attend a sheltered workshop as "denial of the way things are," even though other residents complained about their workshops, too, and even though there was no disagreement among counselors that such programs contributed very little to the independence or employment prospects of residents, not to mention their wallets.

Some of the specific ways Irving acted like staff only confirmed the counselors' concerns. He frequently monitored the health of other residents by telling them what and how much they should eat. One explosive evening, Evelyn ran crying into the staff office because Irving had told her she was too fat to eat the cookies laid out for snack. Daniel and Sally went immediately into the kitchen and told him angrily, "This job doesn't mean that you are allowed to mind other people's business, ya know?" and, "You don't like it when counselors tell you to shower, right? Or to do what you need to do? Why should you do it to other people? You're not staff!" This was unusually public and harsh in tone. Irving simply stared at them as they spoke. When they left the kitchen, he resumed his work sponging down the counter. In the office just afterward, Sally and Daniel accounted for their harshness as necessary to counter the way the job exacerbated Irving's usual problems. The next day, Irving and I talked privately. He was perplexed by their anger, given that "people here have medical problems, diabetes, blood pressure . . . then they just eat too much." I asked, "But why do the staff not like you to tell other residents about that stuff?" He shrugged: "They think I'm too bossy." Their reaction the night before was familiar to him, if harsher than usual, and he was both annoyed and disappointed. Furthermore, he seemed unable to explain why they thought he was bossy. This reaction reflects the paradoxical character of this kind of conduct. Even though Irving was "methodologically" correct when he acted on the conduct of other residents, he did not avoid the unpredictable conflict with counselors. Constantly enjoined to "help" his peers, he used the practical methods observable to him in the counselors' own conduct. His confusion between helping and acting like staff was not a psychological one, as counselors had it, but a practical one produced by their own work.

Counselors were also keenly aware that the work residents did with each other could be functional for the group home. They frequently asked residents to help each other with specific tasks at home. Chris, Mark, or Ruby was often enlisted to take Diane, Donna, and Evelyn on errands, as well as other residents who were able to go out in the community but needed help getting to a specific shop or completing a particular errand. Apart from these overt requests, residents' work with each other made a sizable contribution to the operation of the group home. Irving assisted Ruby by accompanying her to the bank; Evan frequently made lunch for himself and Kenneth on weekend afternoons; Chris took Evelyn for batteries and other items in the neighborhood. Theresa not only kept in view all the evening chores but often figured out how to coordinate and cover the tasks of people who were not home, making sure those tasks were done and not done twice. In the evenings, she knew without being asked to prod David to shower and shave so they could go down for coffee. Counselors relied on Theresa to help David. She was asked to wake him, something she was able to do without incurring the wrath he apparently reserved for counselors, and to help him on Saturdays with laundering, folding, and putting away his clothes.

Counselors also recognized the potentially paradoxical character of this kind of resident work. In a friendly and informal conversation between counselors in the staff office, Maria joked, "Well, you know that Theresa is [David's] *real* counselor; at least he listens to her." That we all chuckled reflected a shared know-how about the potential confusion inherent in the way Theresa and David's relationship was shaped by her work, some of which was at the counselors' request. They recognized that even when personal relationships between residents do not necessarily conform to their ideal notions of peer support, it often eases their work. Nearly every Tuesday, Theresa stepped in to help Evelyn with her laundry when she was lugging her full hamper through the hallway. It so happened that doing laundry independently was one of Evelyn's goals, and her plan laid out in detail how to sort the clothes into light and dark piles, measure the soap, and use the machines, as well as when to seek staff assistance. Theresa's awareness (or lack of it) that Evelyn had a laundry goal had no bearing on how she helped. Evelyn, for her part, was always grateful, and it seemed that the only work she cared about was getting her laundry done, not necessarily getting it done independently. Counselors invariably saw Theresa and Evelyn huddled together over the machine and left them alone to their work. Sometimes they even encouraged them: "Oh, great! Theresa's helping you." Permitting them to do the laundry together was the counselors' situated decision that Theresa was assisting her peer rather than acting like staff. Seeing it as appropriate rather than problem conduct meant the counselors had a little less work to do that day. They knew that at least the laundry would get done properly, even if it meant that Evelyn did not properly work on her goal. In the demanding course of group home work, it would be near impossible for counselors to pass up opportunities that here and there relieved them of certain tasks. Though Theresa's assistance certainly freed up a little extra time, the counselors could never escape, at the end of every Tuesday evening, the task of recording that Evelyn had successfully completed her laundry goal. This was never exactly untrue, of course, because what defined the successful completion of Evelyn's goal was that she did her laundry without *staff* assistance.

When residents help their peers, it is a sign of self-knowledge and independence unless someone determines that they are acting like staff. The line between helping and acting like staff becomes clear only when it is drawn practically. Once it's crossed, peer support is a clinical problem. Residents take for granted and manage routinely the paradoxical outcomes of their own conduct. Though the counselors joked about, for example, Theresa being David's "real" counselor, such acknowledgment by counselors of their reliance on residents did not go further. Perhaps it could not. In a similar way, Gary Kielhofner observed in his study of a classroom for adults with intellectual disability that the teachers' concern with managing trouble resulted in the teaching not of competencies and skills that were expressed goals but of specific incompetencies that maintained the appearance of an orderly classroom. Counselors do not acknowledge the paradox, because, in their view, helping and acting like staff are self-evident and distinct kinds of conduct. Acting like staff is a clinically warrantable problem like any other and indicates a resident's failure of self-management. Yet counselors unwittingly create, in their own conduct, the very conditions for acting like staff. So, time and again residents discover that in their everyday work of helping their peers, the available practical methods they use can at any moment be claimed by counselors as theirs alone.

III. Group Home Technologies

7 EXPERTISE AND THE WORK OF STAFF MEETINGS

THERE WAS A WEEKLY STAFF MEETING at Driggs House every Thursday afternoon, from 2:00 to 5:00. Its length was one indication of the complexity of work coordination and, for both clinical and legal reasons, the value placed on efficient communication and consensus across shifts. Sonia and the main counselors—those who worked the weekday morning and evening shifts—were the regular attendees. The weekend counselors never attended, but the morning and evening counselors all worked one weekend shift, and it was part of their responsibility to convey information from the meeting to weekend staff, who were expected also to review the week's log. There were others who attended the staff meeting often but not regularly: Mike, the regional supervisor; Beth, the nurse; and Cynthia, the behavior specialist.

The overall tone of the meetings reflected the informal camaraderie that generally characterized staff relationships. One of the morning counselors always managed a trip to the store with petty cash to provide soda, chips, dip, and cookies. On special occasions, such as a staff member's birthday, the counselors often provided a proper lunch, bringing homemade dishes or, for the morning staff, using the kitchen between tasks during their shift to prepare a spread for the meeting.

The staff office was barely adequate to contain the eleven or twelve people who assembled regularly. Extra chairs were brought in from the dining room and arranged in a tight circle backed up against the desks, cabinets, and shelves that were lined with the treatment and goal books and other binders of vital group home information. Sonia ran the meetings, often sitting with her back to the closed door because she was usually the last one to arrive from her office down the hall. She had to maneuver her chair or stand up to answer a knock or let people come and go. As the staff gathered, there was always chitchat about movies, politics, sports, or personal issues. If there was an unusual group home issue or brewing controversy, the counselors might already be discussing it before Sonia arrived. She called everyone to order informally as she passed out an agenda that listed the six or seven items she planned to cover.

The way Sonia ran the meetings elicited certain ways of being a counselor: her participatory techniques drew on the very clinical assumptions of group home work, emphasizing the significance of each individual. Sonia continuously encouraged and sometimes required counselors to participate: "Your input is important, because you are the ones who *really* work with the guys." Each counselor's capacities and commitment became visible to Sonia in the collective decision-making work about the work. In fact, it was not all that difficult to mobilize counselors to participate in the work of staff meetings, at least in the talk about clinical work. It was the one regular occasion when counselors were required to discuss clinical issues in a formal, systematic, and collaborative way. And the absence of residents permitted more openness than shoptalk, which, though continuous, was subject to constant interruption and always had to account for residents coming in and out of earshot.

There were three kinds of business conducted at the meetings: employment issues (such as benefits and payroll), administrative issues (staff shift schedules and certain group home procedures), and resident issues (work on conduct and interventions, medical issues, and concerns related to other programs). Resident issues were given the most attention, by far, usually at least two and one-half of the three hours. These issues were dominant, in part, because they comprised the bulk of the work, but counselors were also very invested in discussing them. Clinical matters were the most engaging, if also the most frustrating, because they represented the professional and moral importance of counselor work. Though Sonia at times might use the written agenda to control a meeting's pace, keeping things moving could be a challenge when some counselors were not satisfied with the way a problem had been defined or resolved.

The counselors also understood full well the meeting's crucial organizational function in establishing, week to week, the practical course of their everyday work. The largely friendly, informal, and participatory sensibility of staff meetings in no way precluded the possibility of tension or even outright conflict. In fact, disputes about clinical matters revealed particularly well the intensity of the counselors' investment in their work and the practical know-how that made that work possible. Although Sonia always attempted to achieve consensus, when this appeared too difficult or time-consuming, she might end a discussion by imposing the solution she favored. She described to me what she called a "last-resort way" of managing contention, precluding discussion simply by describing a problem of resident conduct and its solution as a fait accompli.

The Practical Meaning of Disability

In their training, counselors learn about intellectual disability (mental retardation) and the way it is defined by certain intelligence tests and scales of functioning. Counselors also complete qualitative scales of adaptive functioning, acting as "informants" for residents with evaluating psychologists when it comes time to bring up to date the annual documentation required by state regulations.

Other than this, formal diagnostic measures and categories have little practical relevance; during my thirteen months of research, they came up in discussion only twice. The scores become relevant only insofar as they confirm or challenge the counselors' practical sense of a resident's capacities. This happened during my first week, while a few counselors were giving me an informal tour of the treatment books. They described the required psychological evaluations as interesting but "obvious" in the context of their own "relationships with the guys." Miles said that the residents' IQ scores were "irrelevant to what people are really like and really capable of," though in some cases they could be meaningful when one first began working at the group home. Miles found that "with David it [the IQ score] was helpful, because it indicates how smart he really is. You know, he could easily have been placed in a lower house without it." Daniel agreed: "I mean, he has a higher IQ than Irving, but you'd never think that."

It was not until near the end of my time at Driggs House that a diagnostic measure came up again as an issue for counselors. An evaluation of Evelyn by an outside psychologist produced lower scores than previous ones. The staff were "concerned." "These can't be right," they thought, because Evelyn's "doing fine." Some counselors expressed alarm about "what it might mean," so the psychologist was asked to test Evelyn again. The second set of scores was the same but did not generate the same concern. Evelyn's scores were relevant only in that they appeared to be at odds with counselors' practical knowledge of her. In the end, it was this knowledge, which was inseparable from their practical work, that mattered more than her scores and what they might indicate. Evelyn *was* fine, after all. The counselors' description of the general irrelevance of these diagnostic measures echoes the research from the early 1970s about the inadequacy of mental tests in relation to the diagnostic entity "mental retardation" (Braginsky and Braginsky; Mercer). The practical irrelevance of mental tests, however, did not impede the counselors' assumption (at least on the two occasions I have described here) that the scores measured *something*, though that something might not matter to their work.

Counselors may be sensitive to the contextual dimensions of the category of disability that establishes eligibility for services at Driggs House, yet they may also invoke disability as a featureless and encompassing abstraction in order to define a resident *tout cour*. What "disability" means depends on how and when it is used. In some situations, counselors referred to a resident's capacities as immutable to suggest that self-management was impossible. They might explain specific problems of conduct as the manifestation of basic limitations that a resident "can't help": "This is who Johnny is," or, "Paul can't help himself." Counselors sometimes focused on observable conduct to make accountable and confirm what they already knew about a resident's "deeper" or "inner" problems. This is a form of reasoning that Garfinkel (1984a, 78) described as the documentary method of interpretation, because "an actual appearance"—observable conduct—is treated "as 'the document of,' as 'pointing to,' as 'standing on behalf of' a presupposed underlying pattern," and the conduct and underlying problem are used "to elaborate the other." Goffman describes a similar process in *Asylums* (1961, 375), in which mundane conduct is treated pathologically as standing for or concealing an inmate's overall sickness, such as schizophrenia. Though he observed that, in principle, specific conduct cannot explain the "essential character" of an inmate, "in practice these categories become magical ways of making a single entity out of the nature of the patient—an entity that is subject to psychiatric servicing."

Counselors, at other times, invoked disability in the opposite way, by imputing a kind of knowing agency to residents, describing their problem conduct as a refusal to manage themselves: Marty knew how to "push staff's buttons," or Kenneth "makes up issues because he likes counseling." In staff meetings and shoptalk, counselors invoked these contradictory ideas about what distinguished the residents as disabled in order to challenge each others' professional assessments as too clinical or not clinical enough. These ideas provided justification for more or less intervention in disputes, and they provided consolation when a resident was particularly upsetting. Whether a resident couldn't help it or willfully failed to manage him- or herself, counselors used disability in situated ways to express and manage frustration with the persistent failure that is inherent in group home work.

"That's Why He's Here!"

During my thirteen months at Driggs House, Johnny spent two ten-day periods on the psychiatric unit of the local hospital. One of these occasions was related to incidents in which he was physically aggressive in the mornings, especially with Maria, his primary morning counselor. These difficulties were episodic; much of the time, he was outgoing and good-humored and got along well with most of the residents and staff. In the past, however, periodic sullenness, anger, and aggression had been targets of various behavior and goal plans. Two flashpoints with counselors emerged: Johnny's requests for spending money beyond what he "budgeted" (especially in the morning, when as a rule it was distributed in the evening), and his lack of interest in going to work (which was how he referred to his day program). On mornings Johnny decided he didn't want to go, the counselors attempted to persuade him, because they regarded his staying home as both reflecting and exacerbating his "self-esteem problem." The counselors' efforts could make him angry and verbally aggressive, but most of the time, if he did not simply refuse and return to his room, he would relent, and by the time he returned in the afternoon his anger was gone. On a few occasions, however, he became physically aggressive, shoving, hitting, and screaming at counselors.

Monica felt afraid of Johnny at these moments; Angie and Maria said they felt "threatened" but "could handle it." The counselors are trained to deal with "challenging behavior" by taking "positive approaches," encouraging "clients to maintain self-control," and engaging in "proactive and non-aversive methods" (OMRDD 2006, 41;

Baker and Bissmire). SCIP (Strategies for Crisis Intervention and Prevention) training is used internationally but was actually developed by OMRDD in 1988; in 1998, the agency produced a new curriculum, SCIP-R, which further emphasizes positive approaches (OMRDD 2006). SCIP training includes techniques of physical restraint that are meant to reduce potential harm to clients and staff, but one overall objective is to enhance the confidence of staff so they are able to handle these situations more effectively and, in principle, prevent the need for physical intervention (Baker and Bissmire). Sonia had established a protocol for calling 911 if counselors could not subdue Johnny and thought they might be harmed. Sometimes when he appeared to be physically threatening, just picking up the phone and announcing they were calling 911 sent him back to his room. The call was actually placed on several occasions, however, and at these times the police came to the residence. In most instances, Johnny had calmed down sufficiently by the time they arrived, but on one occasion they took him (accompanied by a counselor) to the emergency room, where he was admitted to the psychiatric unit of the hospital.

Some counselors complained that Johnny actually enjoyed the hubbub, which was why he was "always fine" by the time the police arrived. In one staff meeting, counselors were especially upset because he had outbursted twice in the past few days, and one of the incidents uncharacteristically involved another resident. He and Theresa were having a loud argument in the living room (apparently about Johnny's chore). From another part of the house, Daniel followed the shouting. When he appeared and asked what was going on, Theresa abruptly turned and left, but Johnny followed her, screaming and cursing, into her room. Johnny left Theresa's room as soon as Daniel appeared. Daniel believed that if he had not followed them, Johnny would have been physically aggressive. Some counselors emphasized the gravity of the incident by portraying it as an extraordinary violation of privacy that, in combination with the morning incidents, indicated a worsening of his conduct.

All that was going on with Johnny illustrates what Robert Emerson has described as the situated logic of last resort, in which "normal remedies," the routine handling of expected troubles, fail. The morning counselors were especially upset that "nothing was being done." Though they did not minimize the stress of dealing with Johnny in the morning, their emphasis was what Johnny "needed." In this discussion, the morning counselors were explicit in their belief that the evening counselors "didn't understand what he was like in the mornings." This is an example of the very occasional organizational tension between the evening and morning counselors. Although their jobs are different in fundamental ways, they frequently swapped shifts and were intimately familiar with the routines and rhythms of Driggs House work through the day. There was tension between counselors across shifts only in situations like this, when the taken-for-granted coordination of work was challenged and specific claims were made of one shift by the other. The following excerpt from a staff meeting is ostensibly about the 911 protocol but in effect is a heated dispute about who Johnny "really" was.

MARIA: He needs to know the consequences—

MONICA: Pressing charges is the only way. Johnny is a threat to others. Just threatening— . . . 911 is not enough, it's not fair to everyone else! Theresa's family should have pressed charges.

DANIEL: You can't [press charges], because living in a group home already involves accepting some curtailment of rights!

MARIA: He should be taken down to the precinct, just to see the reality of it.

MILES: That's unfair!

DANIEL: Yes, unfair.

MILES: He's mentally incompetent. That's why he's here!

DANIEL: He can't control himself, it's not personal. These are not new behaviors. (Maria and Monica both shake their heads in vigorous disagreement.) The issue is whether he belongs here. Johnny needs to be in an ICF.

MILES: He's not able to verbalize; that means he feels bad and acts out.

(Maria nods in agreement but shrugs to indicate that Miles's point is not relevant to her complaint about the 911 protocol. Several other staff members make sympathetic remarks about how difficult the situation is for Maria, who is always faced with Johnny's temper on the morning shift. She ignores them and responds to Daniel.)

MARIA: That's not the point [whether he belongs at Driggs House]. Calling 911 is not enough—

DANIEL: This is what he's like!—

MARIA: You don't need to tell me what he's like—I work with him every day!

(At this point Sonia ends the discussion, perhaps to halt or diffuse the escalating tension, by assuring everyone that she will think about the problems they raised. She reiterates that, for the moment, the 911 protocol is "still an important resource" when counselors are concerned for their own safety.)

Which is it? Was Johnny unable to "help himself" because of "who he is" and "what he's like"? Or was he capable of learning how to conduct himself differently by "seeing the reality" and facing the consequences from which he was now protected? These are situated questions, and, for this reason, neither the counselors' clinical training about intellectual disability nor their personal experience with Johnny necessarily could produce consensus in the answers. For Daniel and Miles, "who Johnny is" was a criticism of Maria and Monica's presumption that he was capable of understanding and learning from the consequences of his actions. But the morning counselors did not accept Daniel and Miles's characterization of Johnny by refusing their attempt to shift the discussion from the topic of the emergency protocol to the question of whether Johnny should be living at Driggs House or somewhere else. In this staff meeting and in general, the practical meaning that disability has in specific contexts often required no explication. When a meaning was provided, it was often the tautological assertion of positions that follow reflexively from the initial claim. For example, Miles was incredulous when he declared that Johnny was "mentally incompetent." But in this context, the meaning of mental incompetence was the very conduct it was meant to explain. Miles's emphatic use of this stark phrase—one that I had never before heard in the group home and never heard again—expressed the intensity of his opposition to the morning counselors' ideas about Johnny. This staff meeting was among the most heated I observed. In the "micropolitics of trouble" (Emerson and Warren), the counselors took sides by drawing in situated ways on their own ideas about themselves, their work, and the residents. Miles challenged his colleagues' clinical judgment about Johnny, their understanding of intellectual disability, the group home's mission, their role, and, by implication, their moral commitment to fairness, rights, and compassion: "That's unfair! . . . That's why he's here!"

Group Home Know-How and Clinical Expertise

Disputes in meetings were not always between group home staff but could occur as disagreements with absent outside professionals who provided services to the residents in other settings. These were the doctors, psychiatrists, day program teachers, and workshop supervisors scattered across the community. Driggs House functions—much like the weekly staff meeting within the house—to coordinate each resident's dispersed services. Many of the services that residents receive outside require action inside, which becomes an aspect of counselor work. Giving meds is one routine example built into the schedule, but many time-limited tasks, medical and otherwise, arise through outside orders.

When outside assessments are at odds with the way a resident's conduct is known and acted on in the group home, counselors often treat those assessments as criticisms of their own work. Counselors use these contrary accounts at times to preserve and bolster the sense that failure in the group home did not make the work meaningless. As Lipsky (150) described, street-level bureaucrats must "assert discretionary dimensions of their job to a greater degree than called for in theory in order to salvage a semblance of proper client treatment as they define it." Psychiatric expertise posed the emblematic challenge to counselor know-how, because it concerned the aspect of group home work that they regarded as the most interesting and most personally meaningful. Psychiatric hospitalization was uncommon in the group home but, when it occurred, threw into relief the counselors' relationship to contrary outside ideas about the residents.

Marty was the one other resident who spent time on the hospital psychiatric unit, once for ten days and a second time for about two weeks. These hospitalizations were voluntary, at least in the legal sense that Johnny and Marty both consented to the admissions. Counselors frequently disagreed with the hospital psychiatrists' assessments of Marty and Johnny. During their respective hospitalizations, Marty and Johnny were visited daily by a staff member, who always brought back some report, formal or informal, from the unit clinicians and floor staff. Sometimes what hospital staff had to say was "so obvious" that it confirmed for counselors their own clinical skill—"I mean, we could have told them *that*." But when a report contradicted the counselors' ideas, it was seen as a wrench thrown into their already impossible work with Marty and Johnny. Counselors made claims for their knowledge as expertise in its own right that transcended the setting in which they had learned it. At the same time, counselors' claimed the superiority of their judgment on the basis that it was uniquely local. Their regular use of the technical vocabulary and grammar of psy both allowed them to pose challenges to the psychiatrist in his own terms and formed the legitimate professional basis for the ostensibly opposite claim: counselors knew the "real" Marty and Johnny because of their uniquely local expertise, not simply by "looking in the *DSM*. We can do *that!*"[1]

Marty went through a period in which he started to have "episodes" in the mornings. They did not involve falling, but he would be very upset, crying and screaming while still in bed and, at times, banging his head on the headboard. He would repeatedly call out the names of counselors, whether or not they were in the house, and occasionally he called out to residents, but they never responded. Other residents were discouraged by counselors from responding to Marty's cries, told that it wasn't their "responsibility" and that it would only "reinforce" his inappropriate behavior. The residents, in any case, were too annoyed or frightened to enter his room when he was so upset. Counselors were unable to console Marty, and often their presence only made him angrier. His "self-injurious behavior" (SIB) left him with some bruises and cuts on his head. This change in Marty's conduct was serious, because, though his injuries were minor, he posed a physical threat to himself. It was serious also because the group home was not able to manage it. One episode happened to occur on a Thursday morning and dominated that day's meeting. The counselors were very disturbed and saw the recent morning episodes as a sign that Marty's problems were escalating beyond control. Counselors established the "remedial horizon" in their work with Marty beyond which they could not see (R. Emerson). They explained his conduct both as a manipulative expression of his unhappiness with a recently implemented behavior plan and as an indication that the plan was working. His conduct was a calculated response: "He knows what he's doing." Angela said that Marty was "very smart" and knew these episodes were "upsetting to staff." Daniel said that "with Marty, it's a limitless extreme," and that, "with the SIBs, he's upped the ante." Susan described the situation similarly, in terms of Marty's having "discovered self-abuse," which he was using because he "hates" the new plan. Marty had "outsmarted" them.

Within a week of this discussion, Marty went into the hospital for two weeks. But Marty was "fine" in the hospital. That is, he did not try to injure himself, had no falls, and was pleasant and compliant with hospital staff and routines. Counselors were incredulous and angry, because at the hospital they didn't "see the 'real' Marty." On the third day of Marty's hospitalization, Susan and Beth, the nurse, met with the attending psychiatrist. At the staff meeting the next day, Beth took the lead in presenting the report. She began with the psychiatrist's diagnosis of "anxiety disorder and panic attacks." The counselors nodded in agreement. Anxiety was one of the central ways that Marty's conduct was defined and acted on in the group home. But the counselors were filled with a quiet expectation, because they had already heard that the psychiatrist's comments about Marty were "a surprise." Beth continued in a measured tone that indicated her anticipation of their upset and, it turned out, her own disagreement with the report: "He thinks that Marty's smart and should have more independence—" Some counselors sighed, rolled their eyes, looked around, or quietly shook their heads in disbelief. Daniel and Sally both remarked sarcastically, "Oh, right!" Beth continued without acknowledging the counselors' skepticism: "—and that the group home doesn't believe he can do more. I mean, he doesn't think—"

Angela interrupted to ask whether this psychiatrist had talked to Marty's regular psychiatrist, Dr. Nunzio, who was well known to the counselors because a few other residents were also his patients. Belittling Dr. Nunzio in staff meetings was so common as to be unremarkable. The staff was suspicious of him because, though he was "always nice," he was uncooperative about completing the brief report that the group home required for documenting each session. More substantially, they didn't think Dr. Nunzio spent enough time with the residents who were his patients, and some counselors even thought that he was actually "intimidated by the population." In this case, however, he was invoked as an authority to call into question the professional judgment of the hospital psychiatrist. Beth frowned at Angela's question: "No, he hasn't. . . . He also wants to give him an IQ test. Basically, he said we're underestimating Marty, that we don't think he can do more." Susan chimed in incredulously that "the unit [at the hospital] has been giving him passes to go out on his own." Several counselors laughed and said, "Oh, God," and, "I can't believe that!" Miles alone had a positive response—"I think that's good"—which nobody acknowledged. Daniel picked up on Susan's comment with astonishment and disgust: "When he's hospitalized he goes *out* because when he's hospitalized he's *fine!*" Susan followed: "They can't see beyond their noses; they don't listen to us. The person they see is *not* Marty!" The collective exasperation of the staff enabled them to ignore Miles again when, quietly, he suggested in a question he knew would not be answered, "Well, maybe it *is* the group home?"

No Relief

The limited authority counselors have is a frustrating aspect of their work but also provides an account of their disappointment and failure. It was not only in their challenges to outside professional authority but also in relation to the agency that counselors claimed they alone knew what was "really" going on. During these difficult periods, the counselors argued that Driggs House was not a suitable placement for either Marty or Johnny. An important aspect of this line of argument was that such a recommendation was far beyond the sphere of counselor authority. Though the question whether a given resident should actually be living at Driggs House was one over which counselors might have a certain influence, they had no authority to forward such a decision beyond Sonia to the agency. Even formal changes to the resident's services, to increase the degree to which he or she would be structured by group home programs, were something counselors had neither the authority nor the resources to make.

Nevertheless, in relation to Marty's case, some counselors complained that the agency ignored their assessment that an ICF would be more suitable for Marty than Driggs House and that, because of "the idiots at the hospital," they would be even less likely to get a hearing with the agency. Their focus on the issue of placement is an example of what Lipsky (149) called a "defense against discretion." By modifying their scope of responsibility, and in this case by pushing beyond the limits of their authority, counselors could make sense of their failed work with Marty and Johnny.

The counselors' challenges to the psychiatrist's report are a particular kind of work: the work of defending their own practice as credible, if not actual, clinical expertise. In a staff meeting, Daniel challenged the perspective of the hospital psychiatrist by relating Marty's recent SIB and hospitalization to his father's death a few months before. Though he had been estranged from his father since childhood, Marty was very upset by the news and by the funeral, which he attended with his sister. "We know it's his father's death," Daniel asserted confidently. "I mean, for the developmentally disabled or delayed, mourning will be slower and longer. This is the displacement of his father's hatred of him." Whether or not Daniel was correct about bereavement or the impact on Marty of his family relationships, he had invoked crucial local knowledge: what *"we* know" and the psychiatrist "doesn't see." Other counselors heard Daniel's analysis as raising what by then had become a common account of Marty's "real" problem: that the group home was just not suitable for him because it could not provide the structured programming and individual atten-tion he required. The psychiatrist "misunderstood" this and "refused to listen," and if his recommendations were followed, it would only exacerbate Marty's problem conduct. But it would also confirm the counselors' claims and perhaps achieve their objective. Daniel was cynical in his resignation: "Anyway, revolving-door hospitalizations will get him quicker into an ICF."

In ongoing conversations, counselors emphasized Marty's need for "more structure" and a residential environment with "more program-ming." Counselors saw the hospital setting as structured, in contrast to the group home, which required residents to exercise their freedom and be independent. These claims served to affirm that the coun-selors' persistent failure was the result of Marty's overall limitations and Driggs House itself, rather than their misunderstanding of him, lack of commitment, or inadequate skills. Cynthia was incredulous about the psychiatrist's failure to recognize the significance of struc-ture for Marty. "When he's in there," she said, his behavior was not a problem, because "in the hospital, they shave him; it's like ICF struc-tures," which were seen to "automatically increase self-esteem." Miles disagreed with the way Marty's "calmness" in the hospital was pre-sumed to be evidence of the general consensus that what he needed was *more*, not *less*, structure: "You know, there is a different signifi-cance to those things, to ADLs [activities of daily living], outside a CR or ICF."

The following week, Miles and I went to visit Marty in the hospital. He was happy to see us, even cheery. He said that being in the hospi-tal was "helping" and he was "getting better." Our brief, informal report to the staff meeting was met with cynicism and frustration. The counselors extended their resentment of the psychiatrist to Marty in contradictory accounts of his conduct. On the one hand, that Marty was "good" in the hospital affirmed their belief in his need for struc-ture. On the other hand, they characterized him as "manipulative" of them and hospital staff. This is not meant to criticize counselors' clin-ical reasoning but to illustrate how they draw on their clinical know-how to manage the inherent ambiguity and persistent failure of work in a setting where their authority is very limited. They must manage the conflict between the practical limits of their authority and their clinical knowledge: "Our hands are tied."

At a meeting after Marty was home, Sonia was sympathetic to the counselors, but it was not clear to me whether she was actually agreeing or trying to mollify them. If it was the latter, the strategy backfired. Susan said, "Marty doesn't belong here! It's a disservice to have him here; he needs more structure. . . . The anxiety of working with him— I mean, he's not a person anymore, it's just getting worse." Sonia responded sympathetically, "That's why it's so important for staff to document the experiences with Marty, as helping to make this case to the agency." Daniel reacted with indignation: "Documenting *more* to build a case is ridiculous. We already have documentation!" Susan and Angela vigorously agreed. Then Angela, in what appeared to be an effort to diffuse the tension, returned to the practical issues of Marty's conduct. She illustrated how thoroughgoing and fundamental was his incapacity to manage himself by invoking specific skills, and her emphatic tone indicated a certain resignation: "He's here *now,*" so "he must do his hygiene every day. That's the first step!" Miles agreed: "He waits for Daniel [the evenings Daniel works] to shower . . . four days a week. He needs to shave for himself." Daniel sighed: "The severity of the problem is not being recognized." Faced with the seemingly intractable problem of Marty's conduct, a disturbing sign of their own ongoing failure, counselors did the only work they were able to do: limit or deny their own discretion in the clinical terms of group home work.

Such responses result in accounts that are similar to what Goffman (1961, 35) called a "looping effect"—the way a resident's "reaction to his own situation is collapsed back into this situation itself." In a total institution, looping is a feature of the tension between organizational and professional imperatives. In the group home, it can be observed in the counselors' claim that Marty needed more structure—a goal of "treatment" they could not formally pursue. In this case, counselors themselves accounted for his conduct as an organizational feature but then defined and acted on Marty's requests for assistance and attention as a psychological symptom. The practical conditions of counselors' work made it difficult to consider that the psychiatrist might be right and that Marty's falls and self-injury were features of the very group home approach meant to address them. If the group home was already too structured, then it "underestimated" him. Cynthia was indignant that the group home was too *unstructured* for Marty, which was one reason he liked the hospital: "Seeking help is just reinforcing. I mean, the hospital is like a resort. It's a place with no responsibility. Everything is done for him there."

Like that of "disability," the meaning of "structure" is always situated. Initially, the increased structure in the hospital accounted for the reason the psychiatrist and nursing staff didn't see the "real" Marty. Then, counselors began accounting for his "good behavior" by pointing to the hospital routines, which permitted him to work less and provided "relief" from personal care and other responsibilities. Hospital staff might be wrong about Marty's conduct, but the basis of the counselors' claim was that he really needed to be in a more restrictive residence, that he needed more structure. In this sense, perhaps the hospital staff did in fact see the Marty that counselors saw: the one who "can't handle the freedom" and the expectations of group home life. In the counselors' view, the psychiatrist's misjudgment was affirmed, however, by his suggestions that Driggs House was too rigid rather than too free. What Marty's hospitalization confirmed—at least, when Marty was "okay there" instead of "not the real Marty"—was their assumption that he required the more rigorous structure of an ICF. Services in an ICF would more effectively organize him in relation to his own responsibilities, which would reduce his anxiety and his self-injurious behavior. In this sense, for counselors, what indicated that the group home was unable to "help" Marty was his own conduct. They argued that Marty's own capacities—he was smart, articulate, and vastly capable of many everyday life skills—were actually undermined by the group home's individualized and unstructured approach. Marty's inability to "handle the freedom" made Driggs House a serious risk. As Daniel exclaimed, "His living here is like an alcoholic living in a liquor store! It's bad for him."

Counselors similarly accounted for Johnny's problems by comparing the structure of the hospital to the group home. In ongoing staff meeting discussions about the 911 protocol, some counselors suggested that Johnny "wants to be in the hospital"; he "prefers" it to being at home, because "it's a relief from life." That he was at ease with and even interested in the police on the few occasions when they came to the residence was evidence that "he knows what he's doing" and, at the same time, that he was incapable of managing his feelings. For some, it was precisely the calculated character of Johnny's conduct that paradoxically reflected his inability to "manage the freedom of the group home." This is why the 911 protocol "fed into" rather than required him to manage his anger and aggressive impulses in specifically appropriate ways. In one meeting, Maria described as Johnny's "success" the one instance in which the protocol resulted in hospitalization.

Though the issue of psychiatric hospitalization was rare at Driggs House and arose only with Marty and Johnny, it was especially upsetting to the staff. Despite some of their flippant comments, the counselors recognized the gravity of the event, and the decision to encourage a resident to agree to be hospitalized was not taken likely. Cynthia's remark likening the hospital to a resort indicates how fundamental the staff regarded the capacity for freedom to group home work. Her clear assumption, shared by all the staff, was that hospitalization truly was the intervention of last resort (cf. Braginsky, Braginsky, and Ring 1969). And the process by which group home staff made this outcome acceptable reflects the logic of last resort that Robert Emerson described in his observations of decisions about involuntary psychiatric hospitalization. The repeated exhaustion or failure of normal remedies makes hospitalization accountable not as a choice but as the only choice and, in this sense, no choice at all.

The staff was very disturbed when Marty and Johnny were hospitalized because these events forced the staff to acknowledge, in effect, that they just could not provide what these residents needed. Though the counselors really did understand the hospitalizations, at least in one important aspect, as Marty's and Johnny's need for some "relief from life," from the burden of freedom at Driggs House that residents must bear, the counselors also regarded the outcome as an indication of their own limits. The events were treated as a kind of failure from every perspective: the residents', the group home's, and their own. It may be that what made Marty and Johnny disabled was the immutability of their conduct or, conversely, their calculated manipulation, but their hospitalizations indicated that either cause was beyond the scope even of the group home's clinical capacities. Such accounts manage the conflict and disappointment at the same time by locating responsibility in the residents themselves and in the unsuitable placement that is beyond the counselors' control. When failure is accountable by the administrative and clinical decisions of supervisors or the agency, or in challenges to the assessments of outside experts in the experts' own terms, the counselors are able to preserve the legitimacy of their own professional judgment. Even when they attempted to persuade Sonia and each other of the impossibility of certain work, it was always on a clinical basis.

Despite the conflict among staff about Johnny, there was a consensus about the outcome of his hospitalization that Sonia captured in one sympathetic reminder: that counselors did not bear responsibility for Johnny's failure and that, however inadequate the 911 protocol was, "this is what we have to work with. And anyway," she said to close the discussion, "we know that hospitalizing him in this way isn't very therapeutic." This last resort was always a reminder of the failure that counselors daily faced and must manage as an aspect of their work. It is precisely the flexible character of clinical expertise that enables counselors to shape the sphere of their own authority in accountable ways. What Goffman (1961, 370) referred to as the "magical quality" of clinical knowledge endows counselors with a kind of "authority that cannot be discredited"—by residents, each other, or outsiders.

8 PAPER TECHNOLOGIES

Doing and Documenting

> To focus on the technology of an organization is to view the
> organization as a place where some type of work is done, as a
> location where energy is applied to the transformation of
> materials, as a mechanism for transforming inputs into outputs.
>
> —W. Richard Scott,
> *Organizations: Rational, Natural, and Open Systems*

A SUBSTANTIAL PART OF THE WORK AT DRIGGS HOUSE com-
prises the ongoing collection, assessment, and display of data about the
work. The shelves in the staff office are lined with binders that document the lives of residents in multiple ways: daily, weekly, monthly,
annually. These books, and the forms they contain, are more than just
instrumental means of administrative and clinical operation; they are
technologies that organize group home work, in its course, as a central
aspect of that work. They involve many of the techniques for monitoring, assessment, and intervention that shape what counselors can
see, know, and do at Driggs House. I approach records and written
documents as technologies, drawing on a concept of technology developed largely in the social studies of science. I do not understand technology either in opposition to nor as the mere enhancement of cognition
and perception, considered as distinctly human capacities. The technological transformation of human capacity may often involve quantitative enhancement, just as microscopes make it possible to see the
unseen by making the tiny appear large. However, it is largely the
qualities of seeing and knowing in new ways that begin to capture
the complex role technology plays in human life and experience. At
Driggs House, the paperwork that counselors are always rushing to

keep current is central to their work. And though they may regard paperwork as a burdensome, if necessary, distraction, it is actually integral to what they regard as their "real" group home work. As embedded aspects of group home work, paper technologies shape what counselors and residents can know and do. In this chapter, I pick up the discussion about technology from chapter 2, with a brief overview of the concept in various fields. Then I describe how paper technologies at Driggs House organize the work they document and, in multiple ways, translate the ideal of "individualized" service into practical matters of work.

Technology

The distinction between authority based on technical competence and authority based on bureaucratic hierarchy has widely influenced the study of work and organizations. Charles Perrow (1986, 42) argues that this distinction reflects a misunderstanding of Weber's analysis by presuming a narrow concept of expertise that "fails to recognize the technical character of administration." Research on organizational structure has historically defined technology as the apparatuses and processes of production in manufacture. Even conceptual attempts to encompass human knowledge and skill have excluded administrative competence (Perrow 1986; W. Scott). In Perrow's classic paper (1967), he argues that, in order to understand a wide range of work organizations, technology should be defined by the character of the material being worked. This allows for a dynamic classification of organizations based on the relationship to their technology: distinct organizational forms develop in relation to the specific requirements of their unique raw materials. Whether the material is steel, paper, or human conduct, the specific kinds of work each requires are part of the "core technology" of plants, mills, and group homes. Fundamental to the way organizational structure is related to its core technology is the degree to which tasks are routine, and the less routine they are, the more latitude for discretion they require. Despite Perrow's broader concept of technology, as in much organizational theory, records and written documents remain merely "basic coordination mechanisms" (W. Scott, 231). Though documentary practices may reduce the degree of task complexity and uncertainty related to a particular core technology, they are not technologies themselves.

The field of science studies offers a concept of technology that recognizes the multiple functions even of basic coordination mechanisms. Researchers critical of structural and cognitive accounts of the development and use of technology have demonstrated the reflexive relationship between the technologies that are so integral to scientific knowledge and the everyday work of scientists. PET scans, electron microscopes, high-energy physics detectors, and observatory oscilloscopes make visible the activity of brains, cells, atomic particles, and pulsars, but they are more than just neutral instruments. This is not a concern about validity or methodological distortion. The particular kinds of visual products that scientists can make of their work are embedded in and shape the practical problems and processes that organize research.[1] In Latour and Woolgar's study of a biology laboratory, they show that technologies of writing and graphing functioned as more than just tools for the efficient manipulation of vital information. The way data could be used depended on the formats in which they could be made available visually and the standardization and durability of visual display. Photographs, scans, diagrams, graphs, tables, charts, and the like are not simply neutral representational tools but embedded practices that enable the everyday work of science.

Historical research also demonstrates that technology does not just extend but enables new ways of seeing and knowing. John Law (1986a, 1986b, 1987) shows that, in the sixteenth century, the development of Portuguese navigational devices, shipbuilding techniques, and written protocols made possible new modes of communication and new political relationships. New kinds of persons were also both possible and necessary: the emissaries who traveled back and forth, more confident that the crucial knowledge they carried, not to mention themselves, would arrive intact. "Long distance control" (Law 1986a, 1987), or what Bruno Latour describes more broadly as "action at a distance," depends on forms of knowledge that are durable, mobile, standardized, and reproducible. They both enable and require "centers of calculation" where information from afar can be received and evaluated, problems and courses of action assessed, and orders dispensed to be carried out elsewhere.

Conventional causal models of power are unable to account for the novel ways of knowing and acting that are harnessed through and enabled by specific technological innovation. As Latour (6) puts it, for example, "commercial interests, capitalist spirit, imperialism, thirst for knowledge, are empty terms as long as one does not take into account Mercator's projection, marine clocks and their markers, copper engravings of maps, rutters, [and] the keeping of the 'log books.'" For Law (1986a, 236), technologies are "integral" to and "interwoven" with their social, economic, and cultural contexts: the "form" of technologies is "a function of the way in which they absorb within themselves aspects [of] their seemingly non-technological environments." Michel Callon suggests "translation" as a way of understanding the reflexive relationship between technology and social action. Translation refers to the way forms of technical knowledge enable issues or problems to be realized practically and, at the same time, enable institutions and individuals to mobilize the actions of others.

Technologies of Government

In governmentality, technology is used similarly to emphasize the systematic orientation toward individual conduct that is characteristic of liberal societies. For reasons of logistics as well as legitimacy, the state's interest and interventions in spheres of activity, such as the economy or public health, cannot occur through the direct control of citizens. Governing occurs at a distance—Miller and Rose adapt Latour's phrase—by cultivating the capacities of individuals to govern their own conduct freely in relation to specific outcomes, according to the concerns of the state and the larger society. Similar to Perrow's concept, governmentality focuses on the unique character of the material to be transformed: human conduct. In liberal society, human conduct is conceived, in effect, as a resource and, as such, emerges in a reflexive relationship to technologies of government. This "technological orientation to human being," as Dean (1996, 60–61) puts it, requires that the capacities of individuals "be unlocked" and "harnessed"; governing involves the multiple "ways of conducting conduct, ways of acting upon the actions of others."

Conduct can truly become a resource, in this sense, only when the attempts to shape it have the authority of scientific expertise and are rational, systematic, and calculative. Just as technologies of government align individual goals with broader social goals, technology is the "linchpin" that connects the government of conduct and scientific knowledge (Dean 1996, 47). What enabled psy knowledge to become fundamental to different fields was its ability to "cross a technological threshold" (55). Community-based services provide an example, be-cause, in the 1970s, governing individuals with intellectual disability was realized in the translation of the ideals of rights and integration into clinical problems. In the group home, this translation—of rights into the everyday technical work of becoming more independent—reflects the role of psy knowledge in contemporary society in general. This is more than a cultural or ideological matter. As a technology of government, Driggs House is an exemplary instance of the way psy knowledge and techniques have "grafted themselves onto other prac-tices" (Rose 1998b, 87–88).

The weekly staff meeting, for example, should be considered as the gathering together both of the group home's key personnel and of the paper technologies that are embedded aspects of the work they orga-nize and document. In this sense, the meeting functions as the center of calculation and coordination at a distance for all the work being done. The varied technologies of monitoring, assessment, and intervention that establish the conditions of group home seeing and knowing also often organize the work of staff-meeting talk. For example, during a six-week period in which Jennifer's doctor asked that her diabetes be monitored intensively, the staff meetings featured, far more than usual, certain technologies that document the health of residents. A good half hour of each meeting was devoted to the presentation and discussion of data that had been collected, organized, and analyzed over the previous seven days about Jennifer's blood sugar levels, med-ication effects, and vital signs. Aspects of Jennifer's routine conduct that were considered relevant were also monitored and assessed in equally systematic ways: what and how much she ate (that is, her eat-ing behaviors or nutritional choices), how she conducted herself on doctor's visits, her general attitude toward the problem, and so on.

It is worth emphasizing again that technology, in this sense, does not stand in opposition to all that is human. "Quite the reverse," Rose (1998b, 88) explains, because technologies of government are "most frequently the promise of personhood, of being adequate to the real nature of the person to be governed." The term "technology" points to "the characteristic ways in which practices are organized to produce certain outcomes in terms of human conduct: reform, efficiency, edu-cation, cure, or virtue . . . [and to] draw attention to the outcomes—ways of combining persons, truths, judgements, devices, and actions into a stable, reproducible, and durable form." In this sense, the role psychology has played in the community cannot be seen merely as supplanting coercive control in institutions with a normative form of technocratic control. Although Driggs House certainly does "manage" residents, it also enables a kind of psychological personhood (Rose 1998b, 27). The effective operation of the group home depends on the capacities it cultivates in residents to govern themselves freely as selves of endless improvement and potential independence.

To Rose's outcomes of human conduct could be added independence. The promises of personhood translated in the paper technologies of Driggs House make certain persons and problems visible and knowable in everyday group home work.

Records and Written Documents as Paper Technologies

Most social science research on records and written documents has not treated them as social phenomena in themselves.[2] By contrast, ethnomethodology provides an approach to records and written documents much as though they are technologies as I have described: as reflexive, "sense-making procedures" that depend on and shape what can be seen and known in the practical course of work. Ethnomethodologists have sought to understand the unavoidably practical and constitutive character of records in specific settings (Heath and Luff; Parton; Sellen and Harper; Zimmerman 1969a, 1969b). In Garfinkel's well-known paper "Good Organizational Reasons for 'Bad' Clinic Records" (1984b), he argued that when researchers used ideal administrative or clinical standards, the "poor" and "incomplete" quality of psychiatric records was apparent. This wasn't so when they were evaluated in light of the "organizationally relevant purposes and routines" of clinic work. Social science researchers make an error by treating records as "actuarial," because reading them "correctly" relies on the practical know-how that is always a central feature of an organization's everyday work. Tony Hak shows how psychiatric reports reflexively transform the nature of a case in an ongoing process of "reformulation" that depends on the practical methods of both psychiatric and everyday reason.

Dorothy Smith (1990) uses ethnomethodology somewhat differently, to study the ideological function of "textually mediated forms of social organization," which she emphasizes are characteristic of institutional control in contemporary societies. Documentary technologies are the forms of accountability—and, literally, the forms—that are a major part of community services systems. Lipsky argues that in street-level bureaucracies, the compliance function of records is substantial. The increasing emphasis on accountability and bureaucratic rationalization in social services largely reflects ongoing tensions about public resources, but in services for intellectual disability there is an additional political dimension. The extraordinary professional abuse represented by institutions—especially after Willowbrook—resulted in the extraordinary reliance on formal mechanisms of accountability to prevent such abuse and neglect from happening again. At least in New York State, since the 1970s, part of the technical solution of community-based services has been a complex regulatory climate that involves the authority of state and federal agencies over a vast network of both public and private provider agencies and local settings. As Michael Power shows, a "mistrust" is translated in the elaborate audit technologies that are now an aspect of almost all professional service. Audit technologies are the "control of control," governing professional activity, ideally, by making it transparent without undermining its autonomy (Power; Rose 1996). Yet audit technologies also do more, shaping the activities of professionals in particular ways. Lynch, Livingston, and Garfinkel use the term "compliance documents" to describe the organization of scientists' accountability, for example, much as Callon uses "translation" to characterize the relationship between technology and power in terms of the ability to define and mobilize the actions of others.

The ideals of accountability and service converge at Driggs House in the paper technologies that enable it to govern at a distance. "For a domain to be governable," Rose writes, "one not only needs the language to render it into thought, one also needs the information to assess its condition. Information establishes a relay between authorities and events and persons at a distance" (1998b, 73). There is, naturally, a far greater distance between Brazil and Lisbon (especially in the sixteenth-century example cited earlier) than between Driggs House and its parent agency or between that agency, in New York City, and the State Office of Mental Retardation, in Albany. It is the same with the distance between persons: between Mike and Sonia, between Sonia and her counselors, between counselors and residents. Each involved a relationship of government that required the ability to mobilize organizational or individual others indirectly to act in certain ways. The paper technologies enable the government, at a distance, of the relationships they organize between the agency, the group home, the counselors, and the residents, each as a particular kind of self-governing entity.

Translating the Ideal of Individualized Services

In the OMRDD regulations, the "overall" goals of residential habilitation services are to promote and encourage independence, integration, individualization and productivity" (14 N.Y.C.R.R. § 671.1). These goals, abbreviated as 3IP, are expressed broadly in the regulations, which provide only general instructions about habilitation services. They are formulated as ideal goals of service and, at the same time, as "opportunities" to pursue each goal. That is, as guidelines, the 3IP are the opportunities that a service *and* its form of delivery must both provide. Another way of putting it is that the particular "service"— working on personal hygiene, for example—is both the goal *and* the opportunity to pursue it, which means that the form of service delivery itself is a main concern. In this way, a recognition that goals must be translated into practical work is embedded in the regulatory language. Independence is defined by "opportunities to develop capacities that lessen his/her dependence"; integration, by "opportunities to engage in experiences and activities with those who are not disabled"; individualization ensures that in services "the person is given meaningful choices, respected, addressed and provided services in terms of his/her unique and valued individuality"; and productivity is defined by the "opportunities to make an increasingly meaningful contribution to his/her living and community environment" (14 N.Y.C.R.R. § 671.6).

The translation of the ideals of 3IP into everyday work occurs in specific technical ways related to making services accountable for billing and reimbursement under the government-funding program. Habilitation services are funded through a state-federal Medicaid Home and Community Based Services Waiver Program (HCBS). Put simply, state requirements that define "medical" services narrowly are waived. The waiver allows Medicaid funds to be used for the variety of services that enable individuals who do not actually require a nursing facility to live in a community setting. The HCBS waiver was introduced in 1991 as an alternative to earlier Medicaid funding schemes that provided a set amount and standard package of services for each resident.[3] The point of the waiver is to enable an "individualized services environment"

(ISE) by providing separate funding mechanisms for services, on the one hand, and room and board, on the other.[4] In the New York State regulations, an ISE is described as

> a service delivery system in which the person's living arrangement and service delivery . . . are not linked, with services considered discretely rather than in a package. That is, housing and services are mutually exclusive considerations, as is the selection of specific services from the list of available approved services. The individualized services environment is in distinct contrast to an overall or comprehensive residential services model, in which housing and some services are intrinsically linked (i.e., where a person lives determines the services received). In the individualized services environment, where a person lives has no necessary connection to the services received, even those which may be received at the housing site. The administrative separation of housing from service, and the separation of services from categorical groups, is the keystone of the individualized service environment structure. It is this feature which makes it possible to achieve the goal of designing completely individualized service plans. (14 N.Y.C.R.R. § 635-99.1)

An ISE, in principle, must be assembled for each resident service by service. And because each habilitation service must be billed separately, the funding mechanism shapes how the ideal of individualized services is translated into group home work.

The waiver program requires that each resident have a "service coordinator" in addition to and independent of group home staff. The purpose of the service coordinator is to ensure the resident's adequate participation in planning his or her services, that those services are implemented as planned, and that "comprehensive coordination" is provided, which means the service coordinator's work encompasses all the settings (both for services and living arrangements) in which the resident is involved (14 N.Y.C.R.R. § 671.1). To ensure independence from group home services, residents have the right to select their own qualified service coordinator. However, many agencies, including the parent agency of Driggs House, now have separate service coordination departments, which assign service coordinators unless a resident specifically requests one from elsewhere. This arrangement has obvious fiscal and administrative advantages for voluntary agencies. Castellani argues that voluntary agencies benefited in New York from the State's extensive reliance on Medicaid funding schemes from the outset in the late 1970s, which facilitated a rapid expansion of the private-public systems that have characterized community-based services.

Service coordinators are at the group home a few times per month, as well as for case conferences and other special occasions. There is always a potential for conflict with the counselors who provide services daily, because the service coordinator is central to the planning and implementation of group home work and is in a position to question or challenge counselors' work there. In practice, however, service coordinators and counselors perceive each other as colleagues, and they share the basic overall goal of work: to help the residents become more independent. There are occasions when service coordinators ask counselors to explain why a resident's goal was discontinued or how a resident's complaints have been addressed. And it happens, though rarely, that counselors describe service coordinators as posing obstacles in their work, much of which actually overlaps in complementary ways. Although counselors recognize the general historical and legal reasons for an oversight mechanism such as the service coordination requirement, in some moments they resent the implication of mistrust and describe the requirement as a duplication of the services they themselves provide. What tension arises is mild, however, because of both the complementary overlap of responsibility and the clarity provided by the specific division of labor. Service coordinators, for example, are responsible for arranging any special or unusual activities, such as a resident's vacation with one of the agencies that runs tours for adults with intellectual disability. As the direct-service providers, counselors are responsible for the everyday logistical work of preparation and arrangement for pick-up and drop-off. If a resident is bugging a counselor about whether a trip has been finalized, he or she may be directed to the service coordinator. If the counselor discovers from the service coordinator that such a referral has slipped her or his mind, then the counselor may ask that it be responded to "ASAP," either because it seems unfair to make the resident wait any longer or simply because, as I heard Sally say once, "this needs to be done so Diane'll get off my back."

Paper Technologies: The Organization and Documentation of Accountable Work

The "treatment book," the comprehensive record maintained for each resident, lies at the heart of group home operations. The term "treatment" is oddly anachronistic in community services, notwithstanding the encompassing notion of treatment that emerged in the courts in the early 1970s. At Driggs House, the name "treatment book" does not capture how it figures in counselor work, though it may well reinforce the sense of the clinical importance of the job. Gathered in each resident's treatment book is all the information deemed relevant, for a variety of reasons, to the resident's "placement" in the group home. It is a "master technology," because the treatment book comprises all the documentary technologies that it organizes and monitors. These documentary technologies are the various practices of accountability and knowledge production about group home work that are primary aspects of that work. In the simplest sense, the treatment book functions as a technology because it is a physical object that enables counselors to collect, transport, and store their ongoing work. More than this, the way in which group home work is organized is reflected in the physical organization of the treatment book: it is divided into sections, which, like their contents, are ordered in a standard and specified way.

The treatment book is the material realization of the group home in a single technology. The book's very organization can be understood as a reflexive, technical rendering of group home work. The sections into which it is divided and the standard placement of forms, evaluations, and assessments within it mark out the group home's accountable domains. Inside the cover, preceding the titled sections, is the face sheet, which makes readily available a resident's most basic information: name, date of birth, government-issued identification, diagnoses and special medical issues, and family and emergency contacts. Following the face sheet are the agency forms regarding placement and services (which include signed consents), the OMRDD assessment, and other eligibility instruments that establish diagnoses, personal abilities, level of care, and so forth. After this initial section are titled sections that contain the specific documentation pertaining to each: psychological, medical, vocational, and financial, among others. Each section is indicated by a divider and includes the various reports, assessments, and evaluations, whether required or otherwise, that document the specified aspect of the resident and his or her group home life in the ways identified as important to the overall goal of services and as auditable by the State of New York.

The OMRDD establishes minimum criteria for the annual and semiannual "documentation [affirming] that services are necessary to meet the person's needs" and that they are being met, but exactly how the treatment book is ordered and what it contains is up to the service provider (14 N.Y.C.R.R. § 671.6). In fact, an agency providing services has a great deal of discretion over the design and use of its own paperwork systems. As long as they meet the state's minimum criteria, documentary practices may reflect the specific commitments or services of particular programs and may even be designed for internal monitoring and accountability. These documentary technologies function as specifically "auditable" practices of group home compliance. This regulatory strategy—"to set forth the specific minimum requirements and standards" (14 N.Y.C.R.R. § 633.1)—reflects how New York State authority operates over these services. OMRDD regulations are not unusual in the latitude that state agencies allow voluntary service providers. One explanation of this latitude is that it reflects trends in neoliberalism and privatization. As Castellani argues, New York's public-private services system originated in the state's use of Medicaid funding in deinstitutionalization, which expanded the role of established parent-based and other voluntary service providers. However, the latitude can also be understood in terms of how services on this scale must be governed at a distance, something which no doubt both reflects and shapes the changing role of the state. Such regulatory latitude permits, even encourages, agencies to translate general principles of compliance into their own technical systems to reflect a variety of circumstances and philosophies of service practice (cf. Argent).

The service coordinator's chief task is to prepare annually each resident's Individual Service Plan (ISP). The ISP is a comprehensive descriptive evaluation of an individual, his or her needs, and the services being provided. Service coordinators are "responsible for assisting the person . . . as needed, in creating and sustaining an individualized service environment by developing, implementing, reviewing and revising the [ISP]" (14 N.Y.C.R.R. § 671.1). Central to the provision of services, it is the technology that organizes a resident's annual case conference: a new ISP is prepared based on the decisions made at the case conference, though service coordinators actually prepare it ahead in consultation with the resident and his or her primary counselor. At the conference, the new ISP is signed by everyone in attendance.

Service coordinators maintain their own master technology for each resident—the service coordinator's book—which is kept in the staff office. It is best understood as the documentary equivalent to the group home's treatment book in a parallel system of accountability.

The service coordinator's book contains the ISP, notes on discussions with the resident, both scheduled and unscheduled, and notes on the special services arranged, usually with outside providers (such as holiday agencies). For the service coordinators, the book on each resident documents what it organizes: the ongoing monitoring of the ISP's implementation. Though the ISP, which I will describe in more detail, is the responsibility of the service coordinator, it requires and depends on six paper technologies that are a main part of a counselor's work. These six technologies involve the actual provision of habilitation services: the "activities, interventions and therapies" that promote each resident's "independence, individualization, integration and productivity" (14 N.Y.C.R.R. § 671.1). Together, they translate the ideal of individualized service into the everyday work they document. They are assembled in the "Progress" section of the treatment book (which is second, after "Psychology").

"Progress" contains the following: a copy of a resident's Individual Service Plan (ISP) and the counselors' six technologies that form a network that translates the ideals of independence, integration, individualization, and productivity into actual everyday work. What makes them a network is that each is designed in relation to the technical requirements of one or more of the others. Each technology makes habilitation services accountable in different ways, furnishing specific documentary procedures of defining, collecting, formulating, analyzing, and displaying knowledge about the residents' services. The knowledge produced by each technology is usable for its own specific purposes, one of which is always the ongoing transfer of knowledge to or from other technologies in the documentary network. This involves the standardization characteristic of all technical forms of knowledge, especially procedures of simplification that permit ease of circulation and administration in ways that preserve a recognizable object (Knorr-Cetina; Latour; Star). As work tasks that are also durable forms of knowledge, these technologies can be physically gathered and brought to meetings, and are available to staff not copresent, across shifts, and up and down the chain of command. This network forms the technical basis for the ongoing government of group home work at a distance by organizing several relationships of accountability at once: between the group home and the OMRDD; between counselors and their supervisors; between residents and their counselors; and between group home workers and themselves.

THE ONGOING FLOW AMONG THE NETWORK OF
DOCUMENTARY TECHNOLOGIES OF HABILITATION SERVICES

The network of counselors' paper technologies

- *Residential Plan of Services*: lists a resident's "identified needs" and services—all the "activities, interventions and therapies"—by allowable category in the group home and elsewhere

- *Annual Summary of Services*: indicates all services a resident has received during the year and a description of his or her progress

- *Monthly Progress Notes*: list a resident's current services and indicate whether they are effective

- *Goal Plans*: the clinical plans written for individual residents to address specific aspects of conduct

- *Data Collection Technologies*: the variety of technologies used, usually daily but sometimes weekly, to monitor the progress of each goal

- *Habilitation Services Billing Form*: documents monthly the resident's services for which provider agencies will claim government reimbursement

These six technologies, which are the responsibility of counselors, all determine and are determined by the ISP. The ISP is often more than ten pages long and contains an abundance of factual information about financial entitlements, names and addresses of service providers, day treatment programs, a resident's capacity to evacuate in emergencies, and more. But a documentary emphasis does not encompass the function of the ISP; it also contains narrative descriptions meant to capture the individuality of a resident. Service coordinators are urged to understand an individual's preferences and personal goals in terms of the 3IP. According to an OMRDD training manual for service coordinators (2000), the ISP is meant to reflect every aspect of a resident's life and "to help the consumer achieve his or her Individualized Services Environment."

The ISP is the waiver program's central technology and translates the regulatory ideals embodied in the concept of the ISE.[5] In the regulations, "ISP" sometimes refers to a single documentary technology:

> [The ISP is] . . . the written document that is developed . . . [that] describes the services, activities and supports, regardless of the funding source which constitutes the person's individualized service environment. The goal of the individualized service plan is to ensure the provision of those things necessary to sustain a person in his/her chosen environment and preclude movement to [a more restrictive setting]. These services, activities and supports, identified in the individualized service plan, are to reflect the preferences, capabilities and capacities of the person and emphasize the development of self-determination (i.e., making personal choices), independence, productivity, and integration into the community. (14 N.Y.C.R.R. § 686.99)

But "ISP" also refers to the system (or what I call the network) of technologies that it coordinates and on which it depends:

> [The ISP is] a written person-oriented record system . . . which documents the process of developing, implementing, coordinating, reviewing and modifying . . . [the system itself]. It is maintained as the functional record indicating current assessments, all planning activities as well as services (i.e., activities, therapies and interventions), and interventions provided to the person. . . . It constitutes the main portion of the clinical record. (14 N.Y.C.R.R. § 671.99)

The ISP translates the ideal of individualized services into everyday work for counselors and residents: the documentary tasks and goals of conduct, each of which is a service. The waiver funding mechanism requires that each service be billed separately, which enables the ISE to be more than rhetoric. The ISE for each resident realizes technically the combination of customized services and outcomes. Professional expertise, the state-federal waiver funding mechanism, and provider accountability all come together in the selection of "allowable" services, which are formulated in the state regulations as categories of "skills training" to "promote" or "maximize" a resident's 3IP.[6] Specifying categories of allowable services in the regulations is about not delimiting but enabling the nature of clinical problems, providing a mechanism by which the everyday clinical work of service selection automatically produces standardized accountability in other systems. Thus, "individualizing" services makes certain aspects of providers' clinical work specifically auditable across the network of six technologies outlined earlier.

The ISP is the central coordinating technology in habilitation services, but it is the residential plan of services that is at the center of the counselors' documentary network. The residential plan of services specifies a resident's chosen habilitation service outcomes, developed at his or her annual case conference and described in the ISP, and incorporates any ongoing modification or substitution of goals. At the case conference, the annual summary of services is used to review a resident's progress in the past year, furnishing, at a glance, eleven months of counselors' documentary work. The summary presents the durable and mobile data that have been collected, organized, and displayed by the monthly progress notes and the often daily documentation of progress with specific goals. Finally, counselors submit monthly the billing form to the supervisor, the information from which is used ultimately by the agency to claim reimbursement under the waiver program.

What Do You Need to Be Working On?

To illustrate the network of documentary technologies, it makes sense to begin with a relatively simple goal plan. Goal plans are the most specific and individualized technology in the group home, because they translate specific individual "needs" and "preferences" into systematic and accountable clinical work. The basic formula of a goal plan includes a concise statement of the plan's outcome(s) of conduct, the plan's rationale, specific techniques for the resident and staff to follow, and procedures for documenting the resident's progress (and sometimes the staff's conduct).

James Franklin Personal Appearance Goal

Driggs House

Start Date: 02/00
Target Date: 02/01

Rationale

James is a 31 year old man with mental retardation. James takes great pride in his appearance and was previously on a daily clean clothes plan. This was discontinued in February of 2000 as James has made great progress on it and the team felt it was no longer necessary. The purpose of this appearance goal and checklist is to help James self monitor his appearance and provide assistance in times when he is having a depressive episode, a time when his personal appearance tends to get neglected.

-The checklist asks the following things:
• Are my clothes clean?
• Do I need to shave?
• Have I brushed my teeth?

Objective: James will monitor his personal appearance daily.

Methodology: James will be presented daily with his personal appearance checklist and will be required to work through it independently.

Data collection and documentation
Staff will document whether James was able to monitor his personal appearance on the data sheet + (yes) or – (no).

Reinforcement
James will be verbally praised for looking well groomed.

James Franklin's personal appearance goal

Driggs House staff developed a "personal appearance goal" for James, because he occasionally neglected his personal appearance and they regarded this as a sign of his depression. It was agreed that the use of a daily checklist would, as the plan reads, "help James self-monitor his appearance and provide assistance in times when he is having a depressive episode." The outcome for James is stated thus: "James will monitor his personal appearance daily."

The goal plan specifies the following procedure: "James will be presented daily with his personal appearance checklist and will be required to work through it independently." When James achieves the outcome, the plan specifies for counselors a technique of reinforcement: "James will be verbally praised for looking well groomed." In the conduct specified for James and the counselors, the goal plan establishes an association between James's depression and managing his appearance.

James Franklin's Appearance Checklist

- Are my clothes clean?
- Do I need to shave?
- Have I brushed my teeth?

James Franklin's appearance checklist

Even though the goal plan names an association between a resident's inner state and conduct that is regarded as its visible manifestation, such a plan cannot be considered simply to have constructed or to be the origin of the association. What the plan does, as it emerges reflexively in the course of counselor work, is to translate a problem into techniques of assessment, intervention, and documentation as part of that work. The goal plan itself—the photocopyable technology— could be said to formalize the practical conditions for certain persons by explicating the possible ways of knowing and acting on them. In this case, those practical conditions are shaped by how the plan organizes contact between James and the counselors and in the relationship it organizes between James and aspects of his own conduct.

Counselors are required to "document whether James was able to monitor his personal appearance on the data sheet + (yes) or – (no)." This daily work of collecting goal data forms the basis of the monthly progress notes. The regulations require that "progress notes shall be recorded, at least monthly, by the staff member(s) having a substantive responsibility for delivering or monitoring delivery of the [residential] plan of services" (14 N.Y.C.R.R. § 671.6). Counselors must complete monthly progress notes for each resident on their caseloads and file them in the residents' treatment books. Only James's personal appearance goal is used here to illustrate the monthly progress notes, which are usually several pages long. (The residential plan and annual summary of services are also illustrated this way here.)

These paper technologies not only organize the services they document but also create certain conditions of accountability within the group home. Certain technologies make aspects of counselor work specifically visible to the supervisor. Just as progress notes can be used to monitor the progress of residents on a monthly basis, for example, they can be used to monitor counselors, because they make visible to the supervisor certain aspects of their work, much of which takes place out of view in individual contact with residents. In this way, the schedule of review and revision of habilitation services required by the state provides technologies for supervision within the group home. The ability to follow instructions and meet simple deadlines, in addition to assessment and writing skills, was available to Sonia as an indicator of the counselors' organizational capacities, knowledge, and commitment to their work. At the end of each month, counselors were required to submit to Sonia the completed monthly progress notes and billing summaries for each resident on their caseloads.

The network of documentary technologies organizes a chain of accountability that stretches from the daily details of a resident's goal work to the performance of individual counselors to the performance of the supervisor (reflected in the data she submits to the agency) and thus to the performance of the group home overall. These relationships of accountability extend indirectly all the way up to the state. It is through the technologies submitted by Sonia that the agency governs her and the group home site at a distance; in turn, the agency must continuously demonstrate to the OMRDD that the standards of certification are being met in each of its facilities in order to operate and therefore to receive reimbursement (14 N.Y.C.R.R. § 635-4.2).

The monthly progress notes show how techniques of collecting data on goals make those data durable and transferable as they move across the network of documentary technologies. The monthly progress notes must identify a resident's specific services, indicate when and how they are delivered, significant events that have occurred in relation to their delivery, and any recommendations for change. The daily monitoring of each goal, the monthly notes that monitor each resident's progress, and the semiannual case conference are aspects of an ongoing, ever-adjustable review process.

The residential plan of services is the technology that reflexively organizes, modifies, and documents this ongoing process by identifying each chosen category of service, the "need" it addresses, and the form of its delivery. The residential plan is used to record any modifications in a resident's service outcomes or services as they occur. Between annual case conferences, each resident has a six-month conference to review his or her goal work and ongoing medical, personal,

DATA SHEET

Name: James Franklin

Month: April 2000

Outcome: James will use his appearance checklist to monitor his appearance with his personal appearance checklist.

Documentation: Staff will document James' success using the following codes:

+ = James successfully monitored his appearance independently using his checklist.

− = James required prompts to follow his hygiene.

	1	2	3	4	5	6	7	8	9	10	11	12	13	14	15	16	17	18	19	20	21	22	23	24	25	26	27	28	29	30
James followed his checklist	+	+	+	+	−	+	−	+	+	+	+	+	+	+	+	−	+	+	+	+	+	+	−	−	+	+	+	+	+	+
Initials	JV	JV	MS	MS	JS	JS	JV	JV	MS	MS	JS	JV	JV	JV	JS	JV	JS	JS	JV	CR	CR	CR	JS	JS	JR	MB	MB	MB		MB

James Franklin's data sheet

Monthly Progress Notes

Name: James Franklin

Mo/Yr: April 2000

Goal Plans

Res. Hab. Service	Outcome	Is it Effective?		Summary (Area of focus, response, follow-up)	Recommendation
		Yes	No		
Functional Skills	James will use his appearance checklist to monitor his appearance daily.	✓		Did a good job this month Jusing his checklist. Most of the time but not always (25/30)	✓ Continue — Revise — Discontinue — Completed
					— Continue — Revise — Discontinue — Completed
					— Continue — Revise — Discontinue — Completed
					— Continue — Revise — Discontinue — Completed

James Franklin's monthly progress notes

or vocational issues. The residential plan of services is central to the six-month case conference, because it reflects, or is amended to include, any changes that have been made since the annual conference. At the annual conference, the annual summary of services is used to make an overall assessment of the resident's habilitation services over the past year. It organizes twelve months of data about services, transferred in

Name: FRANKLIN JAMES
Medicaid # ZX1234Y

Month/Year: April 2000
Facility: Drop House

Habilitation Services Billing Form

Residential Habilitation Services Codes:

AST-assertiveness/self-advocacy skills training svcs
BST-behavior skills training svcs
CIT-community integration/resources utilization
CST-communication skills training svcs
EST-employment skills training svcs
FST-Functional skills training svcs
HST-health skills training svcs
MAT-med self-administration skills training svcs
MST-motor skills training svcs
SST-socialization skills training svcs

Service Delivery: Indicate information as it relates to the goal.

Date of Service	Service Code	Duration* Yes	Duration* No	Description	Outside site**	Initials
4/00	FST	✓		Daily Personal Appearance Goal		JL

* Indicate yes if service is 15 minutes or longer in duration.
** Indicate only if service is delivered outside the residence.

Name: _____ Title: Supervisor

James Franklin's habilitation services billing form

various ways from the monthly notes and goal data where they have been collected, into a form that is easily readable and usable at a glance by the service coordinator and others involved in the annual service-planning process.

As the primary deliverers of service, counselors are responsible for maintaining this network of technologies. They are also responsible

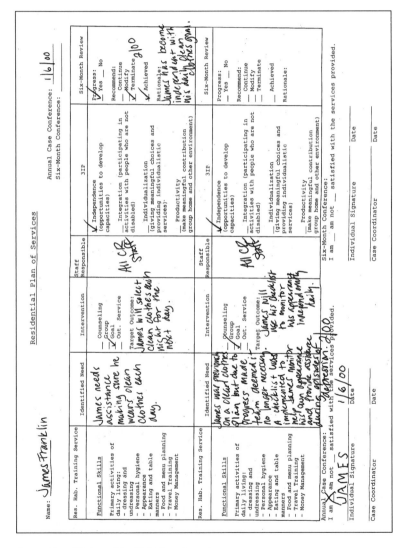

James Franklin's residential plan of services

ANNUAL SUMMARY

Name: James Franklin

Facility: Diggs House

Date: 6/6/2000

Describe the individual's progress over the previous 12 month period in meeting the habilitation service goals defined in the plan of services.

Goal Plans

Res Habilitation Service	Outcome	Progress Summary
Functional Skills	James will monitor his personal appearance daily.	James made a lot of progress with his previous Clean Clothes Plan. When he became independent with it the team implemented a checklist in 2/00 to help him monitor his own appearance
		and assist him during depressive episodes. He has made progress using the checklist. Personal appearance goal should be continued.

James Franklin's annual summary

for coordinating and documenting services provided by others (outside psychotherapists, speech therapists, physicians, and the like). The "description" required of specific services is a distillation of a year's daily and monthly work that is organized by the other technologies.

Conclusion

The paper technologies of habilitation service delivery shape the group home's particular temporality of progress. There must always be measurable progress, even when a resident has made no obvious progress in the simple sense. From the agency's perspective, this is expressed in the emphasis on "continuity" in the clinical work, especially in the continuity of information that counselors can produce in their routine documentary work. As with many voluntary agencies, this one has its own compliance unit devoted to making sure that its various service sites are meeting the OMRDD's basic standards for certification. To ensure that each site is at any time always auditable, the agency periodically audits its own facilities, because the state is entitled to do so randomly. In addition to the agency's self-auditing, staff from the compliance unit periodically attend group home staff meetings to provide training in how to use the paper technologies and to emphasize why they are so important beyond the clinical aims of the group home. The focus of one training at Driggs House was the annual review process. The trainer concluded by summarizing her presentation this way:

> All plans and goals are written with a one year target dated from the Annual Case Conference. At the [six-month] conference, progress is noted in specified sections on the [residential plan of services]. Addenda can be added if there are significant changes. The ISP must contain every plan, activity, or goal that is indicated on the [residential] plan of services or it cannot be billed. This continuity is one of the things that [the compliance unit] looks for. A new ISP must be written every year and there has to be some progress, some growth.

There must *always* be progress, and there *can* be. Progress is possible because of the ways in which the group home's paper technologies organize the work they document. By examining these paper technologies, one can understand how what Latour (3) describes as "the precise practice and craftsmanship of knowing" is accomplished in the group home.

Driggs House does not involve the attention-grabbing, even epoch-making technologies described at the beginning of this chapter. The knowledge produced in and about the group home does not include discoveries of neuronal receptors or celestial objects, and treatment books and goal plans may not be equivalent to PET scanners and observatory scopes. But even the group home can function only by acting at a distance in several ways, all enabled by the paper technologies that translate clinical and administrative ideals into accountable everyday work. As in a scientific laboratory, the production of knowledge about group home work forms an awfully large part of that work. What makes the group home very much like a laboratory is the role its own technologies play in making the objects of its work, and the work itself, knowable, seeable, and doable.

9 GOAL PLANS AND INDIVIDUAL CONDUCT

AT DRIGGS HOUSE, "goal plans" are the technologies at the core of the group home's individual work with residents. Lipsky (15) writes that in "people-processing," work goals in the general sense have "an idealized dimension that make them difficult to achieve and confusing and complicated to approach." Goal plans formalize what conduct can be seen and known, and how it should be acted on, as clinically warrantable conduct, by translating the "needs" of individual residents into practical matters of clinical work. In specified techniques of assessment and intervention, "preferences, capabilities and capacities" become "what residents are working on." For this reason, goals furnish a way of examining how residents and counselors are, to use Hacking's phrase (1986, 1995), "made up" in and through their ongoing work. By specifying psy practices of self-knowledge and accountability, goal plans are technologies of government that at Driggs House shape the practical "conditions of personhood" (Hacking 1986, 225). It's not that goals determine conduct in any simple sense; like all formulated plans, they provide little explanation about how they are implemented, because no plan can ever account fully for the situated character of action (Suchman). My point is that this analysis could be considered an analysis of "kinds," in Hacking's sense, because I treat goal plans as instructable resources, practical everyday instructions in how to be group home persons. My interest is not in whether they are followed "correctly" but in how the clinical vocabulary and techniques that goal plans make available organize the possible relationships that counselors and residents can have to each other and to themselves as certain kinds of group home persons.

Goals as Documentary and Clinical Technologies

A resident's goal plans are filed in the "Progress" section of his or her treatment book. A copy is also filed in the service coordinator's book as documentary support for the individual service plan (ISP). There is also a "goal book" for each resident, a binder that contains the current plans and any related documentary technologies. Though each counselor is responsible for monthly reports on the goal work of the residents on their caseload, all staff contribute to the daily gathering of data on all residents. The technologies for recording the goal work of every resident are assembled together in a single binder, the "data book." There is a practical reason for this: it simplifies the task of documenting the progress of all the residents at the end of each shift for the counselor who happens to be "doing the data."

As clinical technologies, goal plans translate a resident's "needs" into actual work on specific features of conduct. Like all technologies of government, goal plans are based on ostensibly expert knowledge about the nature and needs of the governed. Behavioral psychology furnishes both the outcomes and the techniques of goal plans, locating problems in the sphere of overt conduct even when overt conduct is seen as a sign of something "deeper." The ideals of 3IP are realized in the techniques for achieving the specified outcomes for self-improvement, maximization, and growth: to "lessen dependence or minimize loss of functioning or adaptive capacity" (14 N.Y.C.R.R. § 633.2).

"Behavior plans," which have the same format as goal plans, are designed to act on negative, disruptive, and even dangerous conduct. There is little practical distinction between behavior and goal plans. Both are referred to as "goals" or "plans," and both attempt to cultivate the capacities of individuals to conduct themselves more independently. Even behavior plans intended to reduce or eliminate target behaviors such as verbal and physical aggression aim to enhance a resident's capacity for self-management. All plans specify techniques of conduct that are meant to shape the resident's relationship to his or her own conduct in new ways, as something that can and therefore should be managed. James Franklin's goal plan, described in chapter 8, is one example.

Ruby's Problem with Self-Assertion

When one form of conduct is acted on as a clinical problem, it can frame the way others are understood and addressed. According to

Driggs House staff, Ruby had difficulty asserting and advocating for herself. This was an ongoing problem she "needs to work on" and, thus, the outcome of a goal plan. She also had room cleaning and toothbrushing goals and, at the time of her annual case conference, wanted to continue them. Ruby's case conference began pretty much as they do for all the residents. Ruby's service coordinator, Danielle, who led the conference, asked Ruby, "So, why are we all here?" The answer, in one version or another, which all residents know, is, "To see how I'm doing." This opening gambit, the conference itself, and those who attend all reflect the role that consent and participation must play in the "program-planning process"—the planning of an individual's individualized services (14 N.Y.C.R.R. § 671.6). At Ruby's conference, Cheryl (her primary counselor), Cynthia (the behavior specialist), and I were there, in addition to Ruby and Danielle. (For some residents, family members also attend.) When the discussion came around to her goals for the coming year, Ruby said she just wanted to continue working on the same ones: budgeting, room cleaning, toothbrushing, and self-advocacy, the plan addressing her capacity to assert herself. (Self-advocacy does not refer here to participation in the disabled people's movement, though the movement may well have made the word available in the group home context as shorthand for issues regarding assertiveness, shyness, and the like.) Danielle suggested that because Ruby was already independent with toothbrushing and room-cleaning—that she could do those things without any reminding or assistance—those goals should be continued for another year *only* if they incorporated a self-advocacy component. Ruby quietly agreed.

I later learned from Cynthia that this was essentially a backroom deal struck beforehand between Ruby, Cynthia, and Danielle as they were preparing for the conference, that is, preparing the ISP. Cynthia did not attend annual case conferences as a rule but believed that Ruby "needs encouragement," because she "doesn't want to be independent." Apparently Ruby had occasionally complained to Cynthia and Danielle (but not to Cheryl or other group home staff) that she was annoyed by the staff always "pushing her to be independent." For Cynthia, this was evidence that Ruby was "resistant" to what "she knows she's capable of," the pursuit of independence. Cynthia saw this resistance as a reflection of Ruby's "difficulty . . . asserting her needs."

In fact, Ruby was independent with all personal matters, including some aspects of medical self-care she had to learn (dealing with a

urinary catheter after a surgical procedure, for example). She raised
no behavioral problems and "accessed" the community on her own.
But even a resident like Ruby must have goals. For one, the minimum reimbursement requirements for habilitation services specify
that everyone must have goals. Still, the billing alone does not provide
an adequate explanation. In the group home, there are always aspects
of conduct that could use work, even for Ruby; for conduct that is
unremarkable can be seen in some ways as potentially compromising further progress precisely because it is the desired (or normal or
appropriate) conduct. If Ruby felt frustrated by being pushed by staff,
it may have been that she regarded herself as independent enough.
Requesting that she merely continue the goals she'd been working on
may have been a strategy of participation that required the least
effort. It may have been what some social scientists have interpreted
in other contexts as "resistance" (J. Scott), though not the psychological variety Cynthia had in mind. If Ruby's choice was influenced by
her dissatisfaction, perhaps a more apt description, right out of the
labor movement, is that she was "working to rule." "Not wanting to be
independent" is a problem in itself, but the staff were able to see it
specifically in terms of Ruby's ongoing problem with self-advocacy,
and this suggested a practical course of action. Any aspect of conduct,
however unremarkable or unproblematic, can be transformed into unfinished work by making it a formal goal outcome. And all conduct is
amenable to progress through the techniques of self-management that
goal plans provide. This dynamic relationship between the demands
of the group home and what the residents are working on illustrates
John McKnight's criticism that "need" gets defined in social services
in the very ways that the services can solve; even more, it illustrates
the flexibility and situated character of psy knowledge and practice.

In Ruby's self-advocacy goal plan, the outcome is expressed generally: "Ruby will develop her self-advocacy skills." The plan's rationale
is also a general one: "Ruby is very interested in both the concept and
practice of self-advocacy. . . . She continues to have difficulty in asserting her needs and desires and has therefore requested that she work
on self-advocacy formally. This goal is therefore being implemented to
allow her a more structured plan to address self-advocacy." The plan
specifies meeting weekly to discuss self-advocacy and the specific topics to be covered, with Cheryl (who must keep progress notes): "the
concept of self-advocacy (what it means and why it is important), a

review of rights and responsibilities, the practice of self-advocacy (via Ruby's goals as well as incidentally), assertion, areas wherein Ruby tends to have difficulty (medical issues, peer relations, job issues)."

Although Cynthia's primary role was to develop and write goal plans, it is a collaborative process involving the counselors, because they are responsible for the implementation and monitoring of goal work. In order for plans to become group home practice, counselors must agree with how the outcome and plan are written. In Ruby's case, all the staff agreed she was "resistant" to becoming independent and that continuing her toothbrushing and room cleaning goals should be permitted only if they now incorporated an additional self-advocacy component. Ruby's room cleaning and toothbrushing goals were rewritten as opportunities to "practice" self-advocacy. For example, "Ruby recently requested assistance in maintaining her room. As she has also requested encouragement in regards to self-assertion and advocacy, she will be responsible for alerting staff that it is her day to do room cleaning." The outcome did not change: "Ruby will independently initiate and complete her room cleaning twice a week." But the new plan provided Ruby instructions for conducting herself assertively. First, she was supposed to "alert staff" on her room cleaning days (Tuesdays and Fridays). Then, she was to "complete her room cleaning . . . with supervision and prompts when necessary." A list of specific chores was included, and counselors were required to document whether or not she completed each one, and if so, whether it was independently or with prompts.

It's fair to say that in certain respects Ruby could be described as shy (or reserved or cautious or reticent), but this quality was visible to counselors as a barrier to progress and, for this reason, something she needed to work on. This work was not limited to the goal work, and counselors would routinely require her to practice asserting herself, by joking with her, urging her to speak up, and reassuring her when she seemed reticent or intimidated. In the course of everyday life, the counselors variously encouraged, coaxed, and cajoled Ruby to act on her self as an assertive self.

It appeared to me that self-assertion, as a need, emerged reflexively in relationship to what in another context might very well have been seen, if it was seen at all, simply as shyness. Ruby's treatment book provided little basis for treating a lack of self-advocacy as a problem. A recent annual update of the psychological evaluation written by

Cynthia's predecessor indicated that Ruby was "occasionally non-compliant," something that was "being addressed in counseling" (the weekly meeting between residents and their primary counselors). The same document stated also that Ruby "isolates but is friendly with one other resident." These descriptions of Ruby were the only ones that can be construed as negative among the various documentary technologies throughout her treatment book. Every other indication is that she was a model resident: "engaged," "cooperative," and "a support to peers," with a "good frustration tolerance" and "good impulse control."

Ruby might have been shy, but, as always, the nature of shyness seemed to depend on the company around her. She was certainly comfortable speaking her mind, and could be biting in her sarcasm. In a conversation I had with Ruby and Kenneth about the kinds of things that would help me learn about the residence, both equivocated about goals. I pressed earnestly: "But, I mean, aren't the goals important?" Ruby answered flippantly, "Well, yeah, they run your life." Kenneth nodded in agreement, but beyond a shrug neither would elaborate, either because what she had said was self-evident or perhaps because they thought better of revealing too much, even though at that point I had been in the group home for a long time. Given the available ways of knowing and acting on Ruby, her occasional expression of this sort was plausibly heard by staff as evidence of "non-compliance" or a "bad attitude." By "plausible," I mean Garfinkel's use of "normal and natural" simply as being "in accord with prevailing rules of practice" (1967b, 191). I did not tell Cynthia that when I asked Ruby for permission to attend her annual case conference, she was cavalier: "Sure . . . if it accomplishes anything. I hope it's short." I heard this reply as an expression of mild annoyance with and resignation to the burdens of group home work. However, there was no way for me to know whether I heard this right. Ruby's answer could have been heard just as easily as intimidation or nervousness about the annual review process—or, for that matter, as a way of coping with or concealing her difficulty with self-assertion.

"Jennifer's Doing It for Herself"

Jennifer was quite frank about her lack of interest in and concern for the group home's clinical and administrative requirements and the various niceties they apparently demand. At one point, Beth, the nurse, suggested that Jennifer's personal hygiene was again becoming a problem and posed risks to her health. She suggested trying a behavior plan again. The result was a plan that involved a checklist so that Jennifer could monitor herself. Beyond identifying specific hygiene "responsibilities," the checklist and its prescribed use provided techniques meant to force Jennifer not only to recognize that she had hygiene problems but also to acknowledge them in regular contact with staff. Here was the plan's rationale: Jennifer had a long history of having difficulty maintaining her hygiene. She had worked on numerous hygiene plans over the years with differing reinforcements, but with little success. Jennifer was aware of her personal responsibilities but felt little motivation to participate in them. Although she claimed to dislike staff intervention, she appeared to respond to it, particularly if the intervention was direct, allowed her to choose when to do the hygiene tasks, and was given by one staff member.

All goal plans formulate the mundane work they require of residents as voluntary participation in a quasicontractual form. Jennifer's plan, however, gave special attention to the contractual elements and technical specifications of participation. She was especially immune to the endless group home talk about the importance of "working on yourself," and this posed a particular kind of challenge in counselor work. The plan specified in more detail than usual the kind of counselor conduct, based on what was seeable and knowable about Jennifer, that would increase the likelihood of her successful participation: "Although one staff per shift will be responsible for asking Jennifer if she has completed her hygiene tasks, all staff will directly and honestly comment on her appearance and the consequences. The consequences should be explained honestly and directly but privately and should include issues of health and safety as well as social consequences." Only a regular staff member would know that the primary "consequences" referred to Jennifer's diabetes and history of dermatological problems. The "social consequences" referred to Jennifer's participation in a more general sense—as a group home citizen with responsibilities as well as rights. The presumption that, despite her curmudgeonly attitude, Jennifer wanted to be integrated into group home life is indicated in the prescribed reinforcement: "Staff will praise Jennifer every time she appears and smells clean and invite her to join the conversation." As a technique of inclusion—"the conversation" presumably refers to everyday activities and "hanging out"—this reinforcement establishes the practical conditions for the reverse, but unspecified, intervention: exclusion. Counselors actually raised this possibility in the staff meeting when Beth first suggested that Jennifer needed another hygiene plan. Angela had a unique relationship with Jennifer. She was the only counselor Jennifer claimed to like and the only one in whom she expressed any personal interest or commitment. "Yeah, she's impossible!" Angela said in response to the suggestion that staff exclude or refuse to interact with Jennifer unless she was clean. "Just don't engage with her when she stinks. She really does get the message." This discussion didn't go far because the counselors recognized that this action would be a violation of Jennifer's rights. Besides, the threat of personal exclusion would matter only if it came from Angela.

It was in this meeting that the counselors settled on the use of a checklist. As a documentary technology, it would translate Jennifer's participation—in the plan and in the group home generally—into precise techniques of conduct: deciding whether to do each task of self-care and even whether to use the checklist and initiate contact with staff. Jennifer usually bristled at the degree of attention and monitoring to which she was subjected in the group home (which is why the plan specified that she be approached by only one counselor per shift). The specific documentary work of the checklist functioned daily as the material expression of her contractual arrangement with staff. The voluntary nature of participation was emphasized by providing boxes for Jennifer to mark—it was a literal checklist—and by the formulation of each task, in declarative statements, as her responsibility alone. Contrast this to James's appearance checklist (in chapter 8), whose questions were intended to function mnemonically. The voluntary nature of James's participation was emphasized not by invoking the techniques of a contract so much as by organizing his relationship to his own conduct in a series of self-posed questions. At the bottom of Jennifer's checklist, as with all proper contracts, there was a line for her signature—the most elemental of contractual technologies—so that she might daily acknowledge (or certify or endorse) the basic sentiment that captures what counselors hoped she would come to regard, working on this plan, as not only a regular but a desirable goal of conduct: "I am clean today."

Like all goal plans, Jennifer's hygiene goal ideally cultivated capacities to act freely on her own conduct for her own good. No one was

---

Jennifer Silver's Daily Hygiene Checklist

Date: _____

    1. I showered today.   ____

    2. I washed my hair today.   ____

    3. I brushed my hair today.   ____

    4. I brushed my teeth today.   ____

    5. I wore clean clothes today.   ____

I am clean today.   _____

                                    Signature

Jennifer Silver's daily hygiene checklist

surprised that having a checklist made little difference in the satisfactory accomplishment of her hygiene work. Interestingly, counselors said that she was using the checklist, though never how she used it or to what end. After a month or so, Angela resorted to an informal deal that provided an additional incentive: they would go out to lunch together if Jennifer showered daily for a week. This was one contractual obligation Jennifer was keen to fulfill. One day during that week, Jennifer decided to join me on some errands, because she needed to purchase shampoo. On the way out, we stopped by Sonia's office to get the money for it. The purpose of Jennifer's errand warranted, for Sonia, a query about her hygiene goal; as she was unlocking the metal petty cash box, she asked, "So how is your showering going?" Jennifer replied, "Angela said that if I showered for a week she'd go to lunch with me." Sonia asked, "Well, who are you doing it for?" Jennifer replied matter-of-factly, "Angela." Sonia stood with the bills in her hand, smiled knowingly, and asked, with exaggerated emphasis, "*Only* for Angela?" Jennifer answered without affect: "Yes." Sonia's tone shifted to one of sincerity and concern, asking and then answering her leading question with more leading questions: "What about for *yourself*? To feel *better*? To feel *clean*?" Jennifer again simply said yes. Sonia agreed: "Yes." She was smiling. "Yes! *Always* say that. That's who you're doing it for. *You!*"

Kenneth and the Problem of Problem Solving

I do not claim that goal plans determine the conduct of counselors and residents in any simple sense. Goal plans shape the conditions of knowing, seeing, and acting on matters of work, on what counts as a matter of group home work, by making techniques of conduct available in formats that are standard, durable, and accountable. But how, when, and whether these techniques are actually used depends on the degree to which they relevantly organize experience in and across specific situations. Just adding a new plan to a resident's goal book does not necessarily mean that he or she will conduct him- or herself in the intended ways. The writing of a goal plan occurs in a reflexive relationship to the counselors' ongoing work of defining, assessing, and intervening in a resident's conduct and requires the agreement and some form of participation of the resident. But the agreement to have a new goal does not necessarily result in willing participation, and if a goal turns out to have little practical relevance, it may be ignored by counselors and residents alike. Counselors occasionally discover that they have misjudged a plan's feasibility or the demands it places on their time. Sometimes a new plan must be modified or discontinued because of some unforeseen practical obstacle or unintended consequence, just as a new plan might "work" but not as it was written, or might work on some other aspect of conduct but not the specified target or outcome. For residents, most goal work is done routinely—sometimes with enthusiasm, sometimes as a chore—but what a goal means and how it is done are always situated.

Kenneth's behavior plan to address his "neediness" was carefully wrought and detailed yet rarely used as written. It defined "neediness" as an identifying and specifically identifiable feature of Kenneth's conduct. The plan did not construct a problem that had not existed before; that a behavior plan was considered necessary emerged reflexively from the practical ways in which the counselors and Kenneth already registered his neediness as a problem. The plan translated conduct into actual accountable work by defining "neediness" as a technical problem that counselors and Kenneth could see, know, and act on in systematic and specific ways. Neediness became a formally accountable problem that enabled different kinds of work relationships—between the counselors and Kenneth, and between Kenneth and his own conduct.

The desired outcome in Kenneth's behavior plan was formulated as a matter of problem solving. It specified that Kenneth would discuss certain topics only with his primary counselor and then under particular conditions. It provided a technology for Kenneth himself to use when his counselor was absent but which in effect organized his relationships to all staff, because he was supposed to use his worksheet before approaching them to talk: "Kenneth will independently use his problem solving worksheet when faced with daily challenges and discuss private concerns only with his counselor during scheduled sessions 25/30 days for 3 consecutive months." The plan's rationale acknowledged improvement in the way Kenneth managed his need for staff attention, but of course there was more work to be done:

> Kenneth is a man with mild mental retardation who often presents as emotionally needy and preoccupied with securing attention from direct care staff. He is described as being anxious, having poor impulse control, and poor problem solving skills. In the past, he has displayed a wide range of problem behaviors in his attempts to secure staff attention (ex: physical outbursts, verbal outbursts, property destruction). He is now described as being less aggressive; however, there is concurrent increase [in] other problem behavior. Kenneth will often provoke his peers in an attempt to be made into a "victim," and thus receive supportive attention from staff. In addition, he perseverates on death, dying, and his relationship with various family members. There is some basis in history for these concerns, and Kenneth is currently in psychotherapy to resolve issues related to his family, disability, and previous losses. On rare occasions, Kenneth will mimic the problem behavior of peers in the residence in an attempt to secure attention. The purpose of this plan is to teach Kenneth how to solve his own problems, decrease his dependency on direct care staff, encourage using appropriate forums for getting his emotional needs met, and reinforce progress toward these goals.

Two target behaviors were specified in the behavior plan:

1. *Perseverating on Negative Topics*: Bringing up either directly or indirectly a depressive/negative topic in an attempt to engage staff in a counseling session.
2. *Provoking Peers*: Making statements towards peers or engaging in provocative behaviors that are known to upset or provoke select peers.

The plan provided two sets of techniques related to the target behaviors. The "proactive" procedures were meant to cultivate Kenneth's capacities to manage his own conduct and included specific techniques both for him and for the counselors. The "reactive" interventions specified how counselors were to conduct themselves when Kenneth's target behaviors occurred. Here are the proactive procedures:

Proactive Procedures and Teaching Component:
1. *Structured Counseling*: Kenneth will have preplanned counseling sessions in order to encourage him to limit his discussions of negative topics to the appropriate time and place (in private, with his counselor). Counseling sessions will occur once a day in the evening. These sessions will be scheduled as at a time that is mutually agreeable to both Kenneth and his counselor. During counseling sessions, Kenneth will receive emotional support and assistance with problem solving in accordance with problem solving methodology (see next section). Staff should also review with Kenneth that he does not need to create negative situations if he would like to talk to staff. Explain to him that staff are always happy to hang out with him and discuss positive events.
2. *Problem Solving Worksheet and Binder*: Kenneth will be provided with a problem solving worksheet and a binder in which to keep old completed worksheets. When the problem solving worksheet is initially introduced to Kenneth, staff should spend sufficient time teaching him how to use it. Once Kenneth understands how to use his worksheet, staff will explain to him the importance of learning to solve his own problems and that before staff will assist him, he must first complete his problem solving worksheet. Kenneth must make an attempt to answer all questions on his worksheet before staff will help him with a problem. When Kenneth presents staff with a completed worksheet, staff will review it with him and assist him with implementing a solution to his problem. Once the problem solving worksheet has been completed, Kenneth will place it in his binder for future reference. He should be encouraged to consult his problem solving binder when confronting future problems.
3. *Reinforcement Procedure*: Verbal praise is highly reinforcing to Kenneth. As such, he will be praised when he engages in positive interactions and uses his problem solving worksheets.

From a clinical perspective, these are attempts to shape Kenneth's conduct by teaching him directly, by requiring that he use the written technology to guide himself through the process of problem solving, and by reinforcing him when he implemented or simply completed the worksheet. Even when such instructions are followed to the letter, their function cannot be understood as mere "procedures" or "rules." Such formalized procedures often function more as what Herbert Blumer called "sensitizing devices," which provide "a general sense of reference and guidance in approaching empirical instances" (148). In this sense, they organize the technical conditions of possibility for certain kinds of time, space, and conduct. For Kenneth, the plan overall enabled new possible kinds of conduct in both his relationship to counselors and to himself.

The problem solving worksheet is properly a data collection technology, but it appears in the plan as an intervention—as an aspect of Kenneth's work—rather than a documentation procedure. The description of the worksheet in the plan indicates that its specific technical requirements are understood to be self-evident. Apart from the copy attached to the plan, the worksheet is mentioned only in the context that "Kenneth must attempt to answer all the questions before staff will help him with a problem." Even though the worksheet is a clinical intervention, how to use it was self-evident to staff because it worked like one of their own documentary technologies. The very fact of the worksheet, its instructable character, and its general purpose— to teach Kenneth how to solve his own problems and the importance of being able to do so independently—shaped the nature of Kenneth's contact and expression. Before seeking support from counselors, he must "use" the worksheet to attempt to solve his "daily challenges" independently. The knowledge about himself that he gathered and evaluated was not the only work of self-intervention; the worksheet also furnished, in a series of questions, the techniques of assessment, reflection, comparison, and decision making that constitute "independent problem solving." The very order of the questions can be seen as a technique, formulating for Kenneth the sequential and cognitive logic of the process of problem solving.

The proactive procedures of Kenneth's behavior plan specified techniques of conduct for Kenneth and the counselors that were meant to teach him new ways to manage himself. The reactive interventions instructed counselors in the ways they should act on Kenneth's target

<u>Kenneth's Problem Solving Worksheet</u>

What is my problem: _____

Have I had this problem before?   Yes or No

How did I solve this problem before? _____

_____

Did my solution work?   Yes or No

One way I can solve this problem: _____

_____

Another way I can solve this problem is: _____

_____

Which solution I think will work better: _____

_____

My plan for solving this problem:

What I will do: _____

With who: _____

    When I will do it: _____

    I need help with: _____

    How did my plan work: _____

Signature: _____   Date: _____

Kenneth's problem-solving worksheet

behaviors in order to shape his relationship to such conduct when it occurred:

Reactive Interventions:

1. *Perseverating on Negative Topics*: When Kenneth is perseverating on negative topics or displaying mild behaviors (hand against face, pouting) attention should be minimal. Remind Kenneth that he does not need to engage in those behaviors and that when he is ready you will give him any assistance he needs. Continue responding in this neutral fashion until Kenneth approaches staff and expresses his concerns appropriately.

2. *Provoking Peers*: When these behaviors occur, Kenneth should not be allowed to assume "victim status" and receive excessive emotional support. He should be encouraged to use his next scheduled counseling session to discuss the incident. During counseling, Kenneth should be assisted in seeing the relationship between his behavior and those of his peers and encouraged to take responsibility for the situation. If indicated, he should make amends to the peer he provoked.

The reactive interventions are explained in instructional scenarios that include descriptions of the target behaviors. For all their detail and repetition, these descriptions presume a reader's specific local knowledge. The format of goal plans reflects a standard behavioral intervention, and at Driggs House they are written for an audience of any professional reader. Accountability is an issue here, because the auditable character of plans depends on how they conform to standard professional practice. No doubt, the possibility that they may be evaluated by outside auditors is one reason that a designated person, Cynthia, was responsible for preparing all goal plans. Their professional character is often achieved, however, by including information that is taken for granted in the group home and by auditors ("Kenneth is a man with mild mental retardation . . ."), or by substituting formal methods for practical ones (as in the documentation requirement for James's goal, which uses + and − instead of "yes" and "no"). Despite the plans' formal appearance and expression, it is their "occasional and elliptical character" (Garfinkel 1967b, 201) that enables them to be relevant and usable in group home work.

In the examples described here, only Jennifer's hygiene checklist emphasizes its contractual function, but the basic formulation of all plans is essentially contractual. Just as Garfinkel described psychiatric records (1984b, 197), the contractual function of goal plans can be observed in the range of accountable ways of knowing and acting that they make possible. In Kenneth's plan, for example, the meaning of "minimal attention," "being ready," and even "assistance" and "emotional support" is not contained within the plan itself, and cannot be. The reactive interventions must be general enough to permit counselors to exercise judgment about when and how the specified techniques are relevant. The plan enables the situated, accountable use of certain kinds of knowledge and conduct that must be expressed in enough detail but not so much that the work of the plan becomes practically impossible. At the same time, the only additional details in the reactive interventions, provided parenthetically to distinguish and define "mild behaviors," function in the reverse, defining certain kinds of conduct as having a fixed meaning. "Pouting" and "hand against face" become specifically seeable kinds of conduct: attention seeking strategies that are evidence of neediness.

What was most significant for Kenneth and took up a good deal of his time in relation to the plan was the problem solving worksheet. For counselors, Kenneth's written technology was not a routine part of their work except on those occasions when they reminded him to use it. Actually, there were no precise instructions about how counselors were meant to "use" the worksheet, other than by teaching *him* how to use it (and to devote "sufficient" time doing so). In the proactive procedures, the implication is that when Kenneth sought staff attention in certain ways, he should be asked to complete the worksheet first. I observed staff use it as a direct intervention all of three times. Two occasions involved Cynthia, who used it to "redirect" Kenneth when he attempted to initiate conversation about a negative topic. Perhaps this reflects Cynthia's position as the clinical "expert" and the plan's primary author. In any case, the plan as written was apparently not practical for the counselors in their routine work. Counselors did, however, identify and act on Kenneth's conduct in ways that were accountable to the plan. Both Susan and Carlos joked and complained, on many occasions, that Kenneth made up problems in order to seek counseling. Once, in the staff office, Susan shooed Kenneth away, saying, "I'm busy and don't have time to talk to you right now." Witnessing this exchange, Carlos laughed and said to me, "He makes up issues because he likes to get counseling. You know, he comes and tells things he's done wrong and stuff so that he'll get counseling." Susan affirmed this defiantly: "When he's like that, I just won't talk to him." How Susan and Carlos acted reflects the plan's formulation of Kenneth's conduct and the general logic of intervention. The fact that there was a plan provided a kind of license for counselors to act on Kenneth's behavior as neediness and attention seeking in accountable ways regardless of the prescribed clinical techniques.

For Susan and Carlos, the informal management of Kenneth's conduct often appeared to be a strategy of rationing service. Redirecting him by asking that he complete a worksheet was actually an implied contract, stipulating the conditions that would permit him to make a claim on them later that day. This was a commitment they might not be willing to make; as a practical matter, Kenneth's conduct might be much easier to manage by simply dismissing him than by initiating the plan's systematic and calculative techniques. As with all goal plans, the counselors had to document Kenneth's target behaviors—perseveration on negative topics and provoking peers—if they occurred. Monitoring Kenneth's progress in the data book during each shift required counselors to indicate whether Kenneth had "used" the worksheet. However, the worksheet was not a feature of their own conduct that counselors were required to document. In addition to the usual daily data-collection technology, Kenneth had a "behavior log" for notable or particularly disruptive occurrences of his target behaviors. Although these rarely occurred, Kenneth's potential for negative conduct apparently warranted this additional technology to monitor his conduct in greater detail. The behavior log required a narrative description of the target behavior, its antecedents, and "how counselors responded"—which is the one place where counselors were required to monitor their own conduct in relation to the behavior plan.

The behavior plan also did not capture how the worksheet actually shaped Kenneth's own practical, everyday work. According to the counselors, Kenneth never mentioned the worksheet and was even "secretive" about it, keeping the binder hidden in his room. Carlos told me that Kenneth sometimes "acts surprised" when the worksheet was mentioned and "seems to think that staff do not know about it." In my own many casual conversations with Kenneth, he mentioned the worksheet regularly and, when he did, he seemed to me to be expressing his capacity for solving problems *without* staff—using the worksheet without using one, so to speak. Kenneth also used the worksheet's techniques of evaluation and assessment in conversation:

You know, I have this problem a lot. . . . I've had this problem before. . . .
I worry too much. . . . I don't want to bother staff. . . . Once I talked to Sonia
and she told me . . . I told Daniel about it and he helped me. . . . I'll tell you
what I'm gonna do to stop worrying . . .

On a few occasions early in the research, I asked Kenneth whether
he would show me his worksheets and explain them. Normally quite
forthcoming and eager to show me things, he always deferred these
requests by saying "Another time" or "Maybe later." Some months
into the research period, Kenneth was upset for a few days about the
planned change of his primary counselor from Lisa, who was leaving
the job, to Daniel, who had been his counselor once before. Kenneth
felt Daniel was "too strict" and also said that his mother did not like
Daniel. Kenneth's worry was compounded by the fact that he had
been informed of the change while his mother and Daniel both happened to be away (his mother, visiting relatives out of town, and Daniel,
on vacation for a week).

One of the times I observed Cynthia using the worksheet as an
intervention was during this period. She, Kenneth, and I were in the
staff office. When Kenneth initiated a conversation about Daniel, she
said, "I'll talk to you about what's bothering you, but you have to fill
out a problem worksheet first." Kenneth agreed and headed toward
his room. Several hours later, after the evening chores were finished, I
was in the living room with Kenneth and some other residents when
he asked to talk with me privately in his room because he was upset.
We sat on the bed, and he raised his concerns about Daniel and his
mother's reaction ("She's gonna be upset when she gets back"). After
a few minutes, I interrupted, telling him I had heard Cynthia mention
filling out a worksheet and wondered if it had helped. He said yes
but continued the conversation without elaborating or extending to
me any kind of permission to pursue it. When he asked, "What do you
think I should do?" I took it as another opportunity: "Well, I really
don't know. But, I mean, you have these worksheets that are supposed
to help. Do they? I don't even know what they look like. Aren't you
supposed to fill one out when you're upset?" Kenneth replied, "They
help a little." Then I asked if he would show me one. "Okay, I'll show
you one as an example." He went into his closet and removed a binder,
and from it a single sheet. It was the sheet he had used earlier that day,
and as I looked at it he read it aloud, letting the questions themselves
serve as techniques of explication:

*What is my problem? Getting a new counselor, and he won't let me talk to
other staff except the boss [the supervisor, Sonia]. Have I had this problem
before? Yes. How did I solve the problem before? Talking to the boss. Did my
solution work? No. One way I can solve this problem. Moving out. My plan
for solving this problem. [Kenneth paused, because the answer was blank.]
What will I do? Talk to the boss.*

Kenneth replaced the sheet in the binder. I said, "Okay, I see how it
works now. Does it help to fill one out when you have a problem?" He
replied simply, "Yes." I persisted: "Why does it help?" He hesitated
and then said, "Umm, when I write out the issues, . . ." before trailing
off. He rose to return the binder to the closet and resumed our conversation by switching topics, asking if I was going down for coffee with
Theresa that night.

Kenneth did not answer my question in detail, it seemed to me,
because my question probably did not make sense. To pose it as I did
assumed that, as an intervention, using a worksheet involved some
describable personal process, what he may have been getting at with
his unfinished answer: "When I write out the issues . . ." Kenneth
apparently did not share this assumption. The technique of ordering
the questions provided but did not require a particular temporal logic.
To the question "How did I solve the problem before?" Kenneth
answered, "Talking to the boss," then indicated that this solution did
not work. Perhaps this is why he left blank his plan for solving the
problem this time. Yet when he arrived at the final question, "What
will I do?" the answer was the same as it was before. The logical relation between his prior, unsuccessful solution and solving the problem
at hand was not reflected in the ordering technique that the worksheet
provided. The situated, practical character of such decision making
means that such a logic often cannot be available—for Kenneth or anyone else. For him, the problem solving worksheets were a kind of work
that made sense only in terms of the specific things that he could use
them to accomplish. Kenneth did not indicate whether he was aware
of this "contradiction." Even if he was, it would not likely trouble him.

At least one of the specific accomplishments that completing the
worksheet afforded was the fulfillment of the contractual arrangements
that entitled, and organized, certain kinds of contact with counselors.
Kenneth was aware that talking about what he called "my problems"
was always potentially annoying to counselors. This awareness was
observable when he managed his conduct in ways that were not about

becoming more independent but about not "getting [the counselors] mad." The counselors' interventions—whether the plan was used or not—translated Kenneth's "talking too much" into clinically warrantable conduct, technically as problems of problem solving, inappropriate attention seeking, neediness, perseveration, and so on. Kenneth managed himself preemptively, one might say, to "miss" the target behaviors, or at least to conceal his aim. One night, Kenneth was annoyed at Evelyn about something she had said to Evan during dinner. He discussed it with me briefly during dinner and again afterward, as he was sweeping the dining room. About an hour later, I was sitting in the staff office, reading the newspaper. Carlos was helping Donna on the computer. Kenneth came in, slid into the chair next to me, and said, sotto voce: "I'm still upset . . . you know . . . about what we talked about." On another occasion, he and I were standing in the doorway to the kitchen one afternoon as I was cooking dinner. I had my back to the hall, and he was talking about something at workshop that had upset him earlier that day. Kenneth suddenly stopped talking, turned on his heel, and headed through the kitchen toward the dining room. Then I heard Daniel's voice call from behind me: "What's the matter?" Kenneth paused. Daniel continued: "If you have a problem, write about it." Kenneth said, "Right," and proceeded into the dining room and out of sight. This was the only time I ever observed a counselor using the worksheet as the plan implied, although Kenneth was not actually talking to Daniel, who likely did not hear what Kenneth said or even whether he was complaining; for Daniel, Kenneth was "doing what he always does."

Kenneth often openly discussed his problems and how to conduct himself. One afternoon not long after I started spending time at the group home, I was sitting in the dining room, listening to the radio with Chris. Kenneth had come home from workshop and sat nearby, at another table. He was discussing one of his regular problems, the health of an aging aunt. After a few minutes, we talked about Cheryl, who had just started as an evening counselor, and Kenneth raised his problem of talking about problems:

KENNETH: I'm not allowed to talk about my problems with Cheryl.
JACK: Why not?
KENNETH: Only with Sonia and Daniel.
JACK: Who says? Is that a rule?

KENNETH: It's inappropriate to talk about personal problems with people you don't know.

JACK: Oh.

KENNETH: But soon I'll know her.

JACK: Who said so?

KENNETH: My counselor. He said I can't talk to anybody but him. And Sonia too.

JACK: You're talking to me.

KENNETH: That's because you learn things. You learn things from what clients talk about.

"Who Said So?"

I meant "Who said so?" to be a question about whether Daniel had actually prohibited Kenneth from talking to other counselors or whether Kenneth simply interpreted the plan this way. If Daniel had made such a rule, it would have been informal (and even so, certainly an abuse of Kenneth's rights) and, in practice, unenforceable. What I imagine is that Kenneth formulated, as a rule for me, some advice or a suggestion from Daniel about how to act. In any case, Kenneth referred not to the goal plan but to his practical knowledge about inappropriate conduct—to whom he was and was not permitted to talk about his problems. The residents' ability to know and act on their own need is, in part, shaped reflexively by the kinds of conduct that goal plans enable. Counselors and residents do not question that everyday life in the group home is organized by their own ongoing clinical work. Taken-for-granted clinical ideals must be translated in actual work, but even when goal plans are not followed, they provide a good many of the practical techniques that enable both counselors and residents to act on conduct—their own and each other's. Each plan translates the overall goal of independence into particular problems of individual conduct. Difficulty with self-assertion, poor hygiene, neediness, and attention seeking are a few examples of the way everyday conduct takes shape as work to become more independent. But, like plans, procedures, blueprints, and so on, in all workplaces, goals neither determine nor explain in any simple sense how the work actually gets done (Suchman). How, when, and why plans are used in everyday life are matters that do not necessarily follow directly from the plans themselves, and if goal plans restrict the conduct of counselors and residents too much, then they are not practical and usable resources in their work.

All residents have goals, because work on conduct is never done. There is also the matter of reimbursement, of course, the organizational need to generate enough services to fulfill minimum billing requirements. However, this is something only Cynthia and Sonia are likely to keep in mind. For the counselors, it is simply a fundamental clinical assumption that there is always work to be done. To say that counselors and residents both took for granted the clinical organization of everyday life is not to say they did not criticize and complain about it: residents expressed frustration with the burden of the endless work they must do on themselves, and counselors balked at the clinical judgment of their colleagues and complained about the residents, each other, and Sonia.

Whether a plan seeks to cultivate kinds of conduct that are considered positive or reduce those considered negative, the focus of group home work is normal life and the enhancement of each resident's capacities to manage his or her own routine experience independently. Although the kinds of problems that organize this endless work may appear self-evident to readers, it is only in the group home's specific practical conditions that they are seeable and knowable as clinical problems. The goal plans provide one way of observing the detailed work of governing, because the psy techniques they furnish are the situated and practical resources residents and counselors use to govern themselves in the particular ways that make them group home persons.

IV. At Risk

10   WHAT EVERYBODY KNOWS ABOUT PAUL

WORK AT DRIGGS HOUSE IS NEVER DONE. It is endless because demand is endless, because human conduct is complex, unpredictable material, and because the goal of group home work is itself a process. One aspect of this endlessness is the nature of clinical work in the community: no longer contained within the unifying walls of the institutions, psychiatry and psychology had to adapt in order to function effectively outside the segregated settings that had been its province for so long. By the early 1970s, psy knowledge had already become integral to contemporary culture in many aspects of everyday life (Rose 1999a, 1994, 1998b). About psychiatry in particular, Rose (1998a, 1998b, 1996) argues that, in the context of deinstitutionalization, the field found itself accountable to the public and political concern about whether certain kinds of individuals were capable of freedom in terms of the risks they posed both to themselves and to the community. The assessment and administration of risk became one of the field's central practices and transformed the nature of clinical work (Castel; Rose 1996, 1998).

What occurred in community psychiatry also occurred in the implementation of community services for individuals with intellectual disability. In addition to the practices of accountability that emerged with deinstitutionalization, there was a new division of labor. In the community, the work of diagnosis and the work of treatment are not conducted by the same person or in the same place and, further, do not draw on the same kind of knowledge. For intellectual disability, which is not an illness, what constitutes treatment is not determined simply by the diagnostic classification. In their everyday work, professionals do not administer treatment so much as administer the techniques for assessing and monitoring risk. The ongoing cultivation of capacities that enable residents to govern themselves is about the shaping of conduct in ways that, ideally, allow individuals to manage and reduce the risks they pose to themselves.

This is not an argument about an irreconcilable opposition between substantive clinical knowledge and the administration of services in the community. On the contrary, clinical knowledge was redefined by the problem of government as the practice of risk administration. This requires a different kind of clinical expertise, one that involves systematic attempts to shape conduct in relation to the ongoing assessment of the risks an individual poses to him- or herself and to others. The ideal of autonomy has made clinical work more than ever a general administrative practice rather than separate fields of expertise unique to intellectual disability, mental health, and other areas (Parton; Rose 1998b, 1996). Although Hughes described the risk of mistakes and failure as the burden of all work, the work of group home counselors and other community service professionals is uncertain and prone to failure *by definition*, because it is largely organized by the problem of risk.

What interests me here is how the counselors' work of risk administration creates a constantly transforming field of intervention in which the curtailment of a resident's liberty is to be avoided wherever possible yet provides the one intervention that is seen to reduce risk with any certainty. In this chapter, I use the case of Paul to illustrate how what counselors know and do took practical shape in the endless process of calculating his risk. I describe how Paul's riskiness was assessed and acted on over roughly a six-month period, from June to December. What sets this period apart is not that Paul raised particularly new problems but that counselors identified and acted on him as more at risk than usual. The counselors' heightened concern over this period took shape in relation to the continuous assessment of Paul, and, with each intervention, counselors transformed the very conditions of risk they sought to manage.

Paul

When I began my research at Driggs House, I learned that Paul was already considered a risky individual. The counselors described him to me as full of life and energy but always somehow teetering on the edge of trouble, if not eagerly seeking it out. He was headstrong and intrepid in the pursuit of his daily pleasures, and this was an aspect of the warm and funny personality that counselors truly appreciated. But because a good deal of his preferred activities involved being out in the community on his own, he was, in principle, always putting himself at risk. The focal concerns were Paul's "hoarding behaviors" and "eating behaviors." No doubt Paul's pleasure in being out in the community had to do with his impressive resourcefulness. Paul had a penchant for gathering collectible materials of all sorts, from toys to free catalogs to pens and pencils. He had identified several commercial establishments that provided promotional items such as pens, note-pads, magnets, and drinking cups. He was always scouting for new sources and regularly looked in the paper for giveaways. Whatever the items he found, he intended to keep them all.

By the time I began my research at Driggs House, this had long been identified as a problem, and a behavior plan to address room mainte-nance was a daily aspect of work with and for Paul. The objective of the plan was that Paul evaluate his possessions and keep them in order in a way that neither encroached upon James's side of the room nor posed a risk to either man's health and safety. It was one thing to permit Paul to keep durable items, as long as they were relatively neat, but unwashed paper cups, other "dirty" things, and food were an entirely different matter. To this end, it was "inappropriate" for Paul to clutter the room with all that he collected; his room maintenance plan indicated that he could keep only "appropriate non-garbage items." "Garbage" items were defined as those things that were dirty or dis-posable, and things that he did not "need"—leaflets, paper cups, plas-tic flatware, and the like. Though he might also not "need" toys, key chains, notepads, and pens, he was permitted to keep them on the grounds that he had the right to collect things. Everything else was always vulnerable to the staff's eager inclination toward disposal. Room maintenance occurred every evening and involved a counselor (usually Carlos, Paul's primary counselor) "helping" Paul sort through things he'd collected and put his side of the room in order.

Paul detested room maintenance. Not only did it involve the asser-tion of staff authority over his private area and possessions, it also always involved the loss of various and sundry items that were dear to him. It is not possible to know whether his efforts to hide things from the staff preceded the plan or resulted from it, but, either way, this was a question the counselors did not entertain. The discovery of an unwashed cup in a clothes drawer was simply evidence of hoarding behavior. A few counselors treated uncovering the occasional stash as a kind of sport and as evidence of Paul's compulsive hoarding and his naïveté about what could be kept from counselors. (The small shared bedrooms at Driggs House provided few hiding places.) Room maintenance was such a sore point for Paul that when I asked, after being in the group home for many months, whether I could be there for it, he answered decisively and simply, "No." I never asked again.

Paul's hatred of room maintenance served on a few occasions as a different kind of resource for counselors. My first observation of this was in the office with Carlos and some other staff and residents when Paul came in on his way out of the group home. Carlos asked why he was going out, since it was after dinner, and where could he possibly need to go? Paul said he wanted to buy a toy at a particular store in the neighborhood. Carlos said, "Fine. I'll just do room maintenance without you." Paul was upset. Room maintenance was such an invasion that he chose to forgo his excursion. I regarded it as wrong for Carlos to use room maintenance as a threat in this way. Sonia happened to be present but said nothing and had no obvious reaction to the exchange between Carlos and Paul, which was audible to everyone despite all the activity in the office. From my perspective, this was an overreaching of counselors' authority, because a clinical intervention, a behavior plan, was being used expressly for a purpose not intended, as a method of coercing Paul to remain around the house. In regulatory terms, this might constitute mistreatment rather than outright abuse (14 N.Y.C.R.R. § 624.4), but, whatever the category, the problem seemed self-evident. I presumed Sonia would address it in her weekly individual supervision with Carlos, even though she had no observable reaction to it in the moment. But then I saw Carlos respond to Paul in this way again and, over time, a few other counselors, too, sometimes in Sonia's presence. Clearly, she did not agree that such a response was wrong and considered it, as all the staff apparently did, to be within the legitimate scope of the behavior plan (though the plan itself did not specify this behavior). One defining aspect of a resident's mistreatment is an instance when staff "do not follow accepted treatment practices and standards in the field" (14 N.Y.C.R.R. § 624.4). I mulled over whether I should raise my concern with Sonia. I never did. The infrequent occurrence of such an exchange—it happened a total of five times in my thirteen months at Driggs House—was only part of the reason. Mostly, I thought there was a good chance that Sonia would have perceived me to be challenging her clinical judgment and authority over the counselors, and, frankly, I was afraid this could jeopardize my research by undermining the trust I had worked so hard to establish and maintain.

Though I still believe this use of room maintenance was wrong, the group home's clinical logic did make it an accountable, if unspecified, use of the plan. Counselors seemed to use it as a threat in moments when it appeared to them that Paul was very likely to engage in risky conduct—that is, if he was "manic" (in particularly determined high spirits) or "compulsive" (too eager to go out). The counselors regarded this as a risk-reduction intervention, because if Paul stuck around the house, he wouldn't be tempted to spend money, eat junk food, dig in garbage cans for empties, and whatever else took his fancy. The counselors did not see themselves as threatening Paul just for the sake of it; telling him they'd do room maintenance without him was a method of risk reduction that might help Paul see himself differently. It was an intervention that might assist Paul in being more himself by attempting to realign his risky "behavioral" self with the "real" one who knew the dangers of eating doughnuts and collecting empty cans.

Along with Paul's hoarding behaviors came his risky eating behaviors. He paid little attention to his diet, despite what he knew about the relationship of food, his diabetes, and his blood sugar level. Risky eating behaviors were a larger problem at Driggs House, because the staff took for granted the prevailing assumptions about the relationship between body weight, eating, and health (Campos 2004; Taubes). By the order of Beth, the nurse, eight or nine residents at any given time were subjected to the counselors' dinnertime surveillance by being "on portion control," which meant they could have no seconds except for vegetables. Paul was among this group but appeared immune to the counselors' encouragement to eat more vegetables, fewer starches, and less fat. He was known to try to sneak extra portions and on occasion had been caught eating others' unfinished dinners off the plates piled in the kitchen. The counselors had some impact on what he ate in the house, but they were generally resigned to the idea that Paul did not adequately supervise his own eating out in the community. Counselors often invoked the time some months earlier when Carlos discovered a bag of doughnuts hidden in his dresser. This was also a testament to Paul's resourcefulness, for he had discovered when the local doughnut shop discarded its day-old baked goods and retrieved a few from the dumpster. Sometimes counselors were good-humored about these stories, but at other times they used the very same stories as evidence for their claims about Paul's riskiness, and as proof of what he "definitely" and "obviously" did when he was out on his own.

"More Emotional Lately"

In the second week of June, the idea that Paul seemed "more emotional lately" became a topic of shoptalk. In the staff meeting, Sonia and Carlos, Paul's primary counselor, expressed concern about his "mood swings" and regarded them as something that put him even more at risk. This assessment was accountable in part by the approaching August anniversary of his mother's death, which apparently made summer a difficult time of year. Paul had "a lot going on." The day before the staff meeting, he learned that a first cousin close in age had died suddenly. About midday Thursday, Paul brought me into his room to tell me about it privately. I said, "So that was why [your brother] Henry took you to dinner, I guess. What bad news." He nodded. "Are you going to the funeral?" I asked. "Yesterday," he answered, "it was yesterday." "Oh. . . . Were you close with him?" Paul hesitated, then nodded. Being close with or liking a family member, even one they have grown up with, does not mean intimacy for those residents whose families do not exactly keep them in the loop. Certainly a decision had been made not to bring Paul to the funeral. He was a bit thrown by the news and asked me to tell Sonia. "Haven't you told any of the staff about it?" I asked. When he shook his head, I said, "I will if you want me to. Let's go see if she's here." As we left his room, Sonia was in the hallway, having just arrived. Paul looked at me for a moment and then blurted out, "My cousin died." After learning the details, Sonia asked, "Does this remind you of other things?" He nodded yes. Paul had recently started to mention the anniversary of his mother's death. "The anniversary" functioned as an expression of both the anticipation of sadness and sadness itself. In the staff meeting that day, everyone agreed that "the anniversary" accounted for Paul's recent moodiness. They used the phrase in conversation much as Paul himself did to explain moments of sadness, but for staff it functioned also to indicate what they regarded as an "unhealthy preoccupation" with her death.

That he had been more emotional lately was a topic in shoptalk for only a few days before this meeting occurred. Though there was no disagreement about Paul's emotional state, there was disagreement about what to do. That is, everyone understood that the problem was his riskiness, but there was disagreement about the degree of risk and, as always, how much risk warranted intervention. Sonia made clear that, at the moment, there was nothing to do but be aware of it. Being upset about the anniversary, compounded by the news of his cousin's death the day before, might put Paul more at risk out in the community, but there had been no indication that this would be the case. The opinion of the primary counselor often carried more weight in meetings, but this was not a hard-and-fast rule, because all the counselors were involved with every resident, and all were invested in the way problems got defined and defined their work. Sonia explained that she and Carlos disagreed about what to do. Carlos felt that some action should be taken now, but Sonia believed that since there had been no actual problems, it was important to "allow him his freedom," which she qualified by saying that she did not "endorse" what Paul might do out in the community. Carlos said that although he did believe strongly that Paul was a greater risk to himself, it was true nothing had happened yet. Sonia closed the discussion by reiterating that "we just need to be aware of what's going on with him."

Gone Missing

Usual things began to appear to counselors as problems. Just three days after this meeting, on Sunday afternoon, Miles went out for a walk and to do errands with a few residents, including Paul. On their way back, Paul said he was going to go to the coffee shop and would come home in a little while, something he often did. Miles tried to persuade him to return with the others, because he believed that Paul had been "more emotional lately" and therefore more at risk out in the community. Miles questioned his own concern, however, acknowledging that there was nothing unusual in Paul's wanting to be out on his own, especially at 4:00 on a Sunday afternoon in spring. But Miles continued to feel uneasy and, by 7:00, worried that Paul had still not returned. Being out all day was typical, too, for Paul, but now it seemed different in light of the new perception of the greater risk Paul posed to himself. For Miles to be on edge this way was notable. Of all the counselors, he was generally the most concerned about the group home overstepping its authority and the least likely to favor restrictive interventions. But that Sunday, Miles clearly saw Paul's riskiness as an escalating problem and was worried enough to contemplate calling Sonia to ask whether he should do anything.

Miles was considering this openly with me in the office, where Marty was also present. I suggested that Marty and I go out and look for Paul as an opportunity to put off calling Sonia. Miles thought this was sensible, so Marty and I took a twenty-minute walk in the neighborhood, which started and ended at the coffee shop. But we didn't find Paul. Marty was also worried yet, at the same time, critical of Paul for going out without telling anybody where he was: "It's not right." "But Paul's independent," I replied. "He goes out all the time." Marty said, "I know, but it's still not right, not right to make Miles worry." "Is that what it means to be independent," I asked, "having to tell people where you are all the time?" Marty hesitated. "Yes," he hedged. "I mean, being *out on your own? For so long?*" When we got back, Miles had already given in to his concern. He had spoken to Mike (not having been able to reach Sonia), who was not too worried but suggested that Miles go out and look for Paul. This would not usually have been possible because of the smaller staff on weekends, but Mike said I could serve as unofficial backup for the other counselor in the residence in case of an emergency. As Miles was leaving the building, he met Paul, who was on his way in, and they came into the residence together. Miles was demonstrably relieved. Marty greeted him enthusiastically. Of course, Paul had done nothing out of the ordinary, and if he appeared momentarily confused, he was more than a bit pleased to be fussed over.

Whether Paul had really "gone missing" was never settled, but this is how Miles described the incident in the log notes. In the days following, the counselors talked about it in various ways, all of which added up to confirmation of Paul's diminishing ability to manage himself as the anniversary of his mother's death approached. A little more than a week later, on the last Monday in June, their concern was heightened at the residents' meeting by Paul's excited recounting of his weekend adventures. Not only had he managed to attend a parade in a faraway neighborhood where he had not been known to go regularly, but he had also witnessed an arrest near the group home. Paul's interest in the hubbub with the police was understood by counselors as yet more evidence that he was "drawn to trouble." Just the energetic excitement with which he told the stories confirmed what counselors already saw in Paul as emotional sensitivity and mood swings, sometimes "depressed" and sometimes "manic."

The consensus about Paul's moodiness had been established, but the absence of any definitive "incidents" bred conflict about how exactly to define the problem and what do. Through the last two weeks of June and the first few weeks of July, there were a number of disagreements in shoptalk and staff meetings about "what's really going on with him." These disagreements were actually competing assessments of the kind and degree of risk Paul posed to himself. There was no distinction between Paul's problems and the problem of Paul's riskiness. The counselors' heightened attention, though informal, meant that they were seeing many familiar things in a new way. One was Paul's efforts to collect empty cans and bottles from public wastebaskets to redeem for cash. This had been an issue for years, and group home staff had prohibited it at one point in the past. Now it was talked about as a "relapse," a measure of his increasing riskiness.

In the third week of July, the topic of Paul dominated the staff meeting. Some counselors disagreed with the prevailing psychological explanation. Though they acknowledged the significance of the anniversary, they did not accept it as the primary cause of Paul's problem conduct. The challenge to the strictly psychological formulation rested on an assertion of Paul's general riskiness. Carlos and Daniel argued urgently for intervention. Carlos opened the discussion with the issue of Paul's moodiness and suggested that his dose of Depakote be increased. Depakote was developed as an antiseizure medication for the treatment of epilepsy and, in lower doses, is one of a group of drugs called mood stabilizers, which are prescribed for, among other things, bipolar disorder (of which mood swings are considered a symptom). Paul had received diagnoses of bipolar disorder and obsessive-compulsive disorder before I came to Driggs House, but I had no way of determining when that had happened, only that he had been taking Depakote for at least the three years documented in his treatment book. Nor was I able to know whether the hoarding and mood swings had led to that psychiatric evaluation or followed it.

Carlos argued for increasing Paul's dose of Depakote, as he had done in previous meetings, not on the basis of Paul's actual conduct but on what his moodiness suggested about his possible conduct. That is, Paul's mental state was taken to stand for the probability of prob-lem conduct. Earlier in the week, Paul had run into a counselor while he was carrying empties to the store. This was talked about in the meeting as "his going through the garbage *again*"; counselors did not consider whether Paul had actually been collecting empty cans and bottles all along despite earlier prohibitions. Carlos discussed the issue with a new urgency, because, on the day before the meeting, Paul had cut his finger on a piece of broken glass in a garbage can while looking for empties. For Carlos and some other counselors, this was yet more evidence that Paul was not able to "restrain himself." Angela empha-sized that having diabetes put him at even greater risk if, say, he cut himself again, and Carlos seconded this thought by reminding every-one of Paul's eating behaviors out in the community.

Sonia, however, remained cautious. She disagreed with immediately raising the dose of Paul's medication and, as in the meeting a month earlier, told counselors they were "jumping the gun." She asked the counselors to discuss what they thought were the multiple factors contributing to Paul's conduct and underscored the significance of the anniversary. She told them Paul had "cried with her about it" and "cried on the phone with his brother." Paul had "never cried about it in all these years!" Sonia went on. "So there are positive things happen-ing emotionally, too." Besides, she told them, in the preceding summer Paul had come to her himself and asked whether his Depakote dosage might be raised. Dr. Nunzio lowered it again in May because Paul was "stable," but the counselors discounted the doctor's judgment, describing the decision as "strange" and made "for no reason." Sonia continued: "He [Paul] came last summer and said that he felt out of control. I think we should give him a chance to do that [request a dose increase] on his own." In an effort to persuade Sonia that the dose should be raised "proactively," Daniel again described Paul's psychol-ogy as a predictor of his conduct. Sonia held her ground, and revealed to the counselors that, in fact, she had already spoken to Dr. Nunzio about increasing the dose and he said it would be okay. But, given all the other issues, she wanted to wait before taking that step, indicating that the subject was not off the table. If it was necessary, Sonia said, an increased dose would have an immediate effect, so "we don't have to rush into raising it." Sonia again emphasized Paul's capacity for insight and his ability to ask for help himself. Some counselors seemed unconvinced, but only Daniel persisted: "I don't see any difference between physical and mental illness. He is having a bad time, he's picking through the garbage, and doing things he hasn't done in a long time, so why not just raise it [the Depakote]?" The silence from his colleagues indicated a tacit acceptance of Sonia's position. Only Miles responded, and with impatience: "I don't even think the Depakote will make a difference anyway. There's too much going on."

Sonia then raised the possibility of an entirely different kind of intervention, one that was always in the quiver and had been mentioned here and there since June. She told the staff that, because Paul had cut his finger, she and Carlos had discussed with Paul his behavior out in the community and that if he continued to put himself at risk, they might have to require that he go out only with a counselor. Until then, Sonia had been adamant that restricting him was out of the question. So, telling the staff that she and Carlos had talked to Paul indicated not only that had she come around somewhat to the possibility of increasing Paul's medication but also that it was a viable option. Talking to Paul was also, of course, taken as an intervention in itself. The counselors who felt she hadn't been taking Paul's problems seriously enough appeared to register this as her recognition of their concerns. Sonia used this opportunity to move the conversation toward a close, and it ended with a few staff laughingly discussing Paul's penchant for can collecting with both a kind of affectionate disgust and appreciation for his pleasure in being out and about on his own.

When Paul's increasing risk had become an issue in June, the counselors who felt strongly that something needed to be done immediately argued that his riskiness had already reached perilous levels. Increasing his medication dose and requiring supervision out in the community are different kinds of clinical intervention, but they share a fundamental logic that illustrates how clinical work consists of assessing and acting on degrees of risk. Whether the solution was changing Paul's conduct (which the staff presumed the medication dose would do) or simply controlling his opportunities to engage in certain forms of conduct (by circumscribing his time out in the community), the problem being addressed was Paul's risk.

The Shadow Knows

Sonia's more moderate assessment and decisive insistence from the first discussion in June may have precluded all but the most vigorous opposition. She had never disputed that Paul was at risk, only how much, emphasizing that multiple issues made things too complex to warrant any specific intervention: "Let's wait and see; let's give him a chance." But once the prospect of restricting Paul was on the table, all the counselors—both those who had pushed so hard to intervene and those who had expressed caution and wanted to wait and see—seemed to share a similar assumption about what was going on with Paul and concluded that what was going on required action.

Only a few days later, an intervention not only strengthened this consensus but also transformed the nature and context of the problem. One day during the week following this meeting, as Sally was coming into work, she saw Paul out in the community "picking in the garbage, eating all sorts of stuff, and who knows what." That Thursday, the last in July, Sonia opened the staff meeting by announcing, first, that she had asked Paul whether he'd like his medicine increased and, second, that he needed to be shadowed in the community. By making these announcements, Sonia reduced the possibility of discussion about alternative strategies and, at the same time, formally established Paul's problem as a growing problem of self-management: Paul was an even riskier individual whose freedom of movement had become a legitimate arena for intervention in order to protect him from himself.

In Sonia's statement, "shadowing" meant what it usually does—tailing someone secretly—but staffing at the group home did not permit continuous surveillance, so Paul would be shadowed selectively a few times a week. Counselors did this easily without Paul knowing he was being watched. On occasions when they spoke with Paul or were spotted, the counselors said they had just run into him.

When I arrived on Sunday, in the early afternoon, Paul was not home. Miles soon came in and said he had shadowed Paul to the coffee shop, where he spoke to him. Paul had said he'd come right home, but it was at least an hour before he arrived, and, as soon as he did, he wanted his spending money so that he could go out again for an egg roll and soup. Miles hesitated but gave him his money, reminding him that it was "not safe to eat a lot of junk." While he was waiting, Paul showed me a toy helicopter he had bought earlier that day, but when the money appeared, he was off again. When Miles and I were left alone in the office, I asked whether Paul's medication dose—which had been increased three days earlier, on the day of the meeting—had made a difference. Miles said no and that, if it was to make a difference, it would take a little time despite Sonia's claim that the effect would be immediate. Still, Miles believed that too much had been made of the medication and what it might do, and he reiterated more strongly that "a drug isn't going to solve all the factors involved."

Paul continued to be a main topic of shoptalk. As in meetings, the continuous process of assessing his ever-changing risk was often stimulated by an incident, such as Paul's cut finger, but did not require such an incident. The monitoring in talk of Paul's riskiness included judgments of the efficacy of current, past, and possible future interventions. The counselors discussed every detail of Paul's affect and conduct, interpreting what might or might not be a sign of greater or lesser risk: what he'd eaten at program on a given day; how much and what he said about the anniversary; what particular toy he had purchased; what certain place he had visited. In both staff meeting talk and shoptalk, these discussions were characterized by a sense that there must be some solution, that *something* could be done and, at the same time, that no intervention was fail-proof. The very term "plan" implies the purposive, concerted pursuit of outcomes; in the group home, outcomes are talked about as obvious, definite, clear-cut, yet always uncertain. On those occasions when frustrated counselors would complain that "*nothing* will work with" Paul, Sonia would be encouraging and emphasize that everything was worth trying. However, she also had to stake out the limits of intervention, especially with the counselors who at first had wanted to act urgently, and she was cautious in her assessments of Paul's riskiness. In the group home, there was not quite so sharp a contrast as Robert Emerson (3) found between "the cautious try-all-else attitude toward sanctions of last resort" and "the optimistic, try-it-at-the-first-sign-of trouble" use of routine approaches. As general attitudes, these were not mutually exclusive among staff but depended on the particular context of work. In these discussions about Paul—as in discussion about all the residents—the very nature of staff responsibility and purpose of the group home took shape as the endless monitoring of individual riskiness and the ongoing efforts to act on individuals so that they might reduce the risks they posed to themselves.

A New (Old) Problem, a New Procedure

A week of shadowing confirmed more than the fact that, as Paul made his neighborhood rounds, he regularly collected cans from the garbage and ate food he shouldn't; it also confirmed what counselors already believed about Paul's inability to manage himself. The shadowing actually turned up no new or unusual activities, but given that Sonia and Carlos had already discussed can collecting and eating behaviors with Paul, they now took further license to describe him without qualification as "out of control" and "compulsive." This made it that much easier to talk about who Paul was and could be in narrow behavioral terms that were easily calculable (or, at least, easily articulated) as both risks and risk factors. Still, counselors repeatedly returned to what, as a rule, was particularly frustrating about working with Paul and what made the current situation especially serious: that he was aware of the nature and consequences of his conduct but engaged in it anyway. To the counselors, this was worse than mere compulsion: it was a "contradiction"—one common to a number of residents but especially pronounced in Paul—that made him particularly "resistant" and ever more at risk.

Sonia opened the next staff meeting, the first in August, by asking, "How's Paul doing?" Miles and Carlos both answered that there had been no changes. The observations that the increased medication dose apparently made no difference and that Paul continued to go through garbage cans were taken for granted as evidence of Paul's riskiness. Even so, there were still no crises or consequences related to the behaviors that staff regarded as self-evidently risky. But the fact that he had agreed to stop collecting cans yet was still doing it lent weight to the new, more urgent assessment of riskiness that Sonia had established the week before. Those counselors who had been urging that something be done for nearly two months now made their case again with a different kind of confidence. Angela and Daniel produced a catalog of risks that was decidedly more inclusive than in earlier conversations. Angela said of Paul, "He is given too much freedom and he can't handle it." Daniel followed: "Paul should be monitored more. Things like the amount of ketchup he uses; he eats food in crazy combinations like french fries and chocolate pudding!" Other counselors laughed and shook their heads. Nicky said that "with his garbage picking and hoarding, he seems to feel guilty. He apologizes, is slightly embarrassed, [and] he indicates he knows he's wrong." This acknowledgment of Paul's capacity for insight, for knowing himself—the very reason that since June had been grounds to hold off—at this meeting only bolstered the case for increased intervention.

Angela suggested trying again a plan that had been used two years earlier, which would allow Paul to go out in the community alone but required him, upon returning, to come directly into the office and empty his pockets so that staff could sort the garbage from the nongarbage. This would at least help manage the hoarding problem. The plan also specified what Paul was permitted to carry on his person. His breast pocket alone was always bulging with pens, notepads, and other items, and this was "only the tip of the iceberg." Nicky suggested that they not worry about his pens and stuff but focus on "the garbage," the bits of paper, flyers, cups, and miscellanea that Paul collected "for no reason." Sonia was skeptical about a plan that focused too much on the items he collected, because she was worried about "the material things *and* the impulse problem. . . . He's not happy when he's doing it. I mean, he wants the stuff, but he's not happy when he's doing it." But short of restricting Paul to the residence unless accompanied by a staff member, reinstating this plan to manage his hoarding behavior seemed the only viable option. And *something* had to be done. Everyone agreed that the older plan should be updated and given a try, and Sonia still wanted Paul to be shadowed a few times a week. Despite her point about the emotional component of Paul's risky behaviors, what followed was a detailed conversation about the type and number of items he should be permitted to have in his pockets.

The Next Step . . . and the Next

By the time I arrived on Saturday afternoon, only two days later, the face sheet of the daily log announced, in underlined block letters, PAUL IS NOT ALLOWED OUT WITHOUT A STAFF MEMBER. Earlier that day, Paul had managed to slip into his room without coming into the office for the staff to look at what he had brought home. Because it was the weekend and because what staff called the "search and seizure" plan had just been put in place, Linda felt compelled to call Sonia. The plan depended on Paul's cooperation, and Sonia felt that this offense could not be overlooked. Restricting Paul's movement was talked about as the necessary curtailment of his rights in the name of his health. Perhaps because his diabetes was stable, health had an encompassing psychological dimension. That Paul understood the nature of his diabetes but persisted with unhealthy eating, can collecting, and hoarding behaviors made those behaviors dangerous beyond their compulsive character. Paul's inability to pursue what the staff referred to as "rational choices"—the "*obvious* choices"—was a psychopathology risky in itself, which was only compounded by his medical condition. Prohibiting him from going out without staff was understood fundamentally as a way of limiting his opportunities to eat certain foods, and additionally as a way of identifying to Paul his particular incapacities, that is, what he had to work on in order to manage himself independently out in the community.

The following Thursday, in the second staff meeting in August, Sally was very upset about what Paul had done on Sunday, the day after Sonia decided to restrict him. Sally was out with Paul and a few other residents in the afternoon to do some shopping and poke around the neighborhood. As they were on their way home, Paul announced that he had things to do and he would see the others back at Driggs House. Sally managed, apparently with great effort, to persuade him to return with the group to the house. But, with the restriction in place, the fact that Paul had even considered going off on his own, let alone "giving Sally a hard time," was evidence that he was increasingly incapable of managing himself, because, on top of everything else, he didn't accept staff authority. The ensuing discussion in the staff meeting made sense of this incident as a taken-for-granted indication of Paul's escalating riskiness. Sally was frustrated and said, "We need to talk about what to do if" Paul did this kind of thing again, if "he refuses" to stay with staff. She suggested that perhaps Paul should be allowed to go out not in a group but only alone with a staff member. Sonia asked the staff to entertain the question and decide whether this was a necessary step.

If Paul were considered to be so risky that he could go out only when a staff person was free from other work, he would actually have very few opportunities to leave the residence, which was one of his greatest pleasures. Miles made this point to call into question the basis on which Paul's movement was increasingly being restricted. For the first time in two months of heightened attention to Paul, someone questioned the group home's approach. Miles suggested that perhaps it was unreasonable to prohibit Paul from collecting empty bottles and cans for a little extra cash. "I mean, even if we all think it's gross," Miles conceded, "doesn't he have a right to do it? I mean, a lot of people do the same thing." What had been a more or less settled matter—that

Paul was a risky individual increasingly at risk—was thrown into the air not only as a matter of rights but also as a question about the moral dimensions of the way normalcy is constituted as a clinical matter. Several staff responded forcefully. Cheryl sniped, "Yeah, homeless people do it!" Carlos briefly reiterated that Paul's can-collecting behavior put him at risk for a number of "health and safety issues." For one, Carlos said, "he shouldn't have extra money, because he'll buy sweets." Angela attempted to take the middle ground by asking, "What if he gets bottles from the building or the residence and he can be made to save the money?" Nicky, apparently following Miles, suggested not only that the process of assessing and monitoring Paul's risk was endless but also that counselors now seemed to have lost sight of Paul's problems and their own attempts to address them. He responded to Carlos with a sarcastic rhetorical question: "When would he be able to buy sweets anyway, if he's only out with a counselor?" Angela responded, almost as an aside, "Actually, his sugar levels have been good."

This was another first. In two months of discussion that regularly featured Paul's diabetes as a significant risk factor, there had been no mention of the technology available in the group home that could provide any kind of relatively objective way to monitor Paul's eating behaviors. His blood sugar levels were taken three times a week as part of his routine medical supervision, but nobody had adduced these numbers either for or against the changing definitions of Paul's escalating risk. It was as though, because of the degree of riskiness that had already been established—both generally and in regard to what Paul was likely to eat when out on his own—staff could make claims about the risks he posed to his health independently of the objective evidence they had at their fingertips, so to speak. It appeared to me that it had simply not occurred to the staff that Paul's blood sugar levels could or should be incorporated in their risk assessments, even though his diabetic condition and eating behaviors were major factors in their ongoing calculation. In shoptalk later that day, Angela and Carlos agreed how "funny" this was, especially given that they were the two counselors who almost always took Paul's blood sugar levels. I found this interesting also because only in late January had Beth noted a general but not dramatic increase in Paul's blood sugar levels and stepped up the frequency of the testing from once to three times per week. Clearly, enough time had passed for the new testing regimen to have become taken for granted, especially given that it produced no real news. When Angela, Carlos, and I looked at Paul's medical log, we saw that his blood sugars had been stable all that time, not often exceeding the normal range. Since June, in particular, his sugar levels had not demonstrated the upward trend or spikes that one would expect, given the focus of concern on his risky eating behaviors.

Sally's earlier suggestion that Paul be permitted out in the community alone only with a staff member was largely accepted as "the next step." Though there was some disagreement, the discussion was not at all heated, as earlier ones had been. It is possible that most of the staff didn't share Sally's worry about how to handle Paul if he was out in a group and refused to stay with everyone. Even those who endorsed taking the next step were not especially vigorous in their support, maybe because at this point they didn't need to be. Sonia attempted to use an easy resolution to close the conversation, saying she wanted to think about the staffing issues it raised and, more important, the question of whether it was truly fair at this point to limit Paul's access to the community even further. Miles took this as an opportunity to raise again his question about Paul's rights, which earlier in the meeting had been dismissed almost as though it were a rhetorical point. This time he said that the way staff understood Paul's rights couldn't be separated from how they defined their outcomes for his behavior and the kind of interventions they developed. Miles was frustrated by the inclination to increase control, given the ongoing failure to change Paul's conduct. "I mean, how long? It just seems like it would be impossible to imagine that Paul could be kept from going out for long!" This statement implied several things: that such a serious restriction should not be indefinite, that restricting a resident's movement is always serious but for Paul would substantially affect something that was particularly important to him, and/or that the escalating intervention into Paul's riskiness risked being counterproductive. There may have been other staff who agreed with Miles, but he was the only one who expressed opposition to the logic of their ongoing calculation of and intervention in Paul's risk. Nicky, in this instance, did not respond. Sonia, for her part, made no attempt to defend the assumptions about Paul that Miles called into question but responded by reiterating another familiar clinical logic that precluded pursuing the challenge: "He's benefiting from the structure!" Sonia encouraged everyone. "We're focusing him on the problem; he's feeling the intervention."

Miles later told me privately that what bothered him most about how Sonia ended the discussion wasn't so much that "she just didn't wanna hear it" as that her claim for the staff's success with Paul was simply contrary to the facts.

Endless Work

One of the reasons the group home's clinical work is prone to failure is that it is largely the work of calculating and managing something ultimately incalculable: each resident's risk. The very rhetoric and techniques of risk imply that something *must* be done. Even when there is no warrant for intervention, the work of assessment never ends, because, as group home residents, they are, by definition, "at risk." It's just a question of how risky each case is, a question for which the answer always changes, and of course the answer always changes for the same risky individual. Though the work of risk management never ends, the problem of riskiness that is fundamental to group home work provides an account of the work's failure in the uncertainty of outcomes. Uncertainty is a burden of counselor work. It is a source of conflict among them, because the idea that something can and must be done is a fundamental organizing assumption of the group home setting. Uncertainty is also their consolation. Counselors produce litanies of the risks that are a feature of their ongoing assessment work and that change as their definition of risky changes. That clinical work is actually risk administration returns us to the practical flexibility of counselors' expertise. In other words, what counselors know and do emerges in the course of their work identifying and managing risk, and this very work reflexively transforms how and why certain persons and behaviors can be seen as risky.

In Paul's case, references to diabetes invoked a range of risks to health and safety. His penchant and enthusiasm for collecting toys, giveaway promotional items, pens, and so forth, were adduced as evidence of compulsion. That he didn't pay much attention to what he ate despite what he knew was invoked as a "refusal to regulate his eating behaviors," which were, on the one hand, compulsive and, on the other, a measure of willfulness, denial, and other ostensibly psychological issues that limited his potential for independence.

So far I have described how counselors understood and acted on Paul over the first two months in a period of heightened concern about the riskiness of a person who was already considered risky. The every-day consequences of this heightened concern extended beyond the counselors' systematic interventions. The counselors were demonstrably more attentive to monitoring Paul's eating at dinner and snack time, and they were also more inclined generally to see his conduct as problem conduct. One afternoon, for example, Linda, Daniel, and I were in the office when Paul came in with a toy car he had purchased earlier that day when he was out with me. He was torn between the model he had bought and another model in the store, and now decided he'd rather have the other model. He asked if I would go out again with him so he could exchange the cars. When I told him I couldn't, because I was just about to leave, he asked Linda if she would go. Before she could answer, Daniel said, "Paul, you can't go out again today. You've already been out." Paul protested for a moment but then gave up and left the office quickly, as though he knew it would be a futile effort to challenge Daniel's ad hoc rule. As soon as Paul left, Daniel appeared obliged to offer a clinical account: "He just shouldn't go out again, because he's manic and it would reward his behavior."

Paul and I had a very pleasant relationship right from the beginning of the research period. He was good humored and outgoing and recognized that he could elicit in me, in contrast to the counselors, rather a more serious appreciation of his early film serials, collections, and other pleasures. Though Paul was very social, he was also solitary in many of his pursuits. He was selective about the rec trips he went on and was more likely to join spontaneously a group of residents on the way to a matinee. After the film, more often than not, he'd go his own way before coming home. Paul could also easily irk some residents by attempting to watch one of his videos in the living room or by taking his joking and teasing too far.

When the staff decided Paul could not go out unsupervised, he started seeking me out more often. No doubt he saw me as a ticket to go out in the community, knowing that if I wasn't already engaged I'd likely be happy to accompany him as he conducted his neighborhood business. But he could not count on this, as the preceding exchange with Daniel illustrates, so many of his requests involved activities in the house. In August, on the first day I was there after he had been restricted, he found me in the office to ask if I'd help him cut out coupons from the *Daily News* for free hot dogs from Nathan's Famous, the snack bar in Coney Island. He was always combing the paper for such things on his own, and it appeared to me in this instance that he simply wanted company. We clipped the coupons and he asked for a small envelope to keep them in order. Then we went into his room and, in private, I told him that I'd heard he wasn't allowed out without staff. "Why did they decide that?" I asked him. "Because I go in the garbage," he replied. "Oh," I said. "You must be upset about it." He shook his head no. I was surprised: "Really?" He said nothing, and we carried on with the work of organizing his coupons and clippings.

Lessons Learned

Paul's annual case conference was on August 19, just a week after Sonia decided that he could not go out unsupervised. Both Carlos and Paul's case coordinator, Michelle, were there, but Sonia played a larger role in the case conference than usual, which indicated the gravity with which the curtailment of Paul's rights was taken as well as the group home's burden of accountability. The aspects and behaviors that made Paul risky—diabetes, eating in certain ways, eating the wrong foods, hoarding, and can collecting—were all discussed, but at this meeting they were incidental to the primary justification for restricting him: his going through the garbage. "So," Sonia asked Paul, "what are you working on to be able to go out in the community independently again? What are you trying to do?" Paul was serious and contrite: "The garbage. I learned my lessons." Sonia summarized the issue briefly—for Paul, the other attendees (which included his brother and a social worker from his workshop), and no doubt for the record—and explained why it was too risky for him to be out by himself. Then Sonia looked at Paul. He looked up at her in return and, appearing obliged to respond, repeated quietly, "I learned my lessons." In an encouraging tone, Sonia then explained the problem's solution directly to Paul: "Yeah, we are helping you work on not going in the garbage by being with you. It's dangerous."

A noteworthy aside from the case conference was that the workshop social worker's account of Paul's annual progress was at odds with the group home's. According to Driggs House, the summer before, Paul's Depakote was increased at his request because he was upset about the anniversary of his mother's death, he was getting manic, and the drug stabilized him; Dr. Nunzio then reduced the dosage for some reason in May; subsequently, Paul became more emotional and his risky behaviors increased, so the dose was raised again. According to the workshop, after Paul's Depakote was increased last summer the workshop staff noted improvements that Paul had sustained ever since, and the social worker characterized the year overall in very positive terms: Paul was more cooperative, stayed on task, and was always friendly and social. Sonia was sitting next to me at the case conference. At one moment, I saw that she was poised to interrupt but didn't. The social worker, as though to make a point, interrupted herself and addressed Paul directly: "So, you just had the anniversary. How did you deal with it?" "Upset. I was upset," he said. The social worker responded by praising him for the way he had become more "courageous" and showed "more openness" in talking about "the things you feel." Paul now initiated therapy all the time, she told us, and "uses it well." The workshop staff had also noticed an increase in his hoarding behaviors, but they had implemented a behavior plan specifying what he was permitted to carry with him, and it was working. That is, Paul was working on his hoarding. Michelle, the case coordinator, asked Paul, "Do you feel good? Are you proud? You should feel that way." He was silent, so Michelle continued, adding that he should remember "the importance of recognizing your *good* feelings." With a smile she told the group that he had donated at least a hundred pens to the workshop. Everyone smiled, knowing that the pens he hadn't collected on his excursions out in the community were likely swiped from the group home, various doctors' offices, and the workshop itself. When he said he'd donate more, there were chuckles around the room. Michelle said, with affection, that "collecting things just to donate isn't really a good idea."

Part of the work of managing Paul's risk was the conflict among staff over whether his conduct was problem conduct and the kind of interventions it warranted. After a resident had an annual case conference, the primary counselor reported on it at the weekly staff meeting and described new or modified goal plans. In the first staff meeting that occurred after Paul's case conference, it was Sonia who reported to the counselors. She concluded by announcing that, because Paul "learned the lesson" and understood the dangers he posed by his behavior, she had decided he could go out on his own again, though the staff would continue shadowing him. Sonia made a point of noting that Carlos disagreed with her decision (this is likely why she, and not Carlos, reported on the case conference). Noting this disagreement was effectively an invitation to Carlos to say his piece. I had never seen him so upset, in a meeting or otherwise. Carlos recited a litany of all the dangerous things Paul could and would likely do, and all that might happen. Miles responded sympathetically but said that, in retrospect, the whole enterprise of restricting Paul had been wrong: "You know, you might be right, but these possibilities weren't enough to keep him in the house."

The changing nature of Paul's risk not only fostered disagreement but, over time, began to erode the consensus among staff. Though counselors did not talk about Paul's fluctuating risk as it related to their own changing definitions and interventions, it was perhaps the softening consensus that permitted them to ask the occasional question about even what it meant to say that Paul was at risk. The discussions I have described may suggest that the staff regarded Paul's riskiness and the curtailment of his rights as simple and self-evident. However, I must emphasize that for all the staff, including those most strident about intervening, limiting the rights of a resident, even Paul, was never taken lightly and always had a clinical basis, however arguable. In fact, counselors are well aware that curtailing a resident's rights must be formulated clinically as a behavior plan, which always requires a review by the agency administration. The rhetoric of risk, especially in regard to individual conduct, is hard to refute in a setting defined in practice by the effort to maximize the independence of individuals in order to prevent or at least reduce the problems they are likely to cause themselves.

Why Sonia changed her mind about allowing Paul to go out alone in the wake of the case conference I cannot know. At the end of the conference, I asked her what she thought about the workshop social worker's report. She acknowledged that Paul "might be a little better there [at the workshop], but the issues are different from home." She also pointed out that his hoarding had increased at the workshop, too. This is just how she presented Paul's case at the staff meeting: by capping the workshop's generally positive report about Paul with information about his increased hoarding and the plan to manage it. The continuity of an individual's services across providers is made accountable in the documentary practices that are all geared toward the annual review process, the case conference, and the individual service plan (ISP). One could imagine that Sonia changed her mind because curtailing Paul's rights appeared disproportionate in contrast to the workshop's picture of his annual progress. How well the mutual accountability across settings and OMRDD requirements produces continuity in a person's services I cannot say. What I can say is that, at Paul's case conference, Michelle did not register the group home's and the workshop's different perceptions of his risk. In the revised ISP the differences disappeared, because the annual practice of documenting progress in the ISP allows for smoothing over certain kinds of discrepancies or casting them as setting-specific.

Carlos was very upset after the staff meeting. He felt that the group home was failing Paul. A few days later, the building superintendent found Paul collecting recyclables from the sorted bins in the basement. At the next meeting, the first in September, Carlos was adamant: "Paul is really impossible." Cheryl expressed her disapproval of Paul, saying, "That's *not* okay," and, to Sonia, "I think he should be told that the super told you about it." Everyone agreed that this was important. Everyone also seemed to agree that getting cans and bottles from the building was "not okay." Because the incident was taken simply as further evidence of Paul's compulsion, no distinction could be recognized between the contexts of can-collecting behavior. No one disagreed with Carlos when he said that "doing it in the building is just going to lead to trouble. Even when a counselor is with him [in the community], his eyes shift toward the garbage cans." Some counselors chuckled despite Carlos's urgency, because, in fact, it was one of the first staff meetings in some time in which talk about Paul implied some kind of stabilization or diminishing concern. On this jocular note, Sonia expressed a certain disappointment that he'd gotten into some new trouble: "And he's been in a great mood lately." Some of the counselors nodded. Angela told a story about how Paul was cracking everybody up at a doctor's office earlier that week, including two pharmaceutical salespeople who had given him pens, notepads, and "you name it." The staff were laughing, and the story was appreciative of Paul. Angela mockingly threw her hands up and said, "I know he's not supposed to get stuff like that, but I couldn't help it." Sonia then asked whether Paul was just in a manic phase but immediately qualified her question—"I mean, I don't mean to be too . . . you know . . ."—indicating that she was being hasty, looking for the negative, or had introduced (or reintroduced) concerns that were not the focus of the conversation. But it was too late. Miles used Sonia's apparently offhand remark to return to the still-volatile dispute about can collecting, now in the building: "He just can't be restricted for *that*." Cheryl disagreed: "Yes, he can, Miles! Health and safety take priority." Daniel seconded her comment: "It's sometimes necessary to violate a resident's rights," and added mockingly, "his 'sacred' rights." For those counselors who advocated restricting Paul, a tone of exasperated defiance sometimes implied not only the self-evident nature of the problem and the solution but also their own courage in "seeing things for what they are."

Seeing Clearly

Most of the time, we can't help what we see, it seems, because we know what we see when (and as) we see it. One evening after dinner that same week, I saw Paul eating potatoes that were left at the bottom of a pot waiting to be washed. He wasn't aware that I saw him, and I was able to suppress my impulse to say something. The impulse itself surprised me not just because of my committed nonstaff identity but also because the least troublesome aspect of being at Driggs House was my personal relationships with the residents. To say that I never saw them as the group home staff did would be disingenuous, but, especially out of the staff's view, I had experienced almost no conflict about whether to act on a resident's conduct in the expected clinical ways. Later that evening, Paul and I were joking around, when he happened to bring up what we had eaten for dinner. I said, laughing, "Yeah, you liked the potatoes enough to eat the rest from the pot in the sink!" He laughed, too, and then just grinned.

I had a different experience ten days later, when a whole bunch of us were down for coffee one night. I had already gotten Paul to use artificial sweetener by acting as though he had made an innocent mistake as he was about to put sugar in his cup, and handing him the artificial sweetener instead. When Paul finished his roll (with jelly!), he wanted to order a bagel, and I just couldn't help talking him out of it. This didn't take much effort, and our personal relationship allowed it. Giving in to this impulse reflected the trust and comfort between us, and though talking him out of the bagel was a personal reflex, it traded on the staff authority from which I so conscientiously tried to maintain distance. This confusing moment in the management of my personal identity points to my rapport with Paul, but this I soon realized had nothing to do with his easy willingness to forgo the bagel.

When he, Ruby, and I walked to the corner newsstand, I learned that after paying for his roll and coffee, he had a mere thirty-five cents in his pocket. We went to the newsstand because Marty hadn't felt like coming down and asked me to pick up a magazine for him. Ruby was just along for the walk, and Paul wanted mints. Of course, the clerk knew him and was willing to take the thirty-five cents he had in exchange for the seventy-five-cent item he had chosen. I was looking for Marty's magazine when I noticed that Paul had chosen mints with sugar, and, without thinking, I bellowed at him. He smiled—"Okay, okay!"—and took the kind without sugar instead.

The counselors were not wrong that Paul understood his diabetic condition and knew which foods to avoid yet ate them anyway, but they regarded this behavior as either pathological compulsion or willful defiance. I can offer no explanation for why Paul was willing to eat jelly or purchase regular candies when they were available without sugar; but I'm not sure one is required, given that these are the sorts of things people with diabetes do all the time—that is, people with diabetes who do not happen also to be considered intellectually disabled. Yet the counselors' explanations, though unsupportable, were accountable in terms of group home work. Paul's choices were willfully bad or uncontrollable.

Paul was a lively, charismatic man, something the counselors often appreciated. At the same time, these were the very qualities that could be seen as manic, compulsive, devious, and defiant. I was more impressed than the staff were by Paul's resourcefulness, perhaps for the simple reason that I was nonstaff. Miles was the exception. He was the only counselor who had raised questions about whether some of Paul's activities out in the community fell within the bounds of his freedom even if the staff found them risky, not to mention objectionable. Though a few local shopkeepers refused to deal with him, for the most part he was a well-known neighborhood character who had established a kind of credit at many places. He was a skillful negotiator, as it were, in those moments when he was short of money, needed to exchange something, or wanted to maximize his take on free promotional items. Through a combination of humor and sometimes-feigned confusion, he knew full well when he was trading on perceptions of him as a person "from that group home." It seems to me that Paul understood such transactions as a kind of charity (the word is mine) that reflected the personal relationships he had developed around the neighborhood. As for my perception that his confusion with money and making change was sometimes feigned in these situations, my only basis is having observed him many times make purchases, check his change, and appear to calculate prices in ways that implied a facility with money, but I cannot know whether or how he did (cf. Lave). What this actually means I cannot know. I also cannot know whether, in fact, he really did trade on others' perceptions of him as different and therefore "deserving." Once when we were out and Paul had purchased a toy airplane, I asked why he thought the clerk let him buy it even though he was short of the marked price. Paul replied simply, "He's nice. Dunno." If he did work such an angle, he would not likely have discussed it, because it was yet another thing he did on his own out in the community that would have been discouraged by staff as inappropriate (or worse). For this reason, it was not an issue I pressed.

By the end of September, Paul was allowed out again, and additional procedures had been lifted. Staff were still at odds; those who preferred he be restricted argued for the reinstatement of the "search and seizure" plan that, a few weeks earlier, everyone agreed had failed. Paul remained on the radar, but things seemed to settle down, if one indication is the amount of time and intensity devoted to him in shoptalk.

Things were quiet, as it were, until Halloween. I was out in the late afternoon with Marty, Donna, and Evelyn and noticed that all the shops had candy or little toys to hand out to trick-or-treaters. Costumed children were being ushered in groups from store to store. I didn't think twice about this until later that evening, when the group home received a call from the emergency room of the local hospital. Paul had been out in the community and felt dizzy. He saw an ambulance and approached the crew, who were standing around on a coffee break. They took him in. The emergency room staff said that his blood sugar level was slightly elevated but fine. Mike happened to be in the house that night, so he and Miles went to retrieve Paul. Waiting for them to return, the rest of us in the house all assumed that Paul had simply eaten loads of candy. Sally said, "See, I knew he should never have been allowed back in the community." But Paul claimed that he hadn't eaten much candy, and, given his blood sugar levels, it was likely the truth. The counselors acknowledged this but nonetheless regarded the whole episode as evidence of Paul's "drama" and "attention seeking," especially because the ambulance he approached happened to be fewer than two blocks from the residence.

Paul was well aware he had caused a stir. A few hours after he was home, he and I were alone in Sonia's office. He asked me whether he had done the right thing in approaching the ambulance as opposed to coming home. I said yes, especially if he had been unsure about what to do. He was lying down on Sonia's couch, while I was at the desk with my feet up. After a few minutes, he asked me to get a counselor, because he didn't feel well, and he was dizzy again. Sally came in and tested his blood sugar, which was only at the high end of the normal range. He was relieved. He asked Sally, "How will I take my shower if I'm dizzy?" She told him just to wait and see how he felt in a little while. Then, when he said he didn't want to go to work the next day, Sally replied, "Oh, so that's where this is leading."

The result of Halloween was that Paul was once again not allowed out without a staff member. But by late November, the counselors thought Paul did not require such extensive supervision. Angela told Sonia in a staff meeting that "everyone had been talking a lot about Paul" and wondered whether there was any way the restriction could be eased without being lifted completely. She suggested that Paul might be permitted out in the evening with Theresa and David just to go down for coffee. Sonia rejected this idea immediately on the grounds that it would be unfair to Theresa: she would feel responsible, and Paul just couldn't be trusted. It was a risk. Sonia said that things should continue as they were.

And they did—until the second week of December, when Paul managed to slip out the door during the usual afternoon hubbub between 3:00 and 4:00. He returned after an hour or so with a toy car he had been eager to purchase. Sonia was furious, but not with Paul so much as with staff. She devoted most of the next staff meeting to the incident, asking Mike to attend, and led a discussion about how to handle Paul generally. Sonia's reaction to his slipping out unnoticed clearly reflected her sense of accountability as supervisor, but she was somewhat oblique on this point. It seemed to me that she didn't want this fact to appear more important than Paul himself. Sonia was slightly defensive in her tone when counselors didn't see themselves as particularly culpable or regard the incident as posing a new or unique risk. "But this makes us look silly," she said. Mike responded in defense of the counselors but sympathetically to Sonia: "Well, 'silly' *is* too strong. It's not a lockdown facility." Sonia nodded but turned the topic back to Paul, focusing on how potentially serious such an incident could be for him. He lives here "for his own good," she said, and because "we care about him, we need to protect him, because he cannot protect himself." But it's true: Driggs House isn't a lockdown facility, and counselor work does not require, nor would it permit, stationing someone at the front door. Sonia pursued the discussion about Paul, emphasizing the counselors' role by raising another recent incident when Paul got away from staff and other residents out in the community. "We can't be losing him . . . like that," she concluded. Cheryl suggested developing a procedure specifying when and with how many others Paul should be permitted to go out. But it seemed that new ideas about interventions and procedures weren't what Sonia was after, so much as some recognition from the counselors of their responsibility in these matters. She impatiently replied to the group that if any staff "can't handle" going out with him *and* others, then they should postpone the outing: "He'll just have to wait. . . . But he needs our help right now, just be aware."

And So On

The way Paul was acted on as a risky individual over time illustrates how group home work is largely the ongoing reflexive work of risk administration. This was true for all the residents but was especially obvious with Paul, for whom the inherent conflict between supervision and liberty was often particularly acute. What was the group home's role in encouraging Paul to become more independent? What characterizes the expertise that staff use in their work? How is an annual experience of mourning over the loss of an intimate distinguished from a pathological preoccupation with the death? How and when can affect be regarded as a predictor of certain kinds of conduct? When does routine conduct become risky? The work of managing Paul as a risky individual was a practical matter. The factors constituting warrantable risk are ever changing in relation to—or at least are inseparable from—the continuous monitoring and intervention that is fundamental group home work. What determined Paul's level of riskiness was always contingent on the situated ways that counselors could know and act on clinical problems. Even in the absence of problems, reasonable conduct can become a clinical problem simply when its unremarkable aspect is seen as an indication of the probability of problem conduct.

CONCLUSION

Making Life Work

THE RHETORIC OF RISK is terribly compelling in a setting organized to supervise individuals by cultivating their independence. One aspect of this in practice is working to reduce the problems residents are likely to cause themselves. It's not difficult to see how they could be presumed to be always at risk, given that risk administration is a primary function of psychiatry and psychology in the community. Yet, beyond this complex topography, the problem of risk is central to everyday life everywhere. The ways residents govern themselves, however circumscribed by the group home's organizational demands and documentary practices, illustrate the forms that freedom can take in contemporary liberal societies.

Being a resident at Driggs House does make for a different kind of life than the life of those of us who live out in the community on our own, but the pervasive ethic of autonomy makes all of us at risk in one sense or another. Though contemporary society, despite its many problems, may be the safest and healthiest in history, there is a pervasive assumption that the world is fraught with danger, that everyday life poses constant threats to well-being. We see ourselves as always and forever at risk. As Deborah Lupton argues (1993, 1999), in the United States and places like it, much of social and personal life is organized by the practices of identifying and managing risk. The term "risk" itself no longer refers to probability but instead has come to mean danger. Moreover, because of the assumption about the centrality of individual conduct in both posing and managing risk, the term means not only danger but moral danger. In a culture of "healthism," as Monica Greco puts it (357), "the idea [is that] one's health is an enterprise of oneself"—that is, there is a "duty to be well." "To live," she goes on, "is already and ever-increasingly to be at-risk [because] the pathologization of risk goes hand in hand with the perceived need to make every aspect of one's life 'healthy'" (360). The reduction and management of risk is understood as ultimately being within the grasp of individuals alone, because we have come to regard health and happiness as outcomes of personal choice. We all, more or less, believe that we are responsible for the risks we face or, at least, that we can ward them off by the way we choose to conduct ourselves. Moreover, to pursue healthiness in the absence of disease "conveys connotations of alarm and urgency: to 'prevent' becomes . . . to 'cure'" (360). Such a moral imperative makes sense of the claim at Driggs House that "something, *anything*, must be done!"

Risk management always involves psy practice both inside and outside the group home. Rose does not explain the vast diffusion of psy knowledge as a cultural or social problem but approaches it empirically, investigating the use of psy technologies in a range of settings, from the workplace to the work of the therapist's office, and in the everyday techniques of the self that are widely used by individuals to understand and act on themselves. The cultural dissemination of psy was tied initially to discipline formation in psychology. The late-nineteenth-century focus on pathology yielded knowledge about normal life that transformed it. J. G. Morawski (1997, 217) shows that psychology textbooks through the early twentieth century were central to the wide dissemination of new ideas about human emotion and the self, and their complex relationships to the social organization of both academic knowledge production and American life. Textbooks have largely been overlooked by historians of science, because they are a "literary genre . . . regarded as neither wholly scientific nor simply popular," and, for this reason, they bridge the presumed boundaries between science and culture. From within the ostensibly proper domain of psychological work as well, Morawski (1988, 1994) argues that the initial adoption of procedures of experimental method and the organization of research settings fashioned new identities and forms of cognition for subjects and observers in the laboratory and beyond. Rose (1999a, 1985) argues similarly, in his research on feeblemindedness, that various representations (in photos, numerical translations, and spatial arrangement of experimental settings) transformed mothers and babies into technical objects in ways that shaped both foundational assumptions in psychology and basic popular assumptions about normal development and childhood.

CONCLUSION   *245*

Through the twentieth century, the broadening relevance of psychology meant that techniques of psy management were adapted across many spheres of normal life. That normal life required expert attention implied not only that managing pathological difference within society itself was possible but that *preventing* it was, too. As Sol Cohen argues, the personality of the student became a central focus in education by the 1930s. Analogously, in the workplace, the human relations movement saw increased productivity as resulting from the healthy interaction of well-adjusted workers (Rose 1999a).

Insofar as psy provides the ethical basis for autonomy in contemporary societies, the cultural obsession with health and self-improvement that compels group home residents to work on themselves makes them not so very different from the rest of us. As the central theme of this book has shown, resident work throws into relief what we all do in many large and small ways to live right, to live better. Resident work is but one example of the therapeutic ethic that, as Rose describes (1998b, 159), "impels the subject to 'work' on itself, to take responsibility for its life. It seeks to equip the self with a set of tools for the management of its affairs such that it can take control of its undertakings, define its goals, and plan to achieve its needs through its own powers." The equation of autonomy with activity, self-knowledge, and health can be seen in the government of welfare recipients through self-esteem building (Cruikshank) and in employment programs that govern individuals not as unemployed persons but as "job seekers" (Dean 1995). "Self-empowerment," only recently the rallying cry of antiprofessional movements, is now a central objective for all social services (Baistow).

Even getting old is defined by an ethic of activity. The ordinary, occasional difficulty experienced in later life has been taken up by gerontology as a universal problem of adjustment (Katz). Being well adjusted in old age means being "active," and this ideal organizes everyday life itself as the prevention of poor adjustment and its potential consequences: dependence, illness, and loneliness. A similar ethic of activity defines the risks and demands posed by life at its very start. Some of the most influential research in developmental psychology rests on the way laboratory observations of infants reflect cultural aspirations and political ideals of autonomy and the individuated self (Cushman). For parenting experts, by the 1980s, autonomy had become the primary developmental goal, based on the idea that infants require a high level of intellectual stimulation, which in turn requires "active" parenting and "observant" (rather than "passive") care (Wrigley).

Group home residents, too, govern themselves according to an ethic of autonomy that requires them to take their own selves actively as objects of work. It is true that many of my descriptions of Driggs House illustrate the inequality between counselors and residents. No doubt some readers will find certain examples just plain disturbing, but certainly not surprising. Nevertheless, my observations illustrate also the complex character of authority in the group home, and my study neither refutes nor precludes the prescient concerns with the limited rights, as well as outright violations, that remain widespread in community services. Insofar as I have addressed this issue, I have done so indirectly from another angle, by showing how rights and autonomy pose ongoing practical issues that organize Driggs House in fundamentally different ways than does the direct coercion that is characteristic of other settings. What I have shown is that group home work is the work of governing because authority is not simply exercised in opposition to the autonomy of individual residents and, further, that authority seeks to shape the very capacities for autonomy on which the group home depends. At Driggs House, as elsewhere in liberal societies, social regulation depends fundamentally on practices of self-regulation that align the goals and aspirations of free individuals with those of the whole.

About ten years will have passed between the start of my research at Driggs House and the publication of this book. In this time, there have been some regulatory changes, yet they require no particular explication: all aim to further the role of services in fostering the autonomy of individuals and demonstrate the expanding rhetoric of "partnership" and "putting people first" (OMRDD 2008). Also, I have learned anecdotally that across a number of agencies in New York City, "consumer" has finally supplanted "client" in everyday life. Moreover, there have been increasing limits on the maximum number of persons who may live in new community residences (which are now often called "individual residential alternatives"), as well as the development of more programs on an even smaller scale, serving two or three people. By the time I started at Driggs House, its fifteen residents actually exceeded, by one, the maximum number permitted in new facilities; that number is down now from fourteen to eight. Most notably, changes to the Medicaid waiver program enable even more easily the aims of individualized services (OMRDD 2006, 2008). These changes were a response to the criticism in the mid-1900s of, among others, the New York State Commission on Quality of Care for the Mentally Disabled that the HCBS waiver resulted less in truly individualized services than in financial advantages for participating states.

The focus on individualization and participation reflects a trend across all services. Some researchers who value these aims nonetheless see them critically in the context of broad political and economic changes. They argue that acknowledging and incorporating the individuality of individuals became truly possible only in the 1980s, when reductions in government support resulted in the dramatic reorganization of health and social services (Tomes; Yeatman and Penglase). For Nancy Tomes, principles of self-determination and consumer empowerment were largely ignored in the 1970s and cannot be understood as the cause of transformations in services in the United States. On the contrary, these principles could become the measure of an enlightened perspective only as a consequence of the political and economic restructuring of health and social services that began in the 1980s. Yeatman and Penglase point to an emphasis on outcomes in individualized services that involves ever-intensive monitoring not just of service outcomes but also of individual participation. In a way very similar to my description of the role that paper technologies play in group home work, individualized service takes shape "in a continuous and documented process of planning" in which "the documentation becomes a rolling strategic plan in the management" of each individual (Yeatman and Penglase, 237–38). Despite all this, these critics do not dismiss the aims of individualization and self-determination merely because the "emphasis on outcomes fits the current ethos of performance management and results-oriented government" (Yeatman and Penglase, 235). They do not agree with arguments that reduce new service models to mere ideology (Singh and Cowan) and that mistake as a programmatic weakness the "inevitable tension" between self-determination as a service goal and "top down demands" for accountability (Yeatman and Penglase, 244).

From my own perspective, to be quite frank, I thought psy knowledge played a far greater role at Driggs House than seemed necessary to create a supportive residential environment. This could have been due to the quality of training or supervision at Driggs House. Though I did not investigate this possibility, my judgment is that the staff discharged their duties adequately, certainly in the group home's own terms. The plausible explanation is that, in a world organized by a therapeutic ethic of autonomy, any adequate residential setting more than likely relies on the extensive use of psy. This is what I have argued throughout: not only are the dilemmas of freedom posed by the integration of intellectual disability defined and managed as individual clinical problems, but also the very flexibility that allows psy to cross fields as an ethical basis for government makes psy difficult to contain, especially in the intimate setting of a group home, where the beginning and end of work are always situated matters.

On the one hand, I am more than sympathetic to the ideas that challenge the persistence of a professional agenda in the community by increasing the participation and decision-making power of individuals with intellectual disability. On the other, these ideas too often fail to recognize not only that professional authority rests in part on psy knowledge and practice but also that the antiprofessional critiques do, too. It is precisely the ideals of person-centeredness, self-direction, quality of life, and supports (rather than services) that indicate the constitutive role psy authority plays in governing individuals who are free yet somehow incapable of freedom. Duncan Ivison (3) makes an analogous point about the concept of liberty in political theory. Liberty was framed through the late twentieth century by Isaiah Berlin's dichotomous ideas of positive and negative freedom—either freedom *to* or freedom *from* interference—but "liberalism is a complex tradition, and it has been equally concerned, at different times, not only with protecting and securing spheres of individual liberty but with conditioning and structuring the liberties taken therein." The inordinate focus on "the degree to which freedom from interference is a central measure of an individual's liberty" makes it difficult to think about liberty in other ways, especially in terms of the specific contexts and practices that shape our ideas about it at particular times.

Whatever their limits, the increasingly influential approaches that aim to reduce or limit professional authority and to enhance individuality and participation reflect the continuing "governmentalization" of services in the community. These approaches may well resonate with current versions of liberal individualism, but they also provide, in psy practice, a way of managing the inherent tension between liberty and supervision that organizes Driggs House and similar settings. This trend of "responsibilization" (Rose 1999b) extends beyond disability and across social service and policy, requiring individuals to take more and more responsibility for themselves as both subjects and objects of their own expertise in life's ordinary pleasures and sorrows. The trend is hardly unique to social services and the helping professions. It encompasses those of us who live independently but must also govern ourselves more and more by making everyday life work. That group home residents must take their own selves as ongoing projects of independence reflects a therapeutic ethic in contemporary life that urges us all to be working endlessly on ourselves. This concern with ethics is not simply a question about values in the sociological sense; it refers to the way everyday life is pervasively organized by innumerable physical, psychological, and spiritual techniques of the self and the goals of conduct those techniques both translate and pursue: self-improvement, self-knowledge, growth, and health among them. These omnipresent techniques furnish a fundamental know-how in contemporary society, and not only at Driggs House.

To argue that resident work is but one example of broader ethical practices of the self is not to deny that the group home ultimately does make residents' lives profoundly different from everyone else's. The residents do not have certain freedoms most of us take for granted, such as the relative absence of other people authorized to monitor the details of our normal lives. The endless work residents do on themselves may appear vastly different from the work of those who are properly free to choose how to know and act on themselves. The particular conception of freedom this presumes, however, derives from the taken-for-granted everyday practices that equate freedom and choice with autonomy. Freedom from the endless monitoring and assessment of normal life is one freedom that, in principle, certainly should be extended to group home residents. Yet it is difficult to imagine an alternative to psy knowledge as the ethical basis for government in contemporary American society. And aren't we all—as students, employees, family members, citizens—subject to various forms of endless monitoring? Our own ethical practices always occur "under the actual or imagined authority of some system of truth," as Rose puts it (1998b, 29), and these practices are already organized largely as activities of endless *self*-monitoring.

I do not mean to overlook the no doubt wide variation of individual participation in such pursuits, nor do I mean to resort to caricature to make the comparison between group home residents and everyone else. I cannot deny that a resident is, in fact, quite a different kind of person by virtue of his or her group home life. Perhaps this study yields little insight about the ethics of conduct in general, only a reminder that it is not just residents who must govern themselves, or who do so through the endless enhancement of the normal self; self-government in the group home is simply easier to see because of the particular organizational and documentary character of the practices that make residents' lives work. Seen this way, it stands to reason that, whatever the technologies of conduct available, to know and work on one's self as a certain kind of person—as each resident must do—is to reveal what we all do, however unwittingly, to make life work.

NOTES

Introduction

1. This and all subsequent similar citations are to Mental Hygiene Law, Title 14, of the New York Codes, Rules, and Regulations (N.Y.C.R.R.).

2. There is, in addition, a pool of regular substitute counselors, mostly full-time direct-service employees at other facilities in the agency who are well known to the residents. They are also racially and ethnically diverse, are mostly women, and are in their twenties and early thirties.

2. Governing Disability in the Community

1. See, for example, Bercovici; Copp 1998a; Foster; Goode 1983; Goode and Waksler; Heshusius; Johnson; Kielhofner; Kliewer and Drake; Myers, Ager, Kerr, and Myles; Rose-Ackerman; Stroman; Taylor 2001; Taylor, Bogdan, and Lutfiyya; Wing; and Young and Quibell.

2. See, for example, Bogdan and Taylor 1982, 1987, 1989a, 1989b; Gleason; Goode 1983, 1994; Goode and Waksler; Heshusius; Jacobs; Langness and Levine; and Pollner and Goode.

3. See Davis 1995, 1997; Linton; Oliver; and Tremain.

4. See, for example, Angrosino 1997a, 1997b, 1992; Baroff; Bogdan and Taylor 1982, 1987, 1989a; Danforth and Navarro; Devlieger; Dowse; Dudley; Ferguson; Gillman, Heyman, and Swain; Radford; Rapley, Kiernan, and Antaki; Simpson 1996b; Stockholder; Taylor 2000; and Woodill.

5. Some of the areas in which researchers have studied governmentality are accounting (Hopwood and Miller), alcohol regulation and alcoholism (Valverde), child abuse and prevention (Parton), criminology (Smandych), the emergence of economic science and the economy (D. Burchell; Miller and Rose), education (A. Barron), insurance and risk (Ewald), poverty (Procacci), the medical profession (Osborne), community psychiatry (Castel; Rose 1996b, 1998), psychology (Rose 1996a), statistical sciences (Hacking 1986), unemployment (Dean 1995), welfare programs for women (Cruikshank), and transformations in the welfare state (Barry,

Osborne, and Rose; Rose 1999). For comprehensive accounts of the theoretical and empirical contributions of governmentality, see Dean 1999; and Rose 1999.

3. The Work of Everyday Life

1. For studies of work and organizations, see, for example, Garfinkel 1986; Lynch 1985, 1993; Rawls 2008; Suchman; and Orr. Studies on the sociology of deviance and social control include, for example, Sudnow 1965, 1967; and Wieder.

2. See also Mitchell 1983, 1984; and Van Velsen.

7. Expertise and the Work of Staff Meetings

1. The *DSM* refers to the American Psychiatric Association's *Diagnostic and Statistical Manual of Mental Disorders,* which, since the 1980s, has been the diagnostic standard in mental health practice across fields. There was a copy of the *DSM* in the staff office, though I only ever saw Cynthia take it off the shelf, which was notable to me because she was the behavior specialist.

8. Paper Technologies

1. See Beaulieu 2001, 2002; Dumit; Garfinkel, Lynch, and Livingston; Knorr-Cettina and Mulkay; Lynch 1985, 1993; and Traweek.

2. The focus of most social science research has been on the unintended consequences or inappropriate use of records and written documents: as instruments of client control or worker discretion in people-processing work (Goffman 1961; Lipsky; McCleary; Meehan; Prottas), as professional organizational accounts that contrast with the perceptions and experience of crime victims (Fleury, Sullivan, and Bybee) and patients (Weiss), as inaccurate accounts of actual social work practice (Floersch; Monnickendam, Yaniv, and Geva), as evidence of racial and ethnic bias in juvenile justice (Mesch and Fishman) and in hospital (Weiss), or, more broadly, as central to control in organizations historically (Wheeler; Yates).

3. Social Security Act § 1915[c]; U.S. Department of Health and Human Services Health Care Financing Administration, 42 CFR 430.25.

4. I provide here only an overview of the waiver program, and my discussion is limited to those aspects which are relevant to group home work. For example, I do not address the complex calculation of room and board fees, which are paid by a combination of an individual's federal entitlement and OMRDD funds, because this work is done not at Driggs House but at the main office of its parent agency. Since I completed my fieldwork, there have been some changes in the federal funding scheme and OMRDD practice, which I address briefly in the conclusion of the book.

5. The OMRDD is apparently concerned about its own contribution to a bureaucratic climate that discourages participation. One Medicaid Service Coordinator training manual instructs, "Avoid Acronyms. The use of unexplained or

confusing acronyms puts people off, and makes them feel uninformed. It's okay to use acronyms—after you have explained what they mean" (OMRDD 2000).

6. The allowable categories of service are training in health skills, self-administration of medication, socialization skills, communication skills, assertiveness/self-advocacy skills, behavior skills, community integration and resources utilization skills, motor skills, and employment skills (14 N.Y.C.R.R. § 671.5; 14 N.Y.C.R.R. § 635.10-4).

BIBLIOGRAPHY

AAIDD. *See* American Association on Intellectual and Developmental Disabilities.

AAMR. *See* American Association of Mental Retardation.

American Association of Mental Retardation. 1992. *Mental Retardation: Definition, Classification, and Systems of Supports,* 9th ed. Washington, D.C.: American Association of Mental Retardation.

American Association on Intellectual and Developmental Disabilities. 2002. http://aamr.org/Policies/mental_retardation.shtml (accessed May 2008).

Angrosino, M. 1992. "Metaphors of Stigma: How Deinstitutionalized Mentally Retarded Adults See Themselves." *Journal of Contemporary Ethnography* 21 (2): 171–99.

———. 1997a. "The Ethnography of Mental Retardation: An Applied Perspective." *Journal of Contemporary Ethnography* 26 (1): 98–109.

———. 1997b. *Opportunity House: Ethnographic Stories of Mental Retardation.* Thousand Oaks, Calif.: Sage.

Argent, N. 2005. "The Neoliberal Seduction: Governing-at-a-Distance, Community Development, and the Battle over Financial Services Provision in Australia." *Geographical Research* 43 (1): 29–39.

Attewell, P. 1990. "What Is Skill?" *Work and Occupations* 17 (4): 422–48.

———. 1992. "Skill and Occupational Changes in U.S. Manufacturing." In *Technology and the Future of Work,* ed. P. Adler. New York: Oxford University Press.

Baistow, K. 1994. "Liberation and Regulation? Some Paradoxes of Empowerment." *Critical Social Policy* 14 (42): 34–46.

Baker, P., and D. Bissmire. 2000. "A Pilot Study of the Use of Physical Intervention in the Crisis Management of People with Intellectual Disabilities Who Present Challenging Behaviour." *Journal of Applied Research in Intellectual Disabilities* 13:38–45.

Banks, I. 2000. *Hair Matters: Beauty, Power, and Black Women's Consciousness.* New York: New York University Press.

Bannerman, D., J. Sheldon, J. Sherman, and A. Harchik. 1990. "Balancing the Right to Habilitation with the Right to Personal Liberties: The Rights of

People with Developmental Disabilities to Eat Too Many Donuts and Take a Nap." *Journal of Applied Behavior Analysis* 23 (1): 79–89.

Barnes, C., and M. Oliver. 1995. "Disability Rights: Rhetoric and Reality in the UK." *Disability and Society* 10 (1): 111–16.

Barnes, M. 1997. *Care, Communities, and Citizens.* London: Longman.

Baroff, G. 1999. General Learning Disorder: A New Designation for Mental Retardation." *Mental Retardation* (February): 68–70.

Barron, A. 1996. "The Governance of Schooling: Genealogies of Control and Empowerment in the Reform of Public Education." *Studies in Law, Politics, and Society* 15:167–204.

Barron, K. 2001. "Autonomy in Everyday Life, for Whom?" *Disability and Society* 16 (3): 31.

Barry, A., T. Osborne, and N. Rose. 1996. Introduction to *Foucault and Political Reason: Liberalism, Neo-liberalism, and Rationalities of Government,* ed. A. Barry, T. Osborne, and N. Rose. Chicago: University of Chicago Press.

Beaulieu, A. 2001. "Voxels in the Brain." *Social Studies of Science* 31 (5): 635–80.

———. 2002. "Images Are Not the Only Truth: Brain Mapping, Visual Knowledge, and Iconoclasm." *Science, Technology, and Human Values* 27 (1): 53–86.

Becker, H. 1963. *Outsiders: Studies in the Sociology of Deviance.* Glencoe, Ill.: Free Press.

Beckett, A. 2006. *Citizenship and Vulnerability: Disability and Issues of Social and Political Engagement.* London: Palgrave Macmillan.

Bercovici, S. 1983. *Barriers to Normalization: The Restrictive Management of Retarded Persons.* Baltimore: University Park Press.

Berkowitz, E. 1980. "The Politics of Mental Retardation during the Kennedy Administration." *Social Science Quarterly* 61 (1): 128.

Blau, P. 1963. *The Dynamics of Bureaucracy.* Chicago: University of Chicago Press.

Blumer, H. 1969. *Symbolic Interaction.* Englewood Cliffs, N.J.: Prentice-Hall.

Bogdan, R., and S. Taylor. 1982. *Inside Out: The Social Meaning of Mental Retardation.* Toronto: University of Toronto Press.

———. 1987. "Toward a Sociology of Acceptance: The Other Side of the Study of Deviance." *Social Policy* (Fall): 34–39.

———. 1989a. "Relationships with Severely Disabled People: The Social Construction of Humanness." *Social Problems* 36:135–48.

———. 1989b. "What's in a Name?" In *Making Connections: Reflecting on the Lives and Experiences of People with Learning Difficulties,* ed. A. Brechnin and J. Walmsley. London: Hodder and Stoughton.

Braddock, D., R. Hemp, M. Rizzolo, D. Coulter, L. Haffer, and M. Thompson. 2005. *The State of the States in Developmental Disabilities: 2005.* Boulder: University of Colorado, Department of Psychiatry.

Braginsky, B., and D. Braginsky. 1971. *Hansels and Gretels: Studies of Children in Institutions for the Mentally Retarded.* New York: Holt, Rinehart, and Winston.

Braginsky, D., B. Braginsky, and K. Ring. 1969. *Methods of Madness: The Mental Hospital as Last Resort.* New York: Holt, Rinehart, and Winston.

Brockley, J. 1999. "History of Mental Retardation: A Review Essay." *History of Psychology* 2 (1): 25–36.

———. 2004. "Rearing the Child Who Never Grew: Ideologies of Parenting and Intellectual Disability in America." In *Mental Retardation in America,* ed. S. Noll and J. Trent. New York: New York University Press.

Brown, H., and H. Smith. 1992. Introduction to *Normalisation: A Reader for the Nineties,* ed. H. Brown and H. Smith. London: Routledge.

Buck, P. 1950. *The Child Who Never Grew.* Bethesda, Md.: Woodbine House.

Burchell, D. 1998. "'The Mutable Minds of Particular Men': The Emergence of Economic Science and Contemporary Economic Policy." In *Governing Australia: Studies in Contemporary Rationalities of Government,* ed. M. Dean and B. Hindess. Cambridge: Cambridge University Press.

Burchell, G. 1996. "Liberal Government and Techniques of the Self." In *Foucault and Political Reason: Liberalism, Neo-liberalism, and Rationalities of Government,* ed. A. Barry, T. Osborne, and N. Rose. Chicago: University of Chicago Press.

Byrd, A., and L. Tharps. 2001. *Hair Story: Untangling the Roots of Black Hair in America.* New York: St. Martin's.

Callon, M. 1986. "Some Elements of a Sociology of Translation: Domestication of the Scallops and the Fishermen of St Brieuc Bay." In *Power, Action, and Belief: A New Sociology of Knowledge?* ed. J. Law. London: Routledge and Kegan Paul.

———. 1987. "Society in the Making: The Study of Technology as a Tool for Sociological Analysis." In *The Social Construction of Technological Systems: New Directions in the Sociology and History of Technology,* ed. W. Bijker, T. Hughes, and T. Pinch. Cambridge: MIT Press.

Campos, P. 2004. *The Obesity Myth.* New York: Gotham.

Caplan, G. 1961. *An Approach to Community Mental Health.* New York: Grune and Stratton.

Castel, R. 1991. "From Dangerousness to Risk." In *The Foucault Effect: Studies in Governmentality,* ed. G. Burchell, C. Gordon, and P. Miller. Chicago: University of Chicago Press.

Castellani, P. 2005. *From Snake Pits to Cash Cows: Politics and Public Institutions in New York.* Albany: State University of New York Press.

Chadwick, A. 1996. "Knowledge, Power, and the Disability Discrimination Bill." *Disability and Society* 11 (1): 25–40.

Cicourel, A. 1964. *Method and Measurement in Sociology.* Glencoe, Ill.: Free Press.

Cohen, Sol. 1983. "The Mental Hygiene Movement, the Development of Personality, and the School: The Medicalization of American Education." *History of Education Quarterly* (Summer).

Cohen, Stanley. 1985. *Visions of Social Control: Crime, Punishment, and Classification.* New York: Polity.

Cooper, D. 1967. *Psychiatry and Anti-psychiatry*. New York: Ballantine.

Copp, M. 1998a. "Adult-Adolescents: Social Control of Sexuality and Adulthood in People with Developmental Disabilities." *Sociological Analysis* 1 (3).

———. 1998b. "When Emotion Work Is Doomed to Fail: Ideological and Structural Constraints on Emotion Management." *Symbolic Interaction* 21 (3): 299–328.

Coulter, J. 1973. *Approaches to Insanity: A Philosophical and Sociological Study*. New York: Wiley.

Cowden, S., and G. Singh. 2007. "The 'User': Friend, Foe, or Fetish? A Critical Exploration of User Involvement in Health and Social Care." *Critical Social Policy* 27 (1): 5–23.

Cruikshank, B. 1999. *The Will to Empower: Democratic Citizens and Other Subjects*. Ithaca, N.Y.: Cornell University Press.

Cushman, P. 1991. "Ideology Obscured: Political Uses of the Self in Daniel Stern's Infant." *American Psychologist* 46 (3): 206–19.

Danforth, S. 2000. "What Can the Field of Developmental Disabilities Learn from Michel Foucault?" *Mental Retardation* 38 (4): 364–69.

Danforth, S., and V. Navarro. 1998. "Speech Acts: Sampling the Social Construction of Mental Retardation in Everyday Life." *Mental Retardation* 36 (1): 31–43.

Davis, L. 1995. *Enforcing Normalcy: Disability, Deafness, and the Body*. New York: Verso.

———, ed. 1997. *The Disability Studies Reader*. New York: Routledge.

Dean, M. 1995. "Governing the Unemployed Self in an Active Society." *Economy and Society* 24 (4): 559–83.

———. 1996. "Putting the Technological into Government." *History of the Human Sciences* 9 (3): 47–68.

———. 1999. *Governmentality: Power and Rule in Modern Society*. London: Sage.

Dean, M., and B. Hindess. 1998. "Government, Liberalism, Society." Introduction to *Governing Australia: Studies in Contemporary Rationalities of Government*, ed. M. Dean and B. Hindess. Cambridge: Cambridge University Press.

de Swaan, A. 1990. *The Management of Normality: Critical Essays in Health and Welfare*. London: Routledge.

Deutsch, A. 1948. *The Shame of the States: Mental Illness and Social Policy*. New York: Harcourt Brace.

Devlieger, P. 1999. "From Handicap to Disability: Language Use and Cultural Meaning in the United States." *Disability and Rehabilitation* 21 (7): 346–54.

Dexter, L. 1964. *The Tyranny of Schooling: An Inquiry into the Problem of "Stupidity."* New York: Basic.

DiPolito, S. 2007. "*Olmstead v. L.C.*—Deinstitutionalization and Community Integration: An Awakening of the Nation's Conscience?" *Mercer Law Review* 58 (4): 1381.

Donzelot, J. 1979. *The Policing of Families*. New York: Pantheon.

Dordick, G. 2002. "Recovering from Homelessness: Determining the 'Quality of Sobriety' in a Transitional Housing Program." *Qualitative Sociology* 25 (1).

Dowse, L. 2001. "Contesting Practices, Challenging Codes: Self-Advocacy, Disability Politics, and the Social Model." *Disability and Society* 16 (1): 123–41.

Drinkwater, C. 2005. "Supported Living and the Production of Individuals." In *Foucault and the Government of Disability,* ed. S. Tremain. Ann Arbor: University of Michigan Press.

Dudley, J. R. 1983. *Living with Stigma: The Plight of the People Who We Label Mentally Retarded.* Springfield, Ill.: Thomas.

Dumit, J. 2003. *Picturing Personhood: Brain Scans and Biomedical Identity.* Princeton, N.J.: Princeton University Press.

Edgerton, R. 1993. *The Cloak of Competence: Stigma in the Lives of the Mentally Retarded.* Rev. ed. Berkeley and Los Angeles: University of California Press.

Emerson, E. 1992. "What Is Normalisation?" In *Normalisation: A Reader for the Nineties,* ed. H. Brown and H. Smith. London: Routledge.

Emerson, R. 1981. "On Last Resorts." *American Journal of Sociology* 87 (1): 1–22.

Emerson, R., and C. Warren. 1983. "Trouble and the Politics of Contemporary Social Control in Institutions." *Urban Life* 12 (3): 243–47.

Ewald, F. 1991. "Insurance and Risk." In *The Foucault Effect: Studies in Governmentality.* Chicago: University of Chicago Press.

Ferguson, P. 1987. "The Social Construction of Mental Retardation." *Social Policy* (Summer).

Ferguson, P., D. Ferguson, and S. Taylor, eds. 1992. *Interpreting Disability: A Qualitative Reader.* New York: Teachers College Press.

Ferguson, P., M. Hibbard, J. Leinen, and S. Schaff. 1990. "Supported Community Life: Disability Policy and the Renewal of Mediating Structures." *Journal of Disability Policy Studies* 1 (1): 9–35.

Fleury, R., C. Sullivan, and D. Bybee. 1998. "What Happened Depends on Whom You Ask: A Comparison of Police Records and Victim Reports regarding Arrests for Woman Battering." *Journal of Criminal Justice* 26 (1): 53–59.

Floersch, J. 2000. "Reading the Case Record: The Oral and Written Narratives of Social Workers." *Social Service Review* 74 (2): 169–92.

Foster, S. 1987. *The Politics of Caring.* London: Falmer.

Foucault, M. 1965. *Madness and Civilization.* New York: Vintage.

———. 1987. "The Ethic of Care of the Self as a Practice of Freedom: An Interview." In *The Final Foucault,* ed. J. Bernauer and D. Rasmussen. Cambridge: MIT Press.

———. 1988a. "The Political Technology of Individuals." In *Technologies of the Self: A Seminar with Michel Foucault,* ed. L. Martin, H. Gutman, and P. Hutton. Amherst: University of Massachusetts Press.

———. 1988b. "Technologies of the Self." In *Technologies of the Self: A Seminar with Michel Foucault,* ed. L. Martin, H. Gutman, and P. Hutton. Amherst: University of Massachusetts Press.

———. 1991. "Governmentality." In *The Foucault Effect: Studies in Governmentality*, ed. G. Burchell and P. Miller. Chicago: University of Chicago Press. Article originally published 1978.

Freidson, E. 1970. *Profession of Medicine: A Study of the Sociology of Applied Knowledge*. New York: Dodd, Mead.

Garfinkel, H. 1984a. *Studies in Ethnomethodology*. Cambridge: Polity Press.

———. 1984b. "Good Organizational Reasons for 'Bad' Clinic Records." In *Studies in Ethnomethodology*. Cambridge: Polity Press.

———, ed. 1986. *Ethnomethodological Studies of Work*. London: Routledge and Kegan Paul.

———. 2002. *Ethnomethodology's Program: Working Out Durkheim's Aphorism*. Lanham, Md.: Rowman and Littlefield.

Garfinkel, H., M. Lynch, and E. Livingston. 1981. "The Work of a Discovering Science Constructed with Materials from the Optically Discovered Pulsar." *Philosophy of Social Science* 11:131–58.

Garfinkel, H., and H. Sacks. 1970. "On Formal Structures of Practical Action." In *Theoretical Sociology: Perspectives and Developments*, ed. J. C. McKinney and E. Tiryakian. East Norwalk, Conn.: Appleton-Century-Crofts.

Garfinkel, H., and D. L. Wieder. 1992. "Two Incommensurable, Asymmetrical Alternate Technologies of Social Analysis." In *Text in Context: Contributions to Ethnomethodology*, ed. G. Watson and R. Seiler. London: Sage.

Gelb, S. 1995. "The Beast in Man: Degenerationism and Mental Retardation, 1900–1920." *Mental Retardation* 33 (1): 1–9.

———. 2000. "Be Cruel! Dare We Take Foucault Seriously?" *Mental Retardation* 38 (4): 369–72.

Gillman, M., B. Heyman, and J. Swain. 2000. "What's in a Name? The Implications of Diagnosis for People with Learning Difficulties." *Disability and Society* 15 (3): 389–409.

Gleason, J. 1989. *Special Education in Context: An Ethnographic Study of Persons with Developmental Disabilities*. Cambridge: Cambridge University Press.

Gluckman, M. 1956. Foreword to *Schism and Continuity in an African Society*, by V. Turner. Manchester, U.K.: Manchester University Press.

———. 1967. Introduction to *The Craft of Social Anthropology*, ed. A. Epstein. London: Tavistock.

Goffman, E. 1961. *Asylums: Essays on the Social Situation of Mental Patients and Other Inmates*. New York: Anchor.

———. 1963. *Stigma: Notes on the Management of Spoiled Identities*. Englewood Cliffs, N.J.: Prentice-Hall.

Goode, D. 1983. "Who Is Bobby?" In *Health through Occupation*, ed. G. Kielhofner. Philadelphia: Davis.

———. 1994. *A World without Words: The Social Construction of Children Born Deaf and Blind*. Philadelphia: Temple University Press.

Goode, D., and F. Waksler. 1990. "The Missing 'Who': Situational Identity and Fault-Finding with an Alingual Blind-Deaf Child." *Sociological Studies of Child Development* 3:203–23.

Gordon, C. 1991. "Governmental Rationality: An Introduction." In *The Foucault Effect: Studies in Governmentality,* ed. G. Burchell and P. Miller. Chicago: University of Chicago Press.

Gouldner, A. 1954. *Patterns of Industrial Bureaucracy.* New York: Free Press.

Greco, M. 1993. "Psychosomatic Subjects and the 'Duty to Be Well': Personal Agency within Medical Rationality." *Economy and Society* 22 (3): 357–72.

Greenspan, S., and J. Granfield. 1992. "Reconsidering the Construct of Mental Retardation: Implications of a Model of Social Competence." *American Journal on Mental Retardation* 96 (4): 442–53.

Grossman, H., ed. 1983. *Classification in Mental Retardation.* Washington, D.C.: American Association of Mental Deficiency.

Hacking, I. 1986. "Making Up People." In *Reconstructing Individualism,* ed. T. Heller, M. Sosna, and D. Wellbery. Stanford, Calif.: Stanford University Press.

———. 1990. *The Taming of Chance.* Cambridge: Cambridge University Press.

———. 1995. *Rewriting the Soul: Multiple Personality and the Sciences of Memory.* Princeton, N.J.: Princeton University Press.

———. 1999. *The Social Construction of What?* Cambridge, Mass.: Harvard University Press.

Hak, T. 1992. "Psychiatric Records as Transformations of Other Texts." In *Text in Context: Contributions to Ethnomethodology,* ed. G. Watson and R. Seiler. London: Sage.

Hawes, J. 1991. *The Children's Rights Movement: A History of Advocacy and Protection.* Boston: Twayne.

Heath, C., and P. Luff. 2000. *Technology in Action.* Cambridge: Cambridge University Press.

Heritage, J. 1984. *Garfinkel and Ethnomethodology.* Cambridge, U.K.: Polity.

Heshusius, L. 1982 "Sexuality, Intimacy, and Persons We Label Mentally Retarded: What They Think—What We Think." *Mental Retardation* 20 (4): 164–68.

Hewitt, A., and S. Larson. 2007. "The Direct Support Workforce in Community Supports to Individuals with Developmental Disabilities: Issues, Implications, and Promising Practices." *Mental Retardation and Developmental Disabilities Research Reviews* 13:178–87.

Hindess, B. 1986. "Interests in Political Analysis." In *Power, Action, and Belief: A New Sociology of Knowledge?* ed. J. Law. London: Routledge and Kegan Paul.

———. 1996. *Discourses of Power: From Hobbes to Foucault.* Oxford: Blackwell.

Hopwood, A., and P. Miller, eds. 1994. *Accounting as Social and Institutional Practice.* Cambridge: Cambridge University Press.

Hughes, E. 1958. *Men and Their Work.* Glencoe, Ill.: Free Press.

Hutton, P. 1988. "Foucault, Freud, and the Technologies of the Self." In *Technologies of the Self: A Seminar with Michel Foucault,* ed. L. Martin, H. Gutman, and P. Hutton. Amherst: University of Massachusetts Press.

Ingleby, D. 1985. "Professionals as Socializers: The 'Psy Complex.'" *Research in Law, Deviance, and Social Control* 7:79–109.

Ivison, D. 1997. *The Self at Liberty: Political Argument and the Arts of Government*. Ithaca, N.Y.: Cornell University Press.

Jacobs, J., ed. 1980. *Mental Retardation: A Phenomenological Approach*. Springfield, Ill.: Thomas.

Jacoby, R. 1975. *Social Amnesia: A Critique of Conformist Psychology from Adler to Freud*. Boston: Beacon.

Jahoda, A., and M. Cattermole. 1995. "Activities of People with Moderate to Severe Learning Difficulties: Living with Purpose or Just Killing Time?" *Disability and Society*. 10 (2): 203–19.

Jaskulski, T., and W. Ebenstein, eds. 1996. *Opportunities for Excellence: Supporting the Frontline Workforce*. Washington, D.C.: President's Committee on Mental Retardation.

Johnson, K. 1998. *Deinstitutionalizing Women: An Ethnographic Study of Institutional Closure*. Cambridge: Cambridge University Press.

Jones, M. 1953. *The Therapeutic Community: A New Treatment Method in Psychiatry*. New York: Basic Books.

Juravich, T. 2002. "Women on the Line." In *Working in America: Continuity, Conflict, and Change*, ed. A. Wharton. 2d ed. Boston: McGraw-Hill.

Karp, I., and M. Kendall. 1982. "Reflexivity in Field Work." In *Explaining Human Behavior: Consciousness, Human Action, and Social Structure*, ed. P. Secord. London: Sage.

Katz, S. 2000. "Busy Bodies: Activity, Aging, and the Management of Everyday Life." *Journal of Aging Studies*. 14 (2).

Kickbush, I. 1989. "Self-Care in Health Promotion." *Social Science and Medicine* 29 (2): 125–30.

Kielhofner, G. 1983. "Teaching Retarded Adults: Paradoxical Effects of a Pedagogical Enterprise." *Urban Life* 12 (3): 307–26.

Kivett, D., and C. Warren. 2002. "Social Control in a Group Home for Delinquent Boys." *Journal of Contemporary Ethnography* 31 (1): 3–32.

Kliewer, C., and S. Drake. 1998. "Disability, Eugenics, and the Current Ideology of Segregation: A Modern Tale." *Disability and Society* 13 (1): 95–111.

Knorr-Cetina, K. 1981. *The Manufacture of Knowledge*. Oxford: Pergamon.

Knorr-Cetina, K., and M. Mulkay, eds. 1983. *Science Observed: Perspectives on the Social Study of Science*. London: Sage.

Kusterer, K. 1978. *Know-How on the Job: The Important Working Knowledge of "Unskilled" Workers*. Boulder, Colo.: Westview.

Laing, R. D. 1959. *The Divided Self: An Existential Study in Sanity and Madness*. Baltimore: Penguin.

Langness, L., and H. Levine, eds. 1986. *Culture and Retardation: Life Histories of Mildly Mentally Retarded Persons in American Society*. Dordrecht, Neth.: Reidel.

Lasch, C. 1979. *The Culture of Narcissism: American Life in an Age of Diminishing Expectations*. New York: Warner.

Latour, B. 1986. "Visualization and Cognition: Thinking with Eyes and Hands."

Knowledge and Society: Studies in the Sociology of Culture Past and Present 6:1–40.

Latour, B., and S. Woolgar. 1986. *Laboratory Life: The Construction of Scientific Facts*. Princeton, N.J.: Princeton University Press. Originally published 1979.

Lave, J. 1986. "The Values of Quantification." In *Power, Action, and Belief: A New Sociology of Knowledge?* ed. J. Law. London: Routledge and Kegan Paul.

Law, J. 1986a. "On the Methods of Long-Distance Control: Vessels, Navigation, and the Portuguese Route to India." In *Power, Action, and Belief: A New Sociology of Knowledge?* ed. J. Law. London: Routledge and Kegan Paul.

———. 1986b. "Power/Knowledge and the Dissolution of the Sociology of Knowledge." In *Power, Action, and Belief: A New Sociology of Knowledge?* ed. J. Law. London: Routledge and Kegan Paul.

———. 1987. "Technology and Heterogeneous Engineering: The Case of Portuguese Expansion." In *The Social Construction of Technological Systems: New Directions in the Sociology and History of Technology,* ed. W. Bijker, T. Hughes, and T. Pinch. Cambridge: MIT Press.

Light, P. 2002. *The Troubled State of the Federal Public Service*. Washington, D.C.: Brookings Institution.

Linkow, P., and S. Moriearty. 1983. "Everybody Works: Sheltered Work." In *Making Work: Self-Created Jobs in Participatory Organizations,* ed. W. Ronco and L. Peattie. New York: Plenum.

Linton, S. 1998. *Claiming Disability: Knowledge and Identity*. New York: New York University Press.

Lipsky, M. 1979. *Street-Level Bureaucracy: Dilemmas of the Individual in Public Services*. New York: Russell Sage Foundation.

Livingston, E. 1987. *Making Sense of Ethnomethodology*. London: Routledge and Kegan Paul.

Lupton, D. 1993. "Risk as Moral Danger: The Social and Political Functions of Risk Discourse in Public Health." *International Journal of Health Services* 23 (5): 425–35.

———. 1999. *Risk*. London: Routledge.

Lynch, M. 1985. *Art and Artifact in Laboratory Science: A Study of Shop Work and Shop Talk in a Research Laboratory*. London: Routledge and Kegan Paul.

———. 1993. *Scientific Practice and Ordinary Action: Ethnomethodology and Social Studies of Science*. Cambridge: Cambridge University Press.

Lynch, M., E. Livingston, and H. Garfinkel. 1983. "Temporal Order in Laboratory Work." In *Science Observed: Perspectives on the Social Study of Science,* ed. K. Knorr-Cetina and M. Mulkay. London: Sage.

Mandell, N. 1988. "The Least-Adult Role in Studying Children." *Journal of Contemporary Ethnography* 16 (4): 433–67.

Maynard, D., and S. Clayman. 1991. "The Diversity of Ethnomethodology." *Annual Review of Sociology* 17:385–418.

McCleary, R. 1977. "How Parole Officers Use Records." *Social Problems* 24: 576–89.

McKnight, J. 1980. "Nation of Clients?" *Public Welfare* (Fall): 15–19.

McQueen, D. 1989. "Thoughts on the Ideological Origins of Health Promotion." *Health Promotion* 4 (4): 339–42.

Meehan, A. 1993. "Internal Police Records and the Control of Juveniles: Politics and Policing in a Suburban Town." *British Journal of Criminology* 33:504–24.

Mercer, J. 1973. *Labeling the Mentally Retarded: Clinical and Social Systems Perspectives on Mental Retardation.* Berkeley and Los Angeles: University of California Press.

Merton, R. 1957. *Social Theory and Social Structure.* Glencoe, Ill.: Free Press.

Mesch, G., and G. Fishman. 1999. "Entering the System: Ethnic Differences in Closing Juvenile Criminal Files in Israel." *Journal of Research in Crime and Delinquency* 36 (2): 175–93.

Miller, P., and N. Rose. 1990. "Governing Economic Life." *Economy and Society* 19 (1): 1–31.

Mitchell, J. 1983. "Case and Situation Analysis." *Sociological Review,* May, 187–211.

———. 1984. "Case Studies." In *Ethnographic Research,* ed. R. F. Ellen. London: Academic Press.

Monnickendam, M., H. Yaniv, and N. Geva. 1994. "Practitioners and the Case Record: Patterns of Use." *Administration in Social Work* 18 (4): 73–87.

Morawski, J. G. 1988. "Impossible Experiments and Practical Constructions: The Social Bases of Psychologists' Work." In *The Rise of Experimentation in American Psychology,* ed. J. G. Morawski. New Haven, Conn.: Yale University Press.

———. 1994. *Practicing Feminisms, Reconstructing Psychology: Notes on a Liminal Science.* Ann Arbor: University of Michigan Press.

———. 1997. "Educating the Emotions: Academic Psychology, Textbooks, and the Psychology Industry, 1890–1940." In *Inventing the Psychological: Toward a Cultural History of Emotional Life in America,* ed. J. Pfister and N. Schnog. New Haven, Conn.: Yale University Press.

Myers, F., A. Ager, P. Kerr, and S. Myles. 1998. "Outside Looking In? Studies of the Community Integration of People with Learning Disabilities." *Disability and Society* 13 (3): 389–413.

Nettleton, S. 1997. "Governing the Risky Self: How to Become Healthy, Wealthy, and Wise." In *Foucault, Health, and Medicine,* ed. A. Petersen and R. Bunton. London: Routledge.

New York State Commission on Quality of Care for the Mentally Disabled. 1995. *Shifting Costs to Medicaid: The Case of Financing the OMRDD Comprehensive Case Management Program.* Albany: New York State Commission on Quality of Care for the Mentally Disabled.

New York State Office of Mental Retardation and Developmental Disabilities. 2000. *Core Training: New York State Medicaid Service Coordinators.* Albany: New York State Office of Mental Retardation and Developmental Disabilities.

———. 2006. *The Comprehensive Five Year Plan, 2006–2010.* Albany: New York State Office of Mental Retardation and Developmental Disabilities.

———. 2008. *OMRDD Budget Briefing Booklet, Fiscal Year 2008–2009*. Albany: New York State Office of Mental Retardation and Developmental Disabilities.

Noll, S., and J. Trent. 2004. *Mental Retardation in America: A Historical Reader*. New York: New York University Press.

Oetting, J., and M. Rice. 1991. "Influence of the Social Context on Pragmatic Skills of Adults with Mental Retardation." *American Journal of Mental Retardation* 95 (4): 435–43.

Oliver, M. 1996. *Understanding Disability: From Theory to Practice*. London: Macmillan.

OMRDD. *See* New York State Office of Mental Retardation and Developmental Disabilities.

Orr, J. 1996. *Talking about Machines: An Ethnography of a Modern Job*. Ithaca, N.Y.: ILR Press.

Osborne, T. 1993. "On Liberalism, Neo-liberalism, and the Liberal Profession of Medicine." *Economy and Society* 26 (4): 345–56.

Parton, N. 1994. "Problematics of Government: (Post) Modernity and Social Work." *British Journal of Social Work* 24:9–32.

Perlin, M. 2000. "Their Promises of Paradise: Will *Olmstead v. L.C.* Resuscitate the Constitutional 'Least Restrictive Alternative' Principle in Mental Disability Law?" *Houston Law Review* 37:999.

Perrow, C. 1967. "A Framework for the Comparative Analysis of Organization." *American Sociological Review* 32 (2): 194–208.

———. 1986. *Complex Organizations: A Critical Essay*. 3d ed. New York: Random House.

Peter, D. 2000. "Dynamics of Discourse: A Case Study Illuminating Power Relations in Mental Retardation." *Mental Retardation* 38 (4): 354–62.

Pollner, M., and D. Goode. 1990. "Ethnomethodology and Person-Centering Practices." *Person Centered Review* 5 (2): 203–20.

Postman, N. 1982. *The Disappearance of Childhood*. New York: Vintage.

Power, M. 1997. *The Audit Society: Rituals of Verification*. Oxford: Oxford University Press.

Prior, L. 1988. "The Architecture of the Hospital: A Study of Spatial Organization and Medical Knowledge." *British Journal of Sociology* 1:86–113.

Procacci, G. 1978. "Social Economy and the Government of Poverty." *Ideology and Consciousness* 4:55–72.

Prottas, J. 1979. *People-Processing: The Street-Level Bureaucrat in Public Service Bureaucracies*. Lexington, Mass.: Lexington Books.

Radford, J. 1994. "Intellectual Disability and the Heritage of Modernity." In *Disability Is Not Measles: New Research Paradigms in Disability*, ed. M. Rioux and M. Bach. North York, Ont.: Roeher Institute.

Rapley, M., P. Kiernan, and C. Antaki. 1998. "Invisible to Themselves or Negotiating Identity? The Interactional Management of Being Intellectually Disabled." *Disability and Society*. 13 (5): 807–27.

Rawls, A. 2002. Editor's introduction to *Ethnomethodology's Program: Working*

Out Durkheim's Aphorism, by H. Garfinkel. Lanham, Md.: Rowman and Littlefield.

———. 2008. "Harold Garfinkel, Ethnomethodology, and Workplace Studies." *Organization Studies* 29 (5): 701–32.

Rieff, P. 1966. *The Triumph of the Therapeutic: Uses of Faith after Freud.* New York: Harper and Row.

Rivera, G. 1972. *Willowbrook: A Report on How It Is and Why It Doesn't Have to Be That Way.* New York: Random House.

Robillard, A. 1999. *Meaning of a Disability: The Lived Experience of Paralysis.* Philadelphia: Temple University Press.

Rogers, D. 1953. *Angel Unaware.* Westwood, N.J.: Revell.

———. 1963. *Angel Unaware.* Foreword by N. Peale. Westwood, N.J.: Revell.

Rose, N. 1985. *The Psychological Complex: Psychology, Politics, and Society in England, 1869–1939.* London: Routledge and Kegan Paul.

———. 1994. "Expertise and the Government of Conduct." *Studies in Law, Politics, and Society* 14:359–97.

———. 1996. "Psychiatry as a Political Science: Advanced Liberalism and the Administration of Risk." *History of the Human Sciences* 9 (2): 1–23.

———. 1998a. "Governing Risky Individuals: The Role of Psychiatry in New Regimes of Control." *Psychiatry, Psychology, and Law* 5 (20): 177–95.

———. 1998b. *Inventing Our Selves: Psychology, Power, and Personhood.* New York: Cambridge University Press.

———. 1999a. *Governing the Soul: The Shaping of the Private Self.* 2d ed. London: Free Association.

———. 1999b. *Powers of Freedom: Reframing Political Thought.* Cambridge: Cambridge University Press.

Rose-Ackerman, S. 1999. "Mental Retardation and Society: The Ethics and Politics of Normalization." *Ethics* 93 (1): 81–101.

Roth, J. 1963. *Timetables: Structuring the Passage of Time in Tuberculosis Treatment and Other Careers.* Indianapolis, Ind.: Bobbs-Merrill.

Rothman, B. 2005. *Weaving a Family: Untangling Race and Adoption.* Boston: Beacon Press.

Rothman, D. 1971. *The Discovery of the Asylum: Social Order and Disorder in the New Republic.* Boston: Little, Brown.

Rothman, D., and S. Rothman. 1984. *The Willowbrook Wars.* New York: Harper and Row.

Rummery, K. 2002. *Disability, Citizenship, and Community Care: A Case for Welfare Rights?* Aldershot, U.K.: Ashgate.

Sabsay, S., and M. Platt. 1985. *Social Setting, Stigma, and Communicative Competence.* Amsterdam: Benjamins.

Sacks, H. 1972. "On the Analyzability of Stories by Children." In *Directions in Sociolinguistics,* ed. J. Gumperz and D. Hymes. New York: Holt, Rinehart, and Winston.

———. 1975. "Everyone Has to Lie." In *Sociocultural Dimensions of Language Use,* ed. M. Sanches and B. G. Blount. New York: Academic Press.

———. 1987. "On the Preferences for Agreement and Contiguity in Sequences in Conversation." In *Talk and Social Organization,* ed. G. Button and J. Lee. Cambridge: Cambridge University Press.

———. 1992a. *Lectures on Conversation,* ed. G. Jefferson. Vol. 1. Oxford: Blackwell.

———. 1992b. *Lectures on Conversation,* ed. G. Jefferson. Vol. 2. Oxford: Blackwell.

Sacks, H., E. Schegloff, and G. Jefferson. 1974. "A Simplest Systematics for the Organization of Turn-Taking in Conversation." *Language* 50 (4): 696–735.

Sandieson, R. 1998. "A Survey on Terminology That Refers to People with Mental Retardation/Developmental Disabilities." *Education and Training in Mental Retardation and Developmental Disabilities* 33:3.

Scheff, T. 1966. *Being Mentally Il: A Sociological Study.* Chicago: Aldine.

Schegloff, E. 1982. "Discourse as an Interactional Accomplishment: Some Uses of Uh-Huh and Other Things That Come between Sentences." In *Analyzing Discourse: Text and Talk,* ed. D. Tannen. Washington, D.C.: Georgetown University Press.

———. 1987. "Between Macro and Micro: Contexts and Other Connections." In *The Micro-Macro,* ed. J. Alexander, B. Giesen, R. Munch, and N. Smelser. Berkeley and Los Angeles: University of California Press.

Schegloff, E., and H. Sacks. 1974. "Opening Up Closings." In *Ethnomethodology,* ed. R. Turner. Harmondsworth, U.K.: Penguin.

Schutz, A. 1970. *On Phenomenology and Social Relations.* Chicago: University of Chicago Press.

Scott, J. 1985. *Weapons of the Weak: Everyday Forms of Peasant Resistance.* New Haven, Conn.: Yale University Press.

Scott, W. R. 1992. *Organizations: Rational, Natural, and Open Systems.* 3d ed. Englewood-Cliffs, N.J.: Prentice-Hall.

Scull, A. 1977. *Decarceration: Community Treatment and the Deviant—A Radical View.* New York: Prentice-Hall.

Sellen, A., and R. Harper. 2003. *The Myth of the Paperless Office.* Cambridge: Cambridge University Press.

Selznick, P. 1948. "Foundations of the Theory of Organizations." *American Sociological Review* 13:25–35.

Shorter, E. 2000. *The Kennedy Family and the Story of Mental Retardation.* Philadelphia: Temple University Press.

Shriver, E. 1962. "Hope for Retarded Children." *Saturday Evening Post* 235:71–75.

Silverman, D. 1998. *Harvey Sacks: Social Science and Conversation Analysis.* Oxford: Oxford University Press.

Simpson, M. 1996a. "Normalisation and the Psychology of Mental Retardation." *Sociological Review* 44 (1): 99–118.

———. 1996b. "The Sociology of Competence in Learning Disability Services." *Social Work and Social Sciences Review* 6 (2): 85–97.

Siperstein, G. 1992. "Social Competence: An Important Construct in Mental Retardation." *Mental Retardation* 96 (4): iii–vi.

Smandych, R. 1999. *Governable Places: Readings on Governmentality and Crime Control.* Aldershot, U.K.: Dartmouth.

Smith, D. 1990. *Texts, Facts, and Femininity: Exploring the Relations of Ruling.* London: Routledge.

Soodak, L. 1990. "Social Behavior and Knowledge of Social 'Scripts' among Mentally Retarded Adults." *American Journal of Mental Retardation* 94 (5): 515–21.

Stanton, A., and M. Schwartz. 1954. *The Mental Hospital: A Study of Institutional Participation in Psychiatric Illness and Treatment.* New York: Basic Books.

Star, S. 1983. "Simplification in Scientific Work: An Example from Neuroscience Research." *Social Studies of Science* 13:205–28.

Stockholder, F. 1994. "Naming and Renaming Persons with Intellectual Disabilities." In *Disability Is Not Measles: New Research Paradigms in Disability,* ed. M. Rioux and M. Bach. North York, Ont.: Roeher Institute.

Stroman, D. 1989. *Mental Retardation in Context.* Lanham, Md.: University Press of America.

Suchman, L. 1987. *Plans and Situated Actions: The Problem of Human-Machine Communication.* Cambridge: Cambridge University Press.

Sudnow, D. 1965. "Normal Crimes: Sociological Features of a Penal Code in a Public Defender's Office." *Social Problems* 12:255–76.

———. 1967. *Passing On: The Social Organization of Dying.* Englewood Cliffs, N.J.: Prentice-Hall.

Szasz, T. 1960. *The Myth of Mental Illness.* New York: Harper and Row.

———. 1963. *Law, Liberty, and Psychiatry: An Inquiry into the Social Uses of Mental Health Practices.* New York: Macmillan.

Taubes, G. 2001. "The Soft Science of Dietary Fat." *Science,* March 30, 2536–45.

Taylor, S. 2000. "'You're Not a Retard, You're Just Wise': Disability, Social Identity, and Family Networks." *Journal of Contemporary Ethnography* 29 (1): 58–92.

———. 2001. "The Continuum and Current Controversies in the USA." *Journal of Intellectual and Developmental Disability* 26 (1): 15–33.

Taylor, S., R. Bogdan, and Z. Lutfiyya, eds. 1995. *The Variety of Community Experience: Qualitative Studies of Family and Community Integration.* Baltimore: Brookes.

Thompson, D., I. Clare, and H. Brown. 1997. "Not Such an 'Ordinary' Relationship: The Role of Women Support Staff in Relation to Men with Learning Disabilities Who Have Difficult Sexual Behaviour." *Disability and Society* 12 (4): 573–92.

Tomes, N. 2006. "The Patient as a Policy Factor: A Historical Case Study of the Consumer/Survivor Movement in Mental Health." *Health Affairs* 25 (3): 720–29.

Traweek, S. 1988. *Beamtimes and Lifetimes: The World of High Energy Physics.* Cambridge: Harvard University Press.

Treece, A., S. Gregory, B. Ayres, and K. Mendis. 1999. "'I Always Do What They Tell Me to Do': Choice-Making Opportunities in the Lives of Two Older Persons with Severe Learning Difficulties Living in a Community Setting." *Disability and Society* 14 (6): 791–804.

Tremain, S., ed. 2005. *Foucault and the Government of Disability*. Ann Arbor: University of Michigan Press.

Trent, J. 1994. *Inventing the Feeble Mind: A History of Mental Retardation in the United States*. Berkeley and Los Angeles: University of California Press.

Tyor, P., and L. Bell. 1984. *Caring for the Retarded in America: A History*. Greenwich, Conn.: Greenwood.

Valverde, M. 1998. *Diseases of the Will: Alcohol and the Dilemmas of Freedom*. Cambridge: Cambridge University Press.

Van Velsen, J. 1967. "The Extended-Case Method and Situational Analysis." In *The Craft of Social Anthropology*, ed. A. Epstein. London: Tavistock.

Ward, M. 1946. *The Snake Pit*. New York: Random House.

Wehmeyer, M., and M. Schwartz. 1997. "Self-Determination and Positive Adult Outcomes: A Follow-Up Study of Youth with Mental Retardation or Learning Disabilities." *Exceptional Children* 63 (2): 245–55.

Weiss, M. 1997. "For Doctors' Eyes Only: Medical Records in Two Israeli Hospitals." *Culture, Medicine, and Psychiatry* 21 (3): 283–302.

Wheeler, S., ed. 1969. *On Record: Files and Dossiers in American Life*. New York: Russell Sage Foundation.

Wieder, D. 1974. *Language and Social Reality: The Case of Telling the Convict Code*. The Hague, Neth.: Mouton.

Wing, L. 1989. *Hospital Closure and the Resettlement of Residents*. Aldershot, U.K.: Avebury.

Wolfensberger, W. 1972. *Normalization: The Principle of Normalization in Human Services*. Washington, D.C.: National Institute of Mental Retardation.

———. 1989. "Human Service Policies: The Rhetoric versus the Reality." In *Disability and Dependency*, ed. L. Barton. London: Falmer.

———. 1995. "Social Role Valorization Is Too Conservative. No, It Is Too Radical." *Disability and Society* 10 (3): 365–68.

Woodill, G. 1994. "The Social Semiotics of Disability." In *Disability Is Not Measles: New Research Paradigms in Disability*. North York, Ont.: Roeher Institute.

Wrigley, J. 1989. "Do Young Children Need Intellectual Stimulation? Experts' Advice to Parents, 1900–1985." *History of Education Quarterly* 29 (1): 41–75.

Yates, J. 1989. *Control through Communication: The Rise of System in American Management*. Baltimore: Johns Hopkins University Press.

Yeatman, A. 1998. "Interpreting Contemporary Contractualism." In *Governing Australia: Studies in Contemporary Rationalities of Government*, ed. M. Dean and B. Hindess. Cambridge: Cambridge University Press.

Yeatman, A., and J. Penglase. 2004. "Looking After Children: A Case of Individualised Service Delivery." *Australian Journal of Social Issues* 39 (3): 233–47.

Young, D., and R. Quibell. 2000. "Why Rights Are Never Enough: Rights, Intellectual Disability, and Understanding." *Disability and Society* 15 (5): 747–64.

Zetlin, A., and M. Murtaugh. 1990. "Whatever Happened to Those with Borderline IQs?" *American Journal on Mental Retardation* 94 (5): 463–69.

Zimmerman, D. 1969a. "Record-Keeping and the Intake Process at a Public Welfare Agency." In *On Record: Files and Dossiers in American Life,* ed. Stanton Wheeler. New York: Russell Sage Foundation.

———. 1969b. "Tasks and Troubles: The Practical Bases of Work Activities in a Public Assistance Organization." In *Explorations in Sociology and Counseling,* ed. D. Hansen. New York: Houghton Mifflin.

Zola, I. 1983. *Sociomedical Inquiries*. Philadelphia: Temple University Press.

Zuboff, S. 1988. *In the Age of Smart Machines: The Future of Work and Power.* New York: Basic Books.

INDEX

administration: of risk, 214; technical character of, 164. *See also* government

adults, intellectually disabled. *See* intellectually disabled persons

alienists, 23

American Association of Mental Deficiency, 25

American Association on Intellectual and Developmental Disabilities (AAIDD), xix–xx, 34

American Association on Mental Retardation (AAMR), 33

American Psychiatric Association: *Diagnostic and Statistical Manual of Mental Disorders (DSM),* 154, 252n1

Angela (Driggs House counselor), 5; age of, 9; assessment of Marty, 154, 155, 158; assessment of Paul, 222, 226, 227, 229, 230, 236; cooking skills, 15; and Johnny's aggression, 149; work with Jennifer, 196, 197–98; work with Theresa, 72–73

anger: appropriate expression of, 5

ARC v. Rockefeller (1972), 35, 43

Association for the Help of Retarded Children, 27

Association of Medical Officers of American Institutions for Idiotic

and Feebleminded Persons (AOM), 23, 24

authority: bureaucratic, 164; of expertise, 48–49; to govern, 48; in group homes, 46, 53, 57; indirect exercise of, 39, 57; and liberty, 38; of psychiatry, 30; in psy knowledge, 248; in technology, 164–66. *See also* freedom/authority dilemma

autonomy: and clinical work, 214; developmental goal of, 245–46; ethic of, xii, 1, 2, 3, 243, 245–46, 248; of group home residents, xiii, 246; for intellectually disabled persons, 44, 246; personhood as, 124; and professional work, 94–98; rhetoric of, xviii; risk in, 243; of self, 54–55; self-work on, 55; in social services, xviii–xix

Becker, Howard, 30

behaviorism, 50–51; concept of freedom in, 50, 55

behavior plans, 5, 89–90, 154, 194–209; contractual elements in, 196, 203, 205, 207; development of, 97; goals of, 89; intervention in, 201, 203, 204, 206, 217; proactive procedures in, 200; reinforcement of, 128, 200; for risky behavior, 215; sensitizing

JACK LEVINSON is assistant professor of sociology at the City College of New York.